Memory Piano

POETS ON POETRY

David Lehman, General Editor
Donald Hall, Founding Editor

New titles

John Ashbery, *Selected Prose*
Annie Finch, *The Body of Poetry*
Dana Gioia, *Barrier of a Common Language*
Paul Hoover, *Fables of Representation*
Philip Larkin, *Further Requirements*
Alice Notley, *Coming After*
Charles Simic, *Memory Piano*
William Stafford, *The Answers Are Inside the Mountains*
Richard Tillinghast, *Poetry and What Is Real*

Recently published

Thomas M. Disch, *The Castle of Perseverance*
Mark Jarman, *Body and Soul*
Philip Levine, *So Ask*
David Mura, *Song for Uncle Tom, Tonto, and Mr. Moto*
Karl Shapiro, *Essay on Rime*
Charles Simic, *The Metaphysician in the Dark*
Stephen Yenser, *A Boundless Field*

Also available are collections by

A. R. Ammons, Robert Bly, Philip Booth, Marianne Boruch,
Hayden Carruth, Amy Clampitt, Douglas Crase, Robert Creeley,
Donald Davie, Tess Gallagher, Linda Gregerson, Allen Grossman,
Thom Gunn, Rachel Hadas, John Haines, Donald Hall, Joy Harjo,
Robert Hayden, Edward Hirsch, Daniel Hoffman, Jonathan Holden,
John Hollander, Andrew Hudgins, Josephine Jacobsen,
Galway Kinnell, Kenneth Koch, John Koethe, Yusef Komunyakaa,
Maxine Kumin, Martin Lammon (editor), Philip Larkin,
David Lehman, Philip Levine, Larry Levis, John Logan, William Logan,
William Matthews, William Meredith, Jane Miller, Carol Muske,
Geoffrey O'Brien, Gregory Orr, Alicia Suskin Ostriker, Ron Padgett,
Marge Piercy, Anne Sexton, Charles Simic, William Stafford,
Anne Stevenson, May Swenson, James Tate, Richard Tillinghast,
C. K. Williams, Alan Williamson, Charles Wright, and James Wright

Charles Simic

Memory Piano

THE UNIVERSITY OF MICHIGAN PRESS

Ann Arbor

2009   2008   2007   2006   4   3   2   1

A CIP catalog record for this book is available from the British Library.

Library of Congress Cataloging-in-Publication Data

Simic, Charles, 1938–
    Memory piano / Charles Simic.
        p. cm. — (Poets on poetry)
    ISBN-13: 978-0-472-09940-5 (alk. paper)
    ISBN-10: 0-472-09940-X (alk. paper)
    ISBN-13: 978-0-472-06940-8 (pbk. : alk. paper)
    ISBN-10: 0-472-06940-3 (pbk. : alk. paper)
    1. Poetry—History and criticism.   I. Title.   II. Series.

PN1111.S46   2006
809.1—dc22   2005030221

Contents

Asphalt Jungle

The year is 1951. I'm thirteen years old and sitting in a nearly empty movie theater in Belgrade, Yugoslavia. Outside, preparations are being made for the May 1st parade. Huge pictures with faces of our Communist leaders are plastered all over the city. I've skipped school and feel guilty about it and anxious that I may run into someone who'll tell my mother. The theater is an old one smelling of stale tobacco smoke. It has wooden seats that creak at the slightest change of position. I've seen a rat there once run across the stage, so I stir at the slightest rustle at my feet. I know nothing about the film except that it has an intriguing title. I don't even recognize the names of the actors or the director—Sterling Hayden, Louis Calhern, Sam Jaffe, Marilyn Monroe, John Huston—as the black and white credits unroll, but as everyone knows, one sometimes falls in love with a movie or a poem from the first image.

It's early morning in some nameless American city. Over the low rooftops of commercial buildings, I can see part of a bridge and a couple of skyscrapers in the distance blurred by fog. The camera angle is very odd. It's as if someone sprawled in the gutter is holding it up. A police car comes cruising slowly, its radio broadcasting the description of a robbery suspect. Next, we are in a rundown neighborhood where a tall man wearing a hat with the brim pulled down over his eyes hides behind a row of columns as the police car passes by. The camera follows him into a luncheonette with a faded sign, "Home Cooking," over the door. A hunchbacked man, seated behind the counter, is reading a newspaper. The tough-looking stranger comes in and hands him a gun, which the counterman quickly slips into the cash register. At that moment, two cops walk in. They ask the hunchback how long the customer has been sitting there. "Don't ask me, I don't watch the clock. I own the joint," the counterman replies.

I had seen many American films before—westerns, musicals, costume dramas, comedies, even a few tearjerkers with Joan Crawford and Bette Davis—but I never wanted to see one of them again as much as I did this one. What gripped me wasn't so much the film's intricate plot about a failed jewelry store robbery, but the way it was filmed: the desolate streets with their elongated shadows, the windows with their slatted blinds, the dark doorways, the cracked pavements, the stained walls, and the feel of lurking danger and adventure everywhere. There was an explanation for that. For someone already living in the heart of a city, the view of another bigger one is an invitation to daydream. All cities overlap. American movies about rural and small town life looked to me far more foreign. If there were smiling children and friendly neighbors, so much the worse. They scared me more than Frankenstein films. As a war child and a juvenile delinquent, I was already a confirmed pessimist. I preferred trash-strewn subways, tenements with fire escapes, tough guys in nightclubs, children playing baseball in the street. Belgrade with its few flickering neon lights and billboards was already bliss, as far as I was concerned. Times Square on Saturday night, however, was paradise.

Much of the dialogue in *The Asphalt Jungle* was lost on me because of the subtitles, but I remember a woman saying about a police siren going off into the night that it sounded like a soul in hell. After the opening scene, most of the action takes place in poorly lit interiors where the big heist and the various double-crosses are being hatched. I usually hurried out after seeing a movie to tell my friends all about it, but I found myself at a loss for words about this one. I had no vocabulary to explain how people were often photographed from the back so that their most ordinary movements seemed mysterious, or how the camera framed their faces so that the room seemed to be closing in on them. When I tried to describe that, they had no idea what I was talking about or why that should please me, and neither did I. What excited me was the artful way the film was made, but how was I supposed to know that?

I also savored the way the film viewed the characters. These crooks were just ordinary folks trying to make a living. The robbery, calculated down to its minutest detail, is executed perfectly, but then an accident happens and there's a shooting in which a man dies. I was comforted by the movie's underlying message: there is no getting around bad luck. In one of the final scenes the old crook who had masterminded the robbery puts off his escape in order to study a couple of teenagers jitterbugging in a roadside dive. After they run out of money for the jukebox, he drops a handful of coins on their table and watches the pretty girl do a snake dance for him. She lifts her arms, sways them this way and that while snapping her fingers and mincing her steps. Then she bends over, turns, and lifts her ass in its tight little skirt right into his face. At that moment the cops show up and arrest him.

Going over such scenes in my mind, America became a real place for me. When I arrived in New York three years later on a hot August afternoon, not only the skyline, but also the city with its traffic and crowds seemed unexpectedly familiar. Once the night fell and we took a walk in the emptying midtown streets, the movies I had seen came back to me. The moment one left midtown and drifted a few blocks east or west, one found crowded tenements where old people took out their chairs to sit and gossip on the sidewalks and children played in the street. Barely three blocks from elegant Fifth Avenue and the public library, there was a double row of rundown movie houses with huge marquees showing horror films and westerns. There were penny arcades, cheap eating places, and saloons on that stretch of Forty-Second Street. The air smelled of greasy popcorn oil and fried onions. Drunks accosted people asking for a handout. Sailors crowded around the entrance to a dime-a-dance joint. It was both frightening and exhilarating. Right before my eyes was that intangible *something* I could not name, not just what America looks like, but how it feels to be there. The way the light, for instance, glinted off a black car moving down an avenue or the low sound of fine jazz on a radio no one is paying attention to in a candy store. I didn't know what to call it then; now I guess I would call it poetry.

Divine, Superfluous Beauty

It wasn't always so hard making sense of things. When it came to Big Truth it was all settled. There were plenty of little truths for the poets and everybody else to busy themselves with, but they did not have to start from scratch and explain the universe. Then all of a sudden it happened. The silence of the infinite spaces and their own souls made them quake. One may argue about the date when one could no longer formulate with any confidence what the Big Truth was, but already in the nineteenth century, poets as different as Whitman, Dickinson, and Mallarmé found themselves philosophically pretty much on their own. By the time the twentieth century rolled around, the search for a new knowledge of reality and for an authentic self was the burning issue addressed by numerous, otherwise battling poetic movements. While rejecting Christian belief, the not-so-secret ambition of many of these poets was to write a poem about the absolute in an age suspicious of absolutes, and get away with it.

The role of the reader underwent a change too. It was not just a well-turned poem one was expected to admire, but also the homespun metaphysics that came along with it. Given the intellectual ambition and the high stakes, the risk of making a complete fool of oneself was almost guaranteed. Still and all, was it really possible to pretend that the world had not changed, as the aesthetic and political conservatives continue to believe? I mention all this as a way of situating Robinson Jeffers and his work. He is of that same tribe, although his poetry and his own

Review of *The Selected Poetry of Robinson Jeffers* and *The Collected Poetry of Robinson Jeffers*, vol. 5, *Textual Evidence and Commentary*, ed. Tim Hunt. From the *New York Review of Books*, April 11, 2002.

outlook on things ended up being unlike anyone else's among his contemporaries.

Jeffers, who died in 1962 and is little read today, was the author of at least thirteen sizable collections of poetry. This in itself would not be particularly unusual except that, from the 1920s to the 1940s, he was reputed to be one of the greatest poetic voices this country ever produced and was compared to Shakespeare and Homer by critics who loathed modern poetry. After the Second World War, all that changed. Jeffers, who remained a firm isolationist throughout the conflict, began to be thought of as a right-winger of the lunatic fringe. *The Double Axe and Other Poems* came out in 1948 with a publisher's preface disclaiming responsibility for the political views in the book. Not only was Jeffers accused of being a fascist sympathizer—which he was not—but he was also being discarded as a poet. No less an authority than Randall Jarrell thought his poems lacked the exactness and conciseness required of the best poetry. I myself don't remember his name coming up much, if at all, in literary circles in the 1950s and 1960s. We all knew who he was since he was included in all the important anthologies, but his work did not make much of an impression on my generation of poets. Even Frost, thanks to his keen ear for colloquial speech, sounded more like a contemporary. Compared to Eliot and Williams, Jeffers sounded like a provincial windbag. It took a selection of his short poems and an excellent introduction by Robert Hass in 1987 to make me open my eyes and correct some of these misapprehensions.

Not that Jeffers ever made it easy for anyone to like him or that the complaints about his poetry were entirely baseless. Reading his poems one would not know that motion pictures were ever invented or that most Americans lived in cities. What is needed in poems are things that are permanent, he said. Writing an ode to a locomotive, as Whitman did, made no sense to him. He considered most of our modern inventions, good and bad, as passing fads doomed to disappear without trace. It was all right for prose to concern itself with contemporary matters. Poetry for Jeffers had to deal with things that a reader two thousand years from now could still understand and be moved by.

These views of his were not a product of complete ignorance

of modern literature. Jeffers had a thorough knowledge of French poetry, admired it, but thought it was a dead end. Mallarmé's and his followers' dream of divorcing poetry from intelligibility and of bringing it nearer to music seemed to him hopelessly deluded. Their successors in his view could make only further renunciations. "Every advance," he wrote in the introduction to a volume of his poems, "required the elimination of some aspect of reality, and what could it profit me to know the direction of modern poetry if I did not like the direction? It was too much like putting out your eyes to cultivate the sense of hearing, or cutting off the right hand to develop the left."

He disapproved particularly of modern poetry's competition with prose, its desperate attempt, so he thought, to save its soul by sounding as prosaic as possible. "It became evident to me," he writes, "that poetry—if it was to survive at all—must reclaim some of the power and reality that it was so hastily surrendering to prose." Jeffers was not persuaded by the Modernist complaint that the language of poetry needs to renew itself from time to time, that the old ways with words had grown stale, so that poetry as it was being written when he started out had become an embarrassment to any intelligent human being. There was no crisis of language for Jeffers, no likelihood that yesterday's poetic idiom is inadequate to deal with contemporary reality. Given his rejection of every literary fashion of his day, it's not surprising that it took this long for us to begin to see him for what he was, a poet capable of extraordinary originality and beauty.

Everything about Jeffers was out of the ordinary. Even his childhood and upbringing are a puzzle. Born in 1887 in Pittsburgh, he was the first son of a reclusive, eccentric widower who was a minister and professor of Greek and Latin at Western Theological Seminary and his much younger second wife. Dr. Jeffers was over six feet tall, they say, but he went around stooped, giving the impression of a much shorter and much older man. Like his son, he didn't care to meet people or engage in small talk. While Jeffers was growing up, his father kept moving constantly around Pittsburgh. His excuse was that he couldn't find peace to concentrate on his studies because young Robin kept inviting playmates to the house. The insistence on privacy and the formal courtesy with which the family members treated each other are both admirable and a little frightening. For instance, although the family never missed Sunday service, the doctor preferred to worship alone and went to another church. Still, father and son seem to have gotten along despite what Jeffers suggests about their relationship in this early sonnet:

To His Father

Christ was your lord and captain all your life,
He fails the world but you he did not fail,
He led you through all forms of grief and strife
Intact, a man full-armed, he let prevail
Nor outward malice nor the worse-fanged snake
That coils in one's own brain against your calm,
That great rich jewel well guarded for his sake
With coronal age and death like quieting balm.
I Father having followed other guides
And oftener to my hurt no leader at all,
Through years nailed up like dripping panther hides
For trophies on a savage temple wall
Hardly anticipate that reverend stage
Of life, the snow-wreathed honor of extreme age.

What comes as a surprise is that Dr. Jeffers, far from being provincial and narrow-minded, gave his son a broad education. He and his younger brother were sent to study in private schools in Geneva, Lausanne, Zurich, and Leipzig. By the time he was through with high school, Jeffers knew not only French and German but also Greek and Latin. Afterward, he continued his education at Occidental College in California, where the family had moved because of his father's poor health. He got his undergraduate degree in 1905 when he was eighteen and enrolled in the University of Southern California graduate program in literature, where he met his future wife. Mrs. Una Call Kuster, as she was then called, was a married woman. After years of conducting an on-and-off illicit affair, she divorced her lawyer husband and married Jeffers in 1913. He was already writing poems and beginning to think of himself as a poet. He had a small legacy they could live on modestly, so there was no pressing need to worry about making a living.

They planned to go to England but the war interfered and they settled in the village of Carmel in Monterey County. After a few years, they bought a plot of land and erected a stone edifice called "Tor House" and subsequently added a tower which Jeffers built with his own hands with rocks he gathered and dug along the seashore. This is how another California poet, Robert Hass, describes what Jeffers saw when he walked out of his stone house:

> A rocky coast, ridges of cypress and pine, ghostly in the fog. On clear days the Carmel River glittered past the ruin of an old Franciscan mission, and the surf was an intense sapphire, foaming to turquoise as it crested. Gulls, cormorants and pelicans among the rocks, hawks hovering overhead. In the distance, the Santa Lucia Mountains rising steeply from the sea and ranging south toward Big Sur.[1]

Years later, visiting England, Jeffers confessed in a letter that he did not care for trees since they made the landscape soft and fluffy. He liked the violence of the sea, the spectacular cloudbanks at sunrise and sunset that would give the mountainous coast the feel of high drama on any given day. It suited his temperament perfectly. Jeffers was a brooding loner who made even those who knew him well somewhat ill at ease. He never had a single friend as far as I can tell. The local stories and legends he retold in his narrative poems, he heard from his wife, who took the trouble to talk to the neighbors. She often encouraged him to write, answered most of his mail, and was the first reader of all his poems. Una was a strong-willed woman, far more ambitious and opinionated than her husband, and appears to have been as tough to get along with as he was. On one hand, they seem to have lived in near-complete isolation, and then—it doesn't seem so. He read Nietzsche, Vico, Spengler, and psychoanalytic literature. Just as one decides that Jeffers was hopelessly out of touch with intellectual currents of his time, he takes one back by some remarkable insight:

> We obey in fact, consciously or not, two opposed systems of morality. They cannot be reconciled, yet we cling to both of them, and serve two masters. (We have in fact two moralities,

which cannot be reconciled, yet most of us cling to both of them.) We believe in the Christian virtues, universal love, self-abnegation, humility, non-resistance; but we believe also, as individuals and as nations, in the pagan virtues of our ancestors: justice with its corollary vengeance, pride and personal honor, will to power, patriotic readiness to meet force with force. Our conduct almost always compromises between these contradictory moralities. And the great movements of Christianity—the Crusades, for instance, or the great colonizations, or the French and Russian revolutions—are inspired and confused by both of them.[2]

The little prose Jeffers wrote is of the highest quality and the best of it is fortunately included in the back of *The Selected Poetry*. His letters are perhaps not as interesting. A number of them are helpful on matters of his poetry, but the rest tend to be a bit formal and not very forthcoming. His poems are the best clue to what he had on his mind, and that's where the difficulty arises. He wrote so much. *The Collected Poems*, also edited by Tim Hunt, comes in four thick volumes, plus an additional one of textual evidence and commentaries. The new *Selected Poems* is almost 750 pages long, which must be a world record. The volume includes five of his lengthy narrative poems, which take up more than half of the book. I have no objection to including "Tamar" and "Roan Stallion," because they are the best of the lot. Having the others in the book, however, defeats the entire idea of a selection and is bound to scare away many readers. Robert Hass's decision to stick to short poems in his 1987 compilation was wiser in my view.

One can argue, I suppose, that one needs to read a lot of Jeffers to appreciate his range. That includes all the violent, sexually charged, and blasphemous parts of his long, narrative poems that shocked some of his early readers and that one would otherwise miss. No doubt, many individual passages are magnificent poetry, but it's difficult to make a case that they succeed in their entirety as poems. Like many other poets, Jeffers was not content with just his lyrical gift. He wanted some epic sweep so he could dramatize and investigate complex issues like family conflicts and in the process impart momentous wisdom to his contemporaries. He was more than capable of bringing off a dramatic scene or two, but his narrative poems, nevertheless, feel contrived to me. The overbearing presence of a didactic purpose undercuts his characters, who are not very believable to me to begin with. The long poems have their admirers, but I'm not convinced that they belong with his best work.

Jeffers's short poems, on the other hand, pack a lot of power. Here is one of his best-known poems from *Tamar* (1917–23):

Shine, Perishing Republic

While this America settles in the mould of its vulgarity,
    heavily thickening to empire,
And protest, only a bubble in the molten mass, pops and
    sighs out, and the mass hardens,
I sadly smiling remember that the flower fades to make
    fruit, the fruit rots to make earth.
Out of the mother; and through the spring exultances,
    ripeness and decadence; and home to the mother.
You making haste on decay: not blameworthy; life is good,
    be it stubbornly long or suddenly
A mortal splendor: meteors are not needed less than
    mountains: shine, perishing republic.
But for my children, I would have them keep their distance
    from the thickening center; corruption
Never has been compulsory, when the cities lie at the
    monster's feet there are left the mountains.
And boys, be in nothing so moderate as in love of man, a
    clever servant, insufferable master.
There is the trap that catches noblest spirits, that caught—
    they say—God, when he walked on earth.

Jeffers, unlike Auden, thought poems could make things happen. "There is good poetry," he wrote in a letter, "that expresses hatred of injustice, love of freedom."[3] He didn't mean by that some form of propaganda, but a single man's passion to make the world right. While the Modernists were mostly averse to spelling out what the experience in the poem means and allowed the readers to draw their own conclusions, Jeffers, especially in his political poems, liked to mount the soapbox. Nor did he subscribe to Ezra Pound's dictum that the poet must tread in fear of abstractions. He strove to persuade us and move us by the strength of his argument. Like so many other classic American writers, he had a low opinion of what had become of our democracy. He was an old-fashioned Jeffersonian Republican, no friend of progress or empire building, who all his life railed against smugness, greed, and what he called "flunkyism" in our public life. Ordinarily, I don't like being lectured in a poem, but there are numerous passages of his and a few whole poems where his rhetoric turns oracular and ought to strike a chord today:

> The war that we have carefully for years provoked
> Catches us unprepared, amazed and indignant.

The ultimate outcome of our love affair with technology, he thought, would not be comfort or improvement in our lives, but soulless triumphs and unrelieved tragedy. Long before the ecology movement, he warned about elevating our selfish concerns over those of other creatures who share the planet with us. Civilization was the enemy of man, he said again and again. As interesting as this Cassandra side of Jeffers is, his best work lies elsewhere in poems that do not aspire to warn and instruct. Their intentions are much more modest, since they tend to be mostly re-creations of some particular experience where the aesthetic considerations are as important as the ideas and often even more so:

> All the arts lose virtue
> Against the essential reality
> Of creatures going about their business among the equally
> Earnest elements of nature.

There's nothing of Emerson's optimism in Jeffers, as Hass points out. Human consciousness has no special meaning for him. Nor is the presence of a higher, spiritual element in nature a given. He was too much of a materialist for that. What he wanted was a radical philosophical shift in emphasis and significance. Humanity was neither central nor important to the universe. Man in his self-absorption imagined that he was God's favorite, while in all probability he admires the cockroach as much. For Jeffers, as far as I can make out, God is merely a part of creation and certainly no special friend of humanity. "He is like an old Basque shepherd," he wrote in one of his final poems:

> Who was brought to California fifty years ago,
> He has always been alone, he talks to himself,
> Solitude has got into his brain,
> Beautiful and terrible things come from his mind.[4]

He may have been describing himself. "But look how beautiful—are all the things that he does," he continues. He meant a God whose signature was the beauty of things. It's not belief but awe that held Jeffers spellbound, what he called "divinely superfluous beauty." He discerned God's presence in examples of his excesses, the way, for instance, he endowed a seashell on the bottom of the sea with a rainbow. Like countless such examples in nature, the marvel was there long before there were eyes to appreciate it. The heartbreaking beauty of the world has nothing to do with us. It will still be here, he said, when there is no heart to break for it:

Fire on the Hills

The deer were bounding like blown leaves
Under the smoke in front of the roaring wave of the
    brushfire;
I thought of the smaller lives that were caught.
Beauty is not always lovely; the fire was beautiful, the terror
Of the deer was beautiful; and when I returned
Down the black slopes after the fire had gone by, an eagle
Was perched on the jag of a burnt pine,
Insolent and gorged, cloaked in the folded storms of his
    shoulders.
He had come from far off for the good hunting
With fire for his beater to drive the game; the sky was
    merciless
Blue, and the hills merciless black,
The sombre-feathered great bird sleepily merciless between
    them.
I thought, painfully, but the whole mind,
The destruction that brings an eagle from heaven is better
    than mercy.

Czeslaw Milosz in one of the early appreciations of the poet is both attracted by Jeffers's intellectual independence and put off by his terrifying vision of blind necessity. That his "truth" was a harsh one, he himself knew. Now and then we may agree with him, but it's not easy to live with that knowledge. I once looked into the eyes of a hawk sitting on my windowsill in Santa Rosa, California, and the no-nonsense, matter-of-fact astuteness of that gaze is not something I'm likely to forget. For Jeffers, this is what one had to come to terms with. Not turn away from it, as we usually do in life, but act on it and accept the consequences. He had the idea that what is most disliked in his poems is what is most true, and he may have been right about that:

Hurt Hawks

I

The broken pillar of the wing jags from the clotted
     shoulder,
The wing trails like a banner in defeat,
No more to use the sky forever but live with famine
And pain a few days: cat nor coyote
Will shorten the week of waiting for death, there is game
     without talons.
He stands under the oak-bush and waits
The lame feet of salvation; at night he remembers freedom
And flies in a dream, the dawns ruin it.
He is strong and pain is worse to the strong, incapacity is
     worse.
The curs of the day come and torment him
At distance, no one but death the redeemer will humble
     that head,
The intrepid readiness, the terrible eyes.
The wild God of the world is sometimes merciful to those
That ask mercy, not often to the arrogant.
You do not know him, you communal people, or you have
     forgotten him;
Intemperate and savage, the hawk remembers him;
Beautiful and wild, the hawks, and men that are dying,
     remember him.

I'd sooner, except the penalties, kill a man than a hawk; but
    the great redtail
Had nothing left but unable misery
From the bones too shattered for mending, the wing that
    trailed under his talons when he moved.
We had fed him six weeks, I gave him freedom,
He wandered over the foreland hill and returned in the
    evening, asking for death,
Not like a beggar, still eyed with the old
Implacable arrogance. I gave him the lead gift in the
    twilight. What fell was relaxed,
Owl-downy, soft feminine feathers; but what
Soared: the fierce rush: the night-herons by the flooded
    river cried fear at its rising
Before it was quite unsheathed from reality.

Jeffers's philosophy has been called "inhumanism," and yet
what moves us about his finest poems is not only the starkness
of his vision but his genuine compassion. "Throat-bandaged
dogs cowering in cages," he starts a poem about laboratory animals, "still obsessed with the pitiful / Love that dogs feel, longing to lick the hand of their devil." When it came to birds and
animals, he saw clearly and memorably. So unlike us in their
inner strength and heroic resignation to the inevitable, they
represented for him an ethical ideal. He knew it was impossible
to emulate them and then sometimes he pretended that it was.

"Beauty, is the sole business of poetry," we read in a poem.
Most of the time, however, Jeffers did not take his own advice.
The serenity he sought eluded him. He was a tormented man,
as anyone can see reading his late poems. Undoubtedly, they are
more interesting as confessions of a very private man than as poetry. "I seem to hear in the nights many estimable people
screaming like babies," he writes in one of them, suggesting how
far he was from caring only about animals.[5] From what we know
about his life, it's not clear what his own reasons for screaming
were. When he prophesied and rose in wrath against his fellow
human beings, he may have given a temporary rest to these torments, but he generally failed as a poet. He longed for the timeless, but he was at his most poignant when he wrote about the

fleeting moment. The intensity of the experience sharpened his eye and made his language and imagery precise. This, of course, is the paradox of the lyric poem. It has a way of catching the permanent on the wing, as it were, and seemingly without trying. In a dozen or so such poems, when he lets his lyric genius take him where *it* wants to go, Jeffers is peerless, a poet everyone ought to read:

Evening Ebb

The ocean has not been so quiet for a long while; five
    night-herons
Fly shorelong voices in the hush of the air
Over the calm of an ebb that almost mirrors their wings.
The sun has gone down, and the water has gone down
From the weed-clad rock, but the distant cloud-wall rises.
    The ebb whispers.
Great cloud-shadows float in the opal water.
Through rifts in the screen of the world pale gold gleams
    and the evening
Star suddenly glides like a flying torch.
As if we had not been meant to see her; rehearsing behind
The screen of the world for another audience.

NOTES

1. *Rock and Hawk: A Selection of Shorter Poems by Robinson Jeffers,* ed. Robert Hass (Random House, 1987), p. xv.

2. Melba Berry Bennett, *The Stone Mason of Tor House: The Life and Work of Robinson Jeffers* (Ward Ritchie Press, 1966), pp. 135–36.

3. *The Selected Letters of Robinson Jeffers 1987–1962,* ed. Ann N. Ridgeway (Johns Hopkins University Press, 1968), p. 241.

4. *Collected Poetry of Robinson Jeffers,* vol. 3, *1938–1962,* ed. Tim Hunt (Stanford University Press, 1991), p. 454.

5. *Collected Poetry,* vol. 3, p. 448.

The Mystery of Presence

Polish poetry is one of the marvels of twentieth-century literature. As usually happens with work written in one of the less
well-known languages, its many riches were nearly unknown
until fairly recently. Many minor French and Spanish poets were
translated before Czeslaw Milosz and Wislawa Szymborska became widely read in this country. Long before these two received Nobel Prizes for Literature in 1980 and 1996 respectively,
however, there was an anthology, *Postwar Polish Poetry*, edited by
Milosz in 1965. The book introduced a number of other fine
poets, among them Aleksander Wat, Tadeusz Rozewicz, Tymo-
teusz Karpowicz, Jerzy Harasymowicz, and finally Zbigniew Herbert, who ranks among the greatest poets of the last century.
Polish poetry has one rare virtue: it is very readable in a time
when Modernist experiments have made a lot of poetry written
elsewhere difficult, if not outright hermetic. Here's a little prose
poem by Herbert to show what I mean:

The End of a Dynasty

The whole royal family was living in one room at that time.
Outside the windows was a wall, and under the wall, a
dump. There, rats used to bite cats to death. This was not
seen. The windows had been painted over with lime.

When the executioners came, they found an everyday
scene.

His Majesty was improving the regulations of the Holy

Review of *Without End: New and Selected Poems*, by Adam Zagajewski,
trans. Clare Cavanagh, Renata Gorczynski, Benjamin Ivry, and C. K.
Williams; and *Another Beauty*, trans. Clare Cavanagh. From the *New York
Review of Books*, May 9, 2002.

Trinity regiment, the occultist Philippe was trying to soothe the Queen's nerves by suggestion, the Crown Prince, rolled into a ball, was sleeping in an armchair, and the Grand (and skinny) Duchesses were singing pious songs and mending linen.

As for the valet, he stood against a partition and tried to imitate the tapestry.[1]

The accessibility of the poems may have something to do with the country's tragic history. Between 1939 and 1945, both Germany and Russia occupied Poland at different times, its borders were redrawn, and its civilian population was gassed and massacred in large numbers. Afterward, there were more than four decades of communism with their own terrors. Most likely, the pressure of that stark reality made the language games beloved by the avant-garde sound too much like escapism. "There is no bottom to evil," Aleksander Wat says in a poem. The knowledge of the cruelties human beings are capable of inflicting on other human beings is always in the background in these poems, not in theory but as a real possibility. The poets in Milosz's anthology could have been as easily killed as their neighbors were. "Here are people who refused to cheat, who eagerly sought out the truth and shrank from neither poetry nor terror, the two poles of our globe," writes Adam Zagajewski in his memoir, *Another Beauty*. The surprise is not that these Polish poets know all about murder of the innocent but that their vision is often comic. They are funny, skeptical, and sly, as any citizen of a totalitarian country or any prisoner is likely to be.

Zagajewski was born in 1945 and thus missed out on the horrors of the Second World War but he grew up under communism in a country as dreary as the barracks, he tells us. What he shares with the poets of the previous generation is the country's unhappy history of which he himself, too, is the product. "I lost two homelands as a child," he writes. "I lost the city where I was born, the city where countless generations of my family had lived before my birth." Lvov had become a part of Soviet Ukraine, and shortly after his birth his parents were repatriated to Gliwice, a small town in Silesia. He studied philosophy at the Jagiellonian University in Kraków and made his debut in 1972 as one of the leading poets of what was then called the Polish New Wave. An active dissident during the years of the Solidarity movement, he emigrated to Paris in 1982. Since then his work has been translated into most European languages, and there have been three well-received collections of poetry and three books of essays translated into English before the appearance of these two books. Zagajewski is now one of the most familiar and highly regarded names in poetry both in Europe and in this country.

He was not a good philosophy student, he informs us in his memoir. He could not apply himself diligently to the close study of the great works, could not refine a concept or elaborate a new subtlety on the basis of some already existing concept. Without quite realizing it, he was already a poet, happier to make things up as he went along. Teaching Plato and Kant in a police state was an extremely risky occupation. His teachers were mostly frightened men who tried to keep a low profile and only hinted now and then at what they knew. Despite the constraints put on them by the political system and his own diffidence about the subject he was studying, it is clear from Zagajewski's memoir that the study of philosophy nonetheless had a great effect on him. In a poem entitled "Ode to Plurality" he writes:

> . . . Who once
> touched philosophy is lost
> and won't be saved by a poem
> . . . Who once learned a wild
> run of poetry will not taste anymore
> the stony calm of family narratives
> . . . Who has once met
> irony will burst into laughter
> during the prophet's lecture. . . .

Despite their range of subject matter, both *Another Beauty* and *Solidarity, Solitude,* his earlier book of essays, are in truth notes of someone working out a philosophical position in the guise of writing about many other seemingly unrelated things. That a poet may be also a secret metaphysician may strike one as an idle boast, yet if he or she is serious, there is no choice in the matter. The dispute concerning the nature of reality has been a burning issue in both literature and painting at least since the Romantics—if not long before. For someone like Zagajewski, growing up in a country where all questions large and small had already been answered by the official ideology and where each person was obliged to forfeit his right to make up his own mind on any important subject, the search for truth was far more a pressing necessity than it is with us who may feel that we have all the time in the world. In his poetry and his memoir, he asks himself again and again and in a variety of ways about truth. Here is how he describes his predicament:

> I'm not a historian, but I'd like literature to assume, consciously and in all seriousness, the function of a historical chronicle. I don't want it to follow the example set by modern historians, cold fish by and large, who spend their lives in vanquished archives and write in an inhuman, ugly, wooden, bureaucratic language from which all poetry's been driven, a language flat as a wood louse and petty as the daily paper. I'd like it to return to earlier examples, maybe even Greek, to the ideal of the historian poet, a person who either has seen and experienced what he describes for himself, or has drawn upon a living oral tradition, his family's or his tribe's, who doesn't fear engagement and emotion, but who cares nonetheless about his story's truthfulness.

Zagajewski goes on to argue that we are witnessing a revival of literature that serves this very purpose: writers' journals, memoirs, poets' autobiographies that revive an archaic tradition, the writing of history from the viewpoint of what he calls a "sovereign individual." Among the models to emulate he mentions the autobiographical writings of Edwin Muir, Czeslaw Milosz, and Joseph Brodsky, the essays of Nicola Chiaromonte, and the notebooks of Albert Camus. His own memoir clearly belongs in that company, both for the way it is put together and for its high quality. Its clipped, collage-like aspect makes me think of the contents of a photographer's wastebasket. One reaches down and retrieves the torn pieces of photographs one at a time. A life, especially of someone young and still unsure of his identity, does not make for a coherent narrative or picture. One gets at *it*—if at all—by piecing together fragments of a lifetime. Such loose chronology allows Zagajewski to skip from subject to subject as he pleases in his memoir. In *Another Beauty* there are reminiscences of teachers, friends, landladies, uncles, and aunts, lyrical descriptions of Kraków, meditations on music, painting, and philosophical questions, together with short passages that read like prose poems and parables. His prose is dazzling and so is the translation by Clare Cavanagh. Here he is writing about blackbirds:

> The blackbird's song can't be compared with art, with Bach's arias; its sense eludes us completely, and if we listen too long, it may strike us as monotonous. For all this, though, it expresses us, it expresses human beings too. It's a love song, and so it's our song, the song of those who sleep and love, or loved once upon a time. What a pity that we sleep as they sing, that we aren't there to hear it, that our ears are sunk in the pillows' warm substance.
>
> And to think that this frenzied concert, this extraordinary concert full of passion, provoking pity and envy, takes place each day at daybreak from March to June in every European city, London, Munich, Krakow, Arezzo, Stockholm. An unheard concert aimed straight at the sky, unreviewed, unattended, unrewarded, unpaid, with egoless artists.
>
> The poor blackbirds sang most beautifully when no one could hear them except for policemen, milkmen (back when there were still milkmen), janitors scurrying to bureaus and offices, and of course insomniacs. Who knows, perhaps the inhabitants of those cities would be slightly different, a bit more generous, transformed somehow, if they'd heard this concert, which speaks to the human heart even though it's intended in principle for the hearts of small songbirds alone.
>
> When the concert had ended, as it always does, around sunrise, when daylight vanquishes the night's intruders, silence fell, a moment of quiet, which then quickly filled with the following sound: the carefree, silly chattering of sparrows.

The most absorbing questions are the ones we cannot answer, he writes elsewhere in the book. There is something mysterious in the way the earth and things exist, he says. The nothingness that troubles certain thinkers is not their concern. They agree to every kind of light, every kind of weather so that they may seize each moment and exist. They have no time to bother themselves with our ever-changing theories of reality; being in that moment is a serious enough task for them. Zagajewski has in mind something as ordinary as the sight of an apple on the table, except, as he says, there are no ordinary apples for those who open their eyes.

The earliest of his poems translated into English for this new volume are already notable for their polished surface. Most likely, he started out as a poet by critically picking and choosing from the work of his elders and discarding their false notes. If the aesthetic positions available to him ranged roughly from various Polish versions of realism, symbolism, or surrealism, Zagajewski makes a home for them all. His poems have an air of composure that is rarely found in the poetry of the earlier generation.

A number of those poets were fond of striking a cynical, world-weary pose. Not Zagajewski. Still, when it comes to subject matter their influence is very much present in his work. For instance, I can't think of another poetic tradition where there are so many poems about philosophers and their ideas, or poems about paintings and music. What is frequently an almost unfailing poetic recipe for cultural snobbery and irrelevance appears to have worked wonders in Poland. Zagajewski himself has poems about Husserl, Beethoven, Schopenhauer, Kierkegaard, Van Gogh, Schubert, Nietzsche, Morandi, Bruckner, Weil, and a number of other thinkers, musicians, and painters. Again and again he surprises the reader. His philosophical probity and his wit make poetry out of what at first may sound like a mini-essay on an assigned topic. Here is a poem from *Tremor* (1985), his earliest collection in English:

The Self

It is small and no more visible than a cricket
in August. It likes to dress up, to masquerade,
as all dwarfs do. It lodges between
granite blocks, between serviceable
truths. It even fits under
a bandage, under adhesive. Neither customs officers
nor their beautiful dogs will find it. Between

hymns, between alliances, it hides itself.
It camps in the Rocky Mountains of the skull.
An eternal refugee. It is I and I,
with the fearful hope that I have found at last
a friend, am it. But the self
is so lonely, so distrustful, it does not
accept anyone, even me.
It clings to historical events
no less tightly than water to a glass.
It could fill a Neolithic jar.
It is insatiable, it wants to flow
in aqueducts, it thirsts for newer and newer vessels.
It wants to taste space without walls,
diffuse itself, diffuse itself. Then it fades away
like desire, and in the silence of an August
night you hear only crickets patiently
conversing with the stars.

We tend to assume that lyricism has solely to do with some overpowering emotion—and it does—but we forget that it is not only love, grief, or beauty that gives rise to powerful feelings. Abstract ideas can similarly engage the imagination and be a subject of a lyric poem, as Wallace Stevens often demonstrated. The mind in moments of exceptional clarity is where Zagajewski finds his epiphanies. That mind, as we saw already, is steeped in the history and culture of Europe. This may sound pretty obvious, but it turns out not to be. Poets like Rilke, who seem to be at home everywhere and of whom Zagajewski at times reminds me, are not typical. The great poets of any given country are more likely to be proud provincials. It is among the exiles that one usually encounters such a worldly outlook, although with them it is not a matter of choice but of necessity:

A woodpecker cables
an urgent report on the capture of
Carthage and on the Boston Tea Party.

"Man's personality possesses something untamed, mysterious, divine, unhistorical, undomesticated, something that speaks quietly in art, in religion, in the search for truth and it is exactly this delicate something that is the hunted animal, preyed upon by Political Systems and their countless conformities," he writes in one of my favorite passages in *Solidarity, Solitude*. That seems to me as good a reason as I've ever encountered to read the philosophers, look at art, listen to great music, and write about them. Cultural allusions, which in an American poet like Ezra Pound often sound like a high form of tourism, come across as the most natural thing in Zagajewski. The knowledge of arts and music, one ends up feeling, is as much a part of his empirical self as eating bread and drinking water.

Even children ought to know, Zagajewski says, that at least two kingdoms exist and two rulers: history and spirit. In the early Middle Ages, he claims, Western monks occupied themselves intensely with the cultivation of wheat fields and grapevines in addition to contemplation. They were able to be, at one and the same time, mystics and husbandmen. That is the ideal he himself seeks. The poet is a born centrist, he says. This concern on Zagajewski's part for the concrete particulars is a curative against any temptation of pure art. As his poetry makes evident, even his experiences of the sacred come from encounters with things of this world. There are many beautiful poems in *Without End* that dramatize a moment when consciousness expands and time comes to a stop:

It Comes to a Standstill

The city comes to a standstill
and life turns into still life,
it is as brittle as plants in a herbarium.
You ride a bicycle which doesn't
move, only the houses wheel by,
slowly, showing their noses, brows,
and pouting lips. The evening becomes
a still life, it doesn't feel like existing,
therefore it glistens like a Chinese lantern
in a peaceful garden. Nightfall, motionless,
the last one. The last word. Happiness

hovers in the crowns of the trees.
Inside the leaves, kings are asleep.
No word, the yellow sail of the sun
towers over the roofs like a tent abandoned
by Caesar. Pain becomes still life and despair
is only a still life, framed
by the mouth of one passerby. The square
keeps silent in a dark foliage of birds'
wings. Silence as on the fields of Jena
after the battle when loving women
look at the faces of the slain.

Mysticism for Beginners is the title of one of Zagajewski's collections of poetry. How appropriate, one thinks. The poet and the reader are, indeed, both perpetual beginners. In spite of what the scholars tend to believe, the poet has no advance knowledge to impart. Today, certainly, he no longer plays the role of the Romantic or Symbolist seer for whom the heavens open and the vision of ultimate things comes into view. Zagajewski is suspicious of the rhetoric of visionary hype, which is more often a product of the imagination's endless quarrel with reality than of a genuine experience of the sublime. He's equally wary of poets who become poetry's ironic persecutors because it cannot deliver what it promises. Woe to a writer who values beauty over truth, he writes—and woe to the one who only seeks truth, one may add.

"A writer who keeps a personal diary uses it to record what he knows. In his poems and stories he sets down what he doesn't know," Zagajewski observes in his memoir. That makes perfect sense to me. If that were not the case, how would one experience the world anew and stand still in astonishment before that apple on the table? He is very clear about the kind of meaning poetry expresses, if we compare it to history and philosophy. The difference is, he says, that poetry deals with new meanings. It calls to mind the image of a chestnut that has fallen from the tree and lost its husk, stunningly young, pink as a scar. This, if one is honest about it, is about all one can expect from a poem. Poetry never gives answers to philosophical questions, or if it does it can only do so through people and things by reminding us that they cast an odd shadow now and then:

We'd talked long into the night
in the kitchen; the oil lamp glowed softly,
and objects, heartened by its calm,
came forth from the dark to offer
their names: chair, table, pitcher.
At midnight you said, Come out,
and in the dark there we saw the sky of August
explode with its stars.
Eternal, unconfined, night's pale sheen
trembled above us.
The world noiselessly burned,
white fire enveloped it all, villages,
churches, haystacks scented with clover
and mint. Trees burned, and spires,
wind, flame, water and air.
Why is night so silent if volcanoes
keep their eyes open and if the past
stays present, threatening, lurking
in its lair like junipers or the moon?
Your lips are cool, and the dawn will be, too,
a cloth on a feverish brow.

There are times in life when one has the feeling that one has partaken of some larger truth. Only a small part of it, of course, since the whole of it, as Zagajewski says, is mute. The poet can remind us of that experience, as he does in a number of poems. Although he confides to us about such extraordinary moments, we learn little about his private life. The voice of his poems, even when he speaks of works of art and musical compositions that may not be very well-known to the reader, is, nevertheless, intimate. There's some of Whitman's magnanimity in this poet of almost classical elegance and reticence. I'm not telling you anything you already do not have within yourself, he seems to say, so sit back and listen.

I am unable to judge the quality of the translations since I cannot read Polish with confidence, but mostly they sound convincing to me. Zagajewski's poems are visually rich and images as a rule can be translated from one language to another without appreciable loss. He is not the most innovative of poets;

however, his images are often startlingly fresh. This is true of his prose too. He likes to spring a surprise on the reader by cutting—in a cinematic kind of way—from one image to another. A poet has to give the reader the impression that the image both came out of nowhere and is absolutely inevitable. If form is about exercising caution, the image is all about recklessness. It's a gamble, a throw of dice. At the heart of every powerful image there is an incommunicable *something* that can only be conveyed by an image still to come:

Opus Posthumous

The train stopped in a field; the sudden silence
startled even sleep's most ardent partisans.
The distant lights of shops or factories
glittered in the haze like the yellow eyes of wolves.
Businessmen on trips stooped over their computers,
totting up the day's losses and gains.
The stewardess poured coffee steeped in bitterness.
Ewig, ewig, last word. *Song of the Earth,*
it repeats so often; remember how we listened
to this music, to the promise that
we so longed to believe.
We don't know if we're still in Holland,
this may be Belgium now. No matter.
An early winter evening, and the earth hid
beneath thick streaks of dusk; you could
sense the presence of a canal's black water,
unmoving, stripped of mountain currents' joy
and the great amazement of our oceans.
Wolves' yellow eyes were quivering with a nervous
neon light, but no one feared an Indian attack.
The train stopped at that moment when our reason starts
to stir, but the soul, its noble yearning, is asleep.
We were listening a different time to Schubert,
that posthumous quintet where despair declares itself
insistently, intently, almost insatiably,
renewing its assault on the indifference
of the genteel concert hall, ladies in their furs
and the reviewers, minor envoys of the major papers.
And once out walking, midnight, summer in the country,
a strange sound stopped us short: snorting and neighing

of unseen horses in a pasture. As though
the night laughed happily to itself.
What is poetry if we see so little?
What is salvation if there is no threat?
Posthumous quintet! Only music keeps on growing
after death, music and the hair of trees.
As if rivers gave ecstatic milk and honey,
as if dancers danced in frenzy once again

· ·

And yet we're not alone. One day some guitar
worn by time will start singing for itself alone.
And the train moves at last, the earth rocks
underneath its stately weight and slowly
Paris draws close, with its golden aura,
its gray doubt.

Poetry and thinking for Zagajewski have to do with learning
how to see clearly. His poems celebrate those rare moments
when we catch a glimpse of a world from which all labels have
been unpeeled. I imagine he would agree with E. M. Cioran,
who says, "We are born to exist, not to know; to be, not to assert
ourselves."[2] That may not sound like much, but once one gets
over the disappointment and takes stock of what is philosophically possible in a patient and reasonable way, as Zagajewski has,
that may be all we can be sure of in the end. In the meantime,
there's the continuing mystery of presence and these two indispensable books to remind us of it.

NOTES

1. *Postwar Polish Poetry,* ed. Czeslaw Milosz (1965; University of California Press, 1983), p. 141.
2. E. M. Cioran, *History and Utopia* (Seaver, 1987), p. 42.

The Always Vanishing World

Tell me what you see vanishing and I
Will tell you who you are
—W. S. Merwin, "For Now"

The Pupil is W. S. Merwin's eighteenth book of poetry, and that's not counting the four volumes of selected poems that have appeared over the years. He has also published books of prose poems, family reminiscences, collections of miscellaneous prose, and at least twenty books of translations. This is an astounding and probably unequaled body of work among contemporary American poets. I recall an essay by Walter Benjamin in which he lists various available critical approaches and contends that a good essay perhaps could consist entirely of quotations from the author under review. Merwin would be a perfect subject. He has translated from Spanish, French, Italian, Portuguese, and Provençal, the languages he knows well, and with the help of others from Russian, Swedish, Native American languages, Incan, Mayan, Eskimo, Japanese, Sanskrit, Persian, Turkish, Urdu, and a few other languages that I've surely missed. His rendering of *Sir Gawain and the Green Knight* is due out this summer. Being prolific is seldom a guarantee of a consistent quality, but in his case a reader can count on a thorough education in comparative literature and an immense amount of pleasure from his many collections of poetry.

Merwin was born in New York in 1927 and was raised in Union City, New Jersey, and afterward in Scranton, Pennsylvania, in a strict religious household. His father was a Presbyterian minister. He went to Princeton where he studied with R. P.

Review of *The Pupil* and *The Mays of Ventadorn*, by W. S. Merwin. From the *New York Review of Books*, July 18, 2002.

Blackmur and John Berryman and also took courses in Romance languages. In an interview Merwin says, "I went to see Ezra Pound when I was nineteen or so. He told me something that I think I really already knew." In *The Mays of Ventadorn*, Merwin's short history of the beginnings of troubadour poetry in the twelfth century and a delightful memoir of two decades he spent living on and off in a farmhouse in southwest France, he writes about that meeting:

> "If you're going to be a poet," he said, "you have to work at it every day. You should write about seventy-five lines a day. But at your age you don't have anything to write about. You may think you do, but you don't. So get to work translating. The Provençal is the real source. The poets are closest to music. They hear it. They write to it. Try to learn the Provençal, at least some of it, if you can. Meanwhile, the others. Spanish is all right. The *Romancero* is what you want there. Get as close to the original as you can. It will make you use your English and find out what you can do with it."

This is still excellent advice and Merwin followed it. "Translation helps you finish your education," Merwin said in that interview. Indeed. Is there anyone who makes a closer and more empirical study of one's own language than a translator? Translation is one of the very few human activities where the impossible actually occurs on a fairly regular basis. Merwin once said that translation of comedy is one of the great disciplines because in translating jokes, if one gets anything wrong, nothing works. This is true of poetry too, where not only the words have to be translated but also the tone of voice, the prosody with its meaningful pauses, and various other near-intangibles that make a poem or a joke what it is.

Merwin's first book of poems, *A Mask of Janus*, was selected by W. H. Auden for the Yale Series of Younger Poets Award in 1952. What strikes one immediately about the poems is their literary refinement. This young poet has read a lot of literature in several languages and has become skilled in prosody. One can detect the influence of T. S. Eliot, Wallace Stevens, Robert Graves, and Elizabeth Bishop among a few others, but the poet himself is invisible in his poems. He wears masks as he tries different roles and voices. As Pound told him, "it was important to regard writing as not a chance or romantic or inspired (in the occasional sense) thing, but rather a kind of spontaneity which arises out of discipline and continual devotion to something."

In other words, poetry is not about self-expression, but art. The poet owes an unswerving commitment to the poem at hand and nothing else. Like so many pronouncements made about poetry over the centuries, this is both absolutely right and absolutely wrong since poems often tend to be made out of contradictory and to all appearances incompatible impulses.

At that young age, Merwin was perhaps as much a disciple of perfection as young James Merrill was. They shared a love of European literature and had no anxiety whether that made them less American. That identity question was, of course, very much on the minds of Emerson, Whitman, and many of the Modernists, but it ceased to be an issue with these two. While fully recognizing that Americans do have a distinct poetic tradition and a language, Merwin did not have to fret if at times he sounded like François Villon. As Pound had already discovered, there was something unmistakably contemporary about ancient Roman and Provençal poetry. It was their self-consciousness as poets and downright mockery of literary conventions that made them at times sound modern.

Three other volumes of poetry quickly followed *A Mask for Janus*. They are *The Dancing Bears* (1954), *Green with Beasts* (1956), and *The Drunk in the Furnace* (1960). Here's the famous title poem from that book:

The Drunk in the Furnace

For a good decade
The furnace stood in the naked gully, fireless
And vacant as any hat. Then when it was
No more to them than a hulking black fossil
To erode unnoticed with the rest of the junk-hill
By the poisonous creek, and rapidly to be added
To their ignorance,

They were afterwards astonished
To confirm one morning, a twist of smoke like a pale
Resurrection, staggering out of its chewed hole,

And to remark then other tokens that someone,
Cosily bolted behind the eyeholed iron
Door of the drafty burner, had there established
His bad castle.

Where he gets his spirits
It's a mystery. But the stuff keeps him musical:
Hammer-and-anviling with poker and bottle
To his jugged bellowings, till the last groaning clang
As he collapses onto the rioting
Springs of a litter of car seats ranged on the grates,
To sleep like an iron pig.

In their tar-paper church
On a text about stoke holes that are sated never
Their Reverend lingers. They nod and hate trespassers.
When the furnace wakes, though, all afternoon
Their witless offspring flock like piped rats to its siren
Crescendo, and agape on the crumbling ridge
Stand in a row and learn.

Reading this poem I always recall Merwin's hometown, Scranton, with its huge car graveyard visible years ago to anyone driving through town. A junk heap to top all junk heaps, a monument to rust and human futility. The distinguished classicist and translator Dudley Fitts, reviewing the book in the *New York Times Book Review,* was unhappy with the poem and thought it should have been much better. I get the impression that he did not care to see Orpheus compared to a bum. Relegated to a dump next to a polluted creek, this Orpheus makes the best of his predicament living in an abandoned furnace while keeping out of sight. All that's left for him to do is bang with his bottle against the rusty metal and raise hell. Ridiculous, disreputable, someone to warn small children against, he still attracts a youthful following. He is a descendant of Wallace Stevens's "The Man on the Dump." This is our reality, both poems say, the wreckage of things and ideas, where whatever truth is still to be had lies around in irreconcilable bits and pieces.

If Whitman and Dickinson are the prototypes of what an American poet could be, a bard commensurate in optimism with his people versus a recluse and a secret blasphemer, Merwin provides yet another model. As the critic Ed Folsom shrewdly observes, it is with Henry David Thoreau that he sets up his camp. I agree, and would only add, a Thoreau who in the meantime has read Samuel Beckett and the Surrealists. They share a reverence for the natural world, the suspicion of technology, and the ardent wish to live an independent and exemplary existence. Thoreau is also a wonderfully unpredictable thinker and writer. In his journals, alongside many marvelous insights and bits of description, one encounters phrases like "the tiger's musical smile," or "it snowed geometry," that any poet would envy. Rereading Merwin's collection *Lice* (1967), with its poems reduced to bare essentials, I thought of his *Walden* too:

Dusk in Winter

The sun sets in the cold without friends
Without reproaches after all it has done for us
It goes down believing in nothing
When it has gone I hear the stream running after it
It has brought its flute it is a long way

Here is one from *Carrier of Ladders* (1970):

Little Horse

You come from some other forest
do you
little horse
think how long I have known these
deep dead leaves
without meeting you

I belong to no one
I would have wished for you if I had known how
what a long time the place was empty
even in my sleep
and loving it as I did
I could not have told what was missing

what can I show you
I will not ask you if you will stay
or if you will come again

I will not try to hold you
I hope you will come with me to where I stand
often sleeping and waking
by the patient water
that has no father nor mother

Merwin's understanding of the power of individual images to stir the reader's imagination and his unerring ear for language made him pare down the poems to their lyric core. They are unpunctuated, but what in other poets seems like a pointless affectation in his hands becomes an example of formal virtuosity. The poems flow with nothing to arrest their movement. It was hard not to be bowled over by his example. Since autobiography and realistic re-creations of experience tend to be our chief aesthetic strategy, American poets are liable to overwrite. Like William Carlos Williams in an earlier generation, and Robert Creeley among his contemporaries, Merwin reminded us how much can be left out of a poem. He was trying to write directly, he explained, and more succinctly in a way that embodied more the cadence of spoken language. His poetry of this period has a minimum of narrative and depends instead on juxtaposition of images and talismanic repetition of certain key words to suggest content. "The gnostic leap without concern for logic" is how Merwin describes what attracted Pound to Confucius. That's true of him too. The poems, it has been pointed out, sound like fragments of creation myths, riddles, fairy tales, magic incantations, and parables composed by an unknown culture soon to be extinct. This is all correct, although frequently one is also able to detect in the poems unmistakable allusions to more recent history:

Caesar

My shoes are almost dead
And as I wait at the doors of ice
I hear the cry go up for him Caesar Caesar

But when I look out the window I see only the flatlands
And the slow vanishing of the windmills
The centuries draining the deep fields

Yet this is still my country
The thug on duty says What would you change
He looks at his watch he lifts
Emptiness out of the vases
And holds it up to examine

So it is evening
With the rain starting to fall forever

One by one he calls night out of the teeth
And at last I take up
My duty

Wheeling the president past banks of flowers
Past the feet of empty stairs
Hoping he's dead

The apocalyptic tone together with the anonymity of the speaker and the lack of specificity about time and place are both memorable and obscure. Readers and critics of poetry can be classified by how much vagueness they can tolerate in a poem. Undoubtedly, Merwin's images make their impact—like that one about wheeling the president past banks of flowers. "The true poet is the one who inspires," said Paul Valéry. At times more, at times less, the poet in us collaborates with the poet in the creation of such a poem. The poet's imagination temporarily becomes our imagination. It is a powerful experience and one that cannot always be readily accounted for and conceptualized. I may love an image while being clueless about what "my shoes are almost dead" and "waiting at the doors of ice" actually mean. Undoubtedly, this sparse, quasi-symbolist manner was a reaction to more descriptive and more autobiographical earlier poems. Merwin always searched for ways to renew the lyric, and some of these experiments, as one would expect, were more successful than others. Nonetheless, these poems with their teasing ambiguities have, justly or unjustly, become his signature. Some critics don't care for *The Moving Target, The Lice, The Carrier of Ladders,* and *Writing to an Unfinished Accompaniment,* all published between 1963 and 1974; others argue that his best and most original poetry is to be found in these books. I have mixed feelings. There are far stronger poems in his later collections in my view.

The volumes that follow, *The Compass Flower* (1977), *Opening the Hand* (1983), *The Rain in the Trees* (1988), are progressively far more grounded in specific circumstances and narrative. There are poems about his father, about the poets John Berryman and James Wright, about General Sheridan, and about a mugging in broad daylight. Endangered species, forests, and other environmentalist concerns are his themes. Merwin now wishes to make sure we understand the ethical consequences of what he's saying. Like Robinson Jeffers, he is appalled by our bloated self-regard as a species, our conviction that we are all that matters in the universe, able to force nature to change its laws if we so desire. To be aware of the natural world and every living creature in it and to be responsible for their keep is Merwin's hope. I share his alarm and his urgency. At the same time, when his poems become overly didactic, I grow uneasy. I like it better when he lets the particulars of experience work their meanings on their own without pointers along the way.

Merwin has always had a fondness for rustic life and its traditions. Inspecting the sky regarding tomorrow's weather, knowing how to transplant leeks and arrest the tomato wilt, is to him knowledge worthy of profound respect. *The Vixen,* which came out in 1996, is an homage to that vanishing world. It consists of sixty-four poems set in the same village in southwest France as *The Mays of Ventadorn.* In the memoir, he describes the first sight he had of the place in 1953:

> Along the ridge I came to a hamlet surrounded by shaggy fields, orchards, bits of wooded pasture, and I turned off into the long grass beside a wall. I saw the roofs of farms apparently long unused, complete with stone houses and barns, in the massive, elegant rural architecture of the Quercy, which had scarcely changed between the last of the crusades and the First World War. But it was a living village with its own unseen day-life going on, meals at noon in kitchens, smell of oak burning in stoves, hens scratching under walnut trees, sheep in the hillside pastures. The whole of it perhaps quite aware of strangers but seeming to pay no attention as I wandered through it.

The various neighbors and local characters are affectionately described in the poems, their stories and the history of the region and its poets recounted. The vixen of the title appears in several poems and by its mysterious, surprising presence links them together. If Merwin could be chastised for leaving too much out of his poetry in his minimalist phase, here he gets the measure just right. The poems are narrative and lyrical in equal proportion. Fragmentation, ellipsis, and the accompanying inference that words are failing the poet are replaced here by a voice that is unbroken and eloquent. *The Vixen,* as far as I'm concerned, is his finest book. There's not a single poem in it that fails to move me and astonish me by the beauty of its writing. Here's one—although I had a difficult time deciding which one to choose:

Season

This hour along the valley this light at the end
of summer lengthening as it begins to go
this whisper in the tawny grass this feather floating
in the air this house of half a life or so
this blue door open to the lingering sun this stillness
echoing from the rooms like an unfinished sound
this fraying of voices at the edge of the village
beyond the dusty gardens this breath of knowing
without knowing anything this old branch from which
years and faces go on falling this presence already
far away this restless alien in the cherished place
this motion with no measure this moment peopled
with absences with everything that I remember here
eyes the wheeze of the gate greetings birdsongs in winter
the heart dividing and everything
that has slipped my mind as I consider the shadow
all this has occurred to somebody else who has gone
as I am told and indeed it has happened again
and again and I go on trying to understand
how that could ever be and all I know of them
is what they felt in the light here in this late summer

Merwin's voice is far more intimate in *The Vixen.* He wants to draw us and share with us every luminous little detail in that world. Everything matters down to the clack of plates in the kitchen, the feel of the door latch yielding, a bulb in the glass of water at the sunlit window, and countless other realities that fill the lives of these people. His effort in the book, as in this poem, is to recover such ordinary and yet visionary moments when it appears to us as if the world is made of a single instant of time in which all past and future lives come together. To have such an experience does not only mean to taste immortality, as Romantic poets proclaimed, but also to get an inkling of the foundation of moral life. I mean, it's hard to picture one being indifferent to the slaughter of other living creatures and the bulldozing of wilderness afterward, although human beings, of course, are at times perfectly capable of just such monstrous contradictions.

The poems in Merwin's new book, *The Pupil*, although continuing and expanding some of these themes, are not as thematically connected. Their setting is the island of Maui, where Merwin has lived for many years now. The elegiac feel always present in his poetry is now even more pronounced. He recalls in one poem being surprised by his aged face reflected in a train window. He remembers his parents saying how he used to wake up laughing and that he was a happy child. In another poem he defines art. It is a beam of recognition that says that we are who we are individually while having something in common—not just with other men and women, but even with all other living creatures, like that penguin choosing a pebble to offer the lady penguin he hopes to charm.

And then there's this truly lovely poem:

Unknown Bird

Out of the dry days
through the dusty leaves
far across the valley
those few notes never
heard here before

one fluted phrase
floating over its
wandering secret
all at once wells up
somewhere else

and is gone before it
goes on fallen into
its own echo leaving
a hollow through the air
that is dry as before

where it is from
hardly anyone
seems to have noticed it
so far but who now
would have been listening

it is not native here
that may be the one
thing we are sure of
it came from somewhere
else perhaps alone

so keeps on calling for
no one who is here
hoping to be heard
by another of its own
unlikely origin

trying once more the same few
notes that began the song
of an oriole last heard
years ago in another
existence there

it goes again tell
no one it is here
foreign as we are
who are filling the days
with a sound of our own

Birds are many things metaphorically, including being poets.
This bird is like the last speaker of some soon-to-be-extinct language. In a world that is vanishing, it calls in hope that it may be
heard and answered. It will sing or fall silent whether we notice
it or not. And then when we *do* occasionally notice it, the surprise of finding ourselves lifted up by the ears, as it were, is a
sweet wonder. Bird song reminds us that there was always something simpler than we could ever quite believe in and find words

for, something that was always here, unnamed, unknown, and without which we could not go on living.

Like many poets, Merwin sought the authentic first in literature, then in the imaginative space of myth, and finally found it closer to home in the poetry of attentiveness. "We are in danger of forgetting the language which all things and events speak without metaphor," Thoreau wrote. At one time, a poem for Merwin was like the act of taking a rabbit out of a hat, a quest for an astonishing new image. Now it has to do with reverence, a way of finding and praising what has always been here. I imagine he would no longer regard the poet as a marginal figure, someone alternating between silence and banging on the walls of his "bad castle." The most eloquent poems and prose passages in his two new books remind us of our humanity, those little things that give sustenance to our lives: the light of a new day breaking, some unknown bird singing its heart out.

You Can't Keep a Good
Sonnet Down

"Seldom we find," says Solomon Don Dunce
"Half an idea in the profoundest sonnet."
    —Edgar Allan Poe, "An Enigma"

No poem can be more delightful or more idiotic than a sonnet. For every memorable one, thousands of bad ones—and I'm being charitable in my estimate—have been written over the centuries. I recall hearing some years ago of a professor who had composed a long sonnet cycle on the subject of Shakespeare's sonnets. It made me laugh but didn't really surprise me. Sonnets more than any other poems depend on precedent. Anyone writing one most probably has a sonnet he has admired in the back of his mind. At their most successful, they have an uncanny way of saying clever and serious things without sacrificing brevity. Nevertheless, with the ascendancy of free verse in the last hundred years and the Modernist hope to make poems unlike any that came before, the sonnet appeared doomed and in danger of becoming extinct like some rare species of songbird. Happily, as a couple of recent anthologies and these three new collections of poetry show, the form is thriving. In fact, it is recovering some of its old vigor.

A thirteenth-century Italian, Giacomo da Lentini, a notary at the court of Frederick II, wrote the first sonnet, in local Sicilian dialect. It was a new kind of lyric poem, one not supposed to be sung and accompanied by a musical instrument, but meant to

Review of *American Sonnets,* by Gerald Stern; *Swan Electric,* by April Bernard; and *A Short History of the Shadow,* by Charles Wright. From the *New York Review of Books,* September 6, 2002.

be read silently to oneself. It had only fourteen lines and was made up of two asymmetrical parts: a rhymed eight-line stanza and six additional lines with a different rhyme scheme. "Independence from musical performance freed the sonnet to exist as a self-sufficient microcosm, inviting a reader to follow its maze of meaning and sound at whatever pace one preferred," writes Phillis Levin in the recently published *Penguin Book of the Sonnet,* which she also edited.[1] Here then was a small box made of words for that psychological and metaphysical entity we call the self to lock itself in. Sonnets can be about many things, but they are inclined to be introspective. This self-consciousness is present in other lyric poems, but perhaps never to the degree found in a poem with so few lines in which to invent a subject and maneuver it to some sort of closure.

The sonnet craze spread from Italy to almost every other European literature. In the sixteenth century, Sir Thomas Wyatt brought it to the English court where subsequent poets tinkered with its form. Its popularity was due most certainly to its becoming the chief vehicle of love poetry, where argument and counterargument are usually the issue. *I'm madly in love with you,* a sonnet may complain, *while you, for some inexplicable reason, do not care for me. In fact, you hate my guts, but, come to think of it . . .* It's this back and forth leading up to some new insight that is typical of the sonnet. There's a turn in logic and the accompanying shift in tone, mood, and voice. All short poems employ this strategy to various degrees, since without a reversal of some sort and the surprise that comes with it there can be neither emotion nor meaning for the reader.

Gerald Stern is the least likely candidate to be writing a sonnet. The poems in his twelve previous collections sprawl cheerfully over the page. His sense of form is more grounded in narrative than in the elliptical ways of the short lyric poem. He is a monologist who loves to digress, but the kind we forgive because he's entertaining us. There are poets who pare down until they find a bit of language they can play with. With Stern it's the opposite, a wish to be expansive and include everything. "The tale I have to tell" is how he begins a poem in the new book. He tells us about the places where he's lived, friends and lovers he has had, books he's read, meals he's eaten, records he's listened to.

It's a talking voice, friendly and often rambling. His freedom to go wherever his imagination happens to take him gives his poems a feel of adventure that is hard to resist. An extraordinary number of them start with the first-person pronoun and yet what often sounds like a straight confession is clearly a literary ploy. As much as Whitman and Ginsberg, Stern wants to create a persona recognizable from poem to poem.

Son of Jewish immigrant parents, he was born in Pittsburgh in 1925. "I had absolutely no mentors. I came from nowhere," he said in a *NewsHour* interview. The poems give the impression of an unsettled life. His love of poetry kept him spiritually afloat while he went on making a modest living as a teacher. He was almost fifty when he published his first book of poems. "I remember Galileo describing the mind / as a piece of paper blown around by the wind," Stern says in an early poem. His poems have that quality of unpredictability, of skipping from subject to subject. He is a poet of both large cities and small town America who is as much at home in a truck stop diner as he is in the local library. He knows life is tough for most people. In the course of telling us about himself he recounts bits of their stories or he imagines them. Stern has a fondness for visionary states. He savors moments when we step out of our solitude and come together with one another. He wants us to share with him that experience, as in this short poem from *The Red Coal* (1981):

No Wind

Today I am sitting outside the Dutch Castle
on Route 30 near Bird in Hand and Blue Ball,
watching the Amish snap their suspenders at the sunglasses.
I am dreaming of my black suit again
and the store in Paradise where I will be fitted out for life.
A small girl and I recognize each other
from our former life together in Córdoba.
We weep over the plastic tote bags, the apple combs and
    the laughing harmonicas,
and fall down on the hot carpet
remembering the marble forest
of the Great Mosque
and the milky walls
of the Jewish quarter.

I will see her again in 800 years
when all this is sorted out.
I give it that much time,
~~based on the slack mind,~~
the dirty drinking water and the slow decay.
I give it at least that much time
before we lie down again in the tiny lilacs
and paper love houses of the next age.

"I'm quintessentially explaining myself to myself," he says in that same interview, and that is an indispensable trait when it comes to sonnet writing. There are fifty-nine of them in *American Sonnets*. I have no idea if the inspiration for the book came from Billy Collins's poem "American Sonnet," but he would undoubtedly agree with its definition of what we have here. "We do not speak like Petrarch or wear a hat like Spenser / and it is not fourteen lines," Collins writes. Our sonnet, he goes on to say, resembles a picture postcard. On one side there may be a waterfall or a lake and on the other side the space where we condense our impressions and sentiments in a few measured phrases. If compression of feeling and conciseness of vision matter—and they certainly do—the temptation will always be there to write a sonnet. Even Stern, who is ordinarily such a discursive poet, seems happy to place himself under constraints in his new book. His own sonnets range between sixteen and twenty-three lines. Here's what they sound like:

In Time

As far as the clocks—and it is time to think of them—
I have one on my kitchen shelf and it is
flat, with a machine-made flair, a perfect
machine from 1948, at the latest,
and made of shining plastic with the numbers
sharp and clear and slightly magnified in
that heartbreaking postwar style, the cord
too short, though what does it matter, since the mechanism
is broken and it sits unplugged alongside a
cheap ceramic rooster, his head insanely
small and yet his tiny brain alert for
he is the one who will crow and not that broken

buzzing relic, though time is different now
and dawn is different too, you were up all night
and it is dark when he crows and you are waiting
to see what direction you should face and if
you were born in time or was it wasted and what
the day looks like and is the rooster loyal.

The clock is broken, but the imagination works and so the ceramic rooster will crow. It's a nice poem, but is it really a sonnet? As Levin's Penguin anthology demonstrates, there are sonnets missing the required number of lines or having additional ones, skinny sonnets lacking the traditional line length, or having no rhymes at all. What makes them sonnets, I suppose, is the way they impersonate some aspect of the original mode. Fourteen lines is not an arbitrary number. It's near impossible to engage in argument and arrive at a conclusion in ten or twelve lines and make it sound convincing. A different problem occurs when one adds extra lines. The pithiness, which is the soul of a sonnet, is missing and its absence is hard to cover up.

Stern is much too interested in autobiography and narrative to let the tensions between formal restrictions and verbal play configure the meaning on their own. The less space one allows oneself, the more the words on the page take over the poem. The sonnet is more concerned with following its own logic of images and metaphors than with obeying the author's first wishes. That said, the new book has a number of splendid poems. I like "Savel Kliatchko," "Studebaker," "Samaritans," "Spider," and "Sam and Morris." They all do what Stern knows how to do well, and that is make poetry out of good stories.

April Bernard is more interested in prosody and language than Stern is, so her sonnets sound more like the real thing. Accordingly, she's less concerned with what is said than with how it is said. Wit and lightness of touch are her virtues. In *Swan Electric,* her third book of poems, she has ten sonnets and a number of near sonnets, since short poems are her specialty. Affairs of the heart are the concern in several of them, although at times I have no idea who is speaking and about whom—and I don't especially care. The pleasures of her poems lie in details, surprising images, and turns of phrase, each of which has been carefully wrought. Here's an example of what I mean:

English as a Second Language

That voice—from the tv—that voice,
thick smoky cheese, or, no—
dark as burnt flan, sweet,
venison-sweet in the heavy smoke
of a tavern hearth, and hot as brandy.
I served that voice for months,
in a theater on 13th near Third
where losers are the ones who crack first.
I gave you azured hours, nights,
and you placed your soul,
pretty as a dead mouse, at my feet.
Gutturals, the candles guttering backstage.
Your voice went everywhere
you dared not put your hands.

Any poet who can use "azured" and get away with it deserves our admiration. Bernard is primarily a satirist. Her poems may start in the autobiographical mode, but it doesn't take her long before she starts poking fun at herself. "Against Biography" is the title of a poem in her first book. Blurting out confessions is not what she is after. The "I" in *Swan Electric* is a comic persona, a worldly heroine of picaresque urban adventures. There's nothing of the recluse about her and yet Dickinson taught her how to prepare her spare cuisine of beguiling and delectable verbal combinations. With all that lushness of language her poems can at times be hermetic. The sonnets in her new book are in my view far less successful than the memoir sequence about the East Village and New York in the 1980s called "Song of Yes and No." It's the title of a song from *Threepenny Opera*. This turns out to be somewhat misleading. With its erotic and lyric mixture and its assortment of colorful characters, this sequence of fourteen poems partakes more of the spirit of Mozart, whom it evokes repeatedly, than Brecht:

Colossus from a rockabilly float,
piled blonde, plaid blouse cinched into cutoffs,
wiggles, "I need a man, I need a man,
I need a man." Like the old song goes.
Knitting Factory bouncer, House O'Love spy,
double-bottle brunette, cartoon caveman with a jaw like a
    trout,
wolf long as a limo, and don't forget
the ibis that says she's somebody's mother.
You dance close to the tourist whose shaved albino neck
smells of the beer garden, and you realize he's your type.
So maybe you like the scare yourself, de temps en temps.
Some pepper on that?
Fwup, fwup, fwup, shouts the copter
bulging blue head in the inky sky; and lululu,
warbles the auteur. Oh, night is the permeable membrane,
the terrible present tense.

Bernard's poetry can be a lot of fun. Even when she copes with disappointments in love and other daily hassles, she doesn't lose her sense of humor. If a poet is condemned—life being what it is—to say what has already been said thousands of times, then a bit of mischief helps. "I don't know about you, but I've been looking / for a narrative in which suffering makes sense" is how she describes her predicament in one poem. She finds it in a poetic equivalent of a comic opera. I'm happy she does because it inspires her most felicitous flights of imagination. Even with an occasional unevenness, *Swan Electric* is an original and thoroughly enjoyable book of poems by a fine poet.

Charles Wright, too, has a group of sonnets in *A Short History of the Shadow*. As far as I can tell, not since *Bloodlines* (1975) has he written any, although most of the poems in his eight intervening collections tend to run between ten and twenty lines. The unusual aspect of all his poems, long and short, is that they are interconnected and an integral part of a larger body of work, which includes almost everything he has written. In other words, Wright's ambition includes both the individual lyric and the long poem. I'd like to marry Emily and Walt, he has said on

a couple of occasions, and he has certainly tried to do so. Whatever the offspring of that union eventually looks like, here, in
the meantime, is one of his free verse sonnets from the new
book employing his characteristic two-step line:

Citronella

Moonlight blank newsprint across the lawn,
Three-quarters moon, give or take,
            empty notebook, no wind.
When it's over it's over,
Cloud crossing moon, half-clear sky, then
            candle-sputter, shadow-crawl.
Well, that's a couple of miles down the road,
            he said to himself,
Watching the moonlight lacquer and mat.
, Surely a mile and then some,
Watching the clouds come and the clouds go.
Citronella against the tiny ones, the biters,
Sky pewter-colored and suddenly indistinct now—
Sweet smell of citronella,
            beautiful, endless youth.
The book of moonlight has two pages and this one's the
      first one.
Forsake me not utterly,
Beato immaculato,
            and make me marvellous
            in your eyes.

Wright was born in Pickwick Dam, Tennessee, in 1935 and
spent his formative years in rural North Carolina and eastern
Tennessee, where his father was a civil engineer for the TVA.
The U.S. Army sent him to Italy, to which he returned afterward frequently, often for extended visits. Surprisingly perhaps,
there are no Southern poets among his mentors. He's not, as is
typical of that tradition, interested in telling stories. Neither
history nor the Southern Agrarian myth of a lost rural culture
is his subject. From Ezra Pound he learned how to use images,
juxtapose fragments, and quote copiously in his poems. Dante
gave him the idea of making an epic out of a string of lyric

poems. The old Chinese poets taught him not to forget to include in each poem that day's weather report. Wallace Stevens showed him how to read the metaphysics of the natural world and the Surrealists how to trust his imagination and go for broke when making metaphors. "At the heart of every poem is a journey of discovery. Something is being found out," he writes.

True enough, except what is odd about Wright is that the range of his subject matter is exceedingly narrow. This is even truer of his last three books. He is a bit like the Italian painter Morandi, who for most of his life tried to render the same four objects: two olive oil tins, one wine bottle, and one flower vase. For Wright, the trees in his backyard, light and shadow, stars, mountains, the sun and the moon—first in Laguna Beach and now for some twenty years in Charlottesville, Virginia—have served the same function. He pays close attention to them, letting their daily variations in appearance jump-start a poem. One would expect this obsessive single-mindedness to weary the reader after a while, but strangely that is not the case. All things that are the same are also different, Wright proves over and over again. When it comes to describing nature, he is endlessly inventive. "Winter blue moon, light like a wax-thin slice of *finnochio*, / So grainy, so white" comes from "Night Rider" in the new book. There are hundreds of such images throughout his work, risky and often seemingly far-fetched, that turn out to be amazingly precise if we keep our eyes open.

"The poem is a self-portrait / always, no matter what mask / You take off and put back on," he has also said. Pound tried to construct the whole history of the world in his *Cantos* and could not make it cohere. Wright stayed "narrow," but only in the sense that someone like Dickinson or Pascal is narrow. To get a full sense of the complexity of his vision one has to read a lot of his poetry. "There are three things, basically, that I write about—language, landscape, and the idea of God," he has written, only to contradict himself elsewhere by insisting that for him poems are "aesthetic possibilities, objects of beauty and contemplation." Actually, both make sense since Wright's ideas of language, landscape, and divinity are not what one would ordinarily expect:

Even so, I think it's all incomprehensible
Everything that we look at.
Much easier, I think, to imagine the abyss, just there,
The other side of the hedge,
              than to conjure the hedge,
The trees, and time like a puddle of water and not a stream.

When Auden called Van Gogh a "Religious Realist," he could have had Wright in mind. The Dutch painter was a realist, according to him, because he attached supreme importance to incessant study of nature; religious because he regarded nature as the sacramental visible sign of spiritual grace, which it was the artist's aim to reveal to others. Except when it comes to Wright, it gets even more complicated:

I used to think the power of words was inexhaustible,
That how we said the world
              was how it was, and
              how it would be.
I used to imagine that word-sway and word-thunder
Would silence the Silence and all that,
That words were the Word,
That language could lead us inexplicably to grace,
As though it were geographical.
I used to think these things when I was young.
              I still do.

The philosophical quandary for someone like Wright is that he believes in transcendence, but not necessarily in God. How can that be? you ask. To claim mystical states, doesn't one need to believe in the world beyond appearances? Yes and no, as Wright's example shows. Divinity for him resides in the eternal and unsayable reality of the world. His hell, purgatory, and paradiso are all to be found in living and accepting that contradiction. Truth is not stable; it has to be rediscovered and renamed continuously in the light of our experience. Accordingly, the subject of most of his poems is the clock. Time is both the villain and a friend since it gives definition to every moment of our lives. "A moment's monument / Memorial from the Soul's eternity / To one dead deathless hour" is what Dante Gabriel

Rossetti called the sonnet. The mind in the act of finding what will suffice in the face of one's own mortality is Wright's inexhaustible theme.

Short History of the Shadow, together with *Appalachia* (1998), *Black Zodiac* (1997), and *Chickamauga* (1995), contains some of Wright's very best poems. *Country Music,* his selected early poems, and still another selection of poems from 1980 to 1990 called *The World of the Ten Thousand Things* are equally impressive. More than any of his contemporaries I can think of, Wright is capable of saying things memorably. He can write lyrics of great beauty that achieve a level of eloquence where the reader says to himself, if this is not wisdom, I don't know what is. The new book has a number of interesting longer poems, however. With the current strength of the sonnet in mind, I'll conclude with one of his:

On Heaven Considered as What Will Cover Us and
Stony Comforter

The longed-for is tiny, and tenuous as a syllable.
In this it resembles us.
In this it resembles what we've passed on and shucked off.
Interminable as black water,
Irreparable as dirt,
It shadows our going forth and finds us,
                              and then finds us out.

Horizon line like a basted
             slipstitch that shines back,
Seasonal underwork, seasonal blueprint and burn.

Last stop. End of the end. No exit.
Autumn in override,
                    everyone long gone from the garden,
No footprints, wings furled, swords sheathed.
No gears, no wheels. A silence unimaginable.
Saint Sunday, leaves in free-fall,
A little light in the west, a night light,
                              to harry us home.

Reading these three poets, I'm impressed by the resiliency of the sonnet. Even when the poet sets out to break most of its traditional requirements, its presence lingers. That resilience is no mystery. There's nothing comparable to a sonnet in the rest of literature. To write one is to attempt to put into practice the notion that everything that needs saying can be said in a few words. The sonnet is a literary equivalent of an endgame in chess. It is about a series of quick-witted and unforeseen moves within the confines of rigorous rules against an unknown opponent who can be anything or anyone from God to a case of unrequited love. Because we are at our best as poets and philosophers when we are cornered, sonnets continue to be written. In the sonnet's difficulty and downright impossibility lies the secret of its appeal and its hope. A place where one right word or image may take our breath away.

NOTE

1. *Penguin Book of the Sonnet,* 2001.

The Image Hunter

When Diane Waldman selected the pieces for the 1967 exhibition of Joseph Cornell's work at the Guggenheim Museum five years before his death, and wrote for the catalog what was one of the first extensive critical articles on the artist, he was practically unknown. Even the far more wide-ranging retrospective exhibition at MOMA in 1980 and the fine essays and more than three hundred illustrations in the catalog did not make his name much more familiar to the wider public. There was a reason for that. Avant-garde movements, one supposedly more radical than the other, came and went in the years in question, trumpeting other names and competing for attention. If the works themselves and the aesthetic claims made for them were often laughable, it did not seem to matter since they sold for astonishing sums of money.

Then all that gradually changed in the 1990s. Everything that made Cornell a marginal figure—his distance from current fashions and the oddness of his art, with its small-size box constructions in which a variety of inconsequential found objects are assembled—began to attract interest. During the last decade we have had a biography of Cornell, a book of selected diaries, letters, and files, a study of his interest in cinema, a volume on his vision of spiritual order, and several other equally interesting monographs, catalog texts, and isolated essays. Cornell brings out the best in critics and literary historians. He charms them by the way he combines in himself complete ordinariness with high sophistication. They know that even after every aspect of his career and art has been carefully documented, he will re-

Review of *Joseph Cornell: Master of Dreams,* by Diane Waldman. From the *New York Review of Books,* October 24, 2002.

main an enigma. That's why books about him keep being written. When even the most persuasive speculations fail to fully account for the originality of the work, one has no choice but to look again and again.

Long before the Cubists tore up newspaper headlines to make collages and Marcel Duchamp displayed a store-bought snow shovel as a work of art, there was Walt Whitman's poetry with its frequent catalogs of seemingly random images. A "kaleidoscope divine," a "bequeather of poems" is what he called the city of New York and its motley crowds. Street life in all its bustle and variety is one of the great discoveries of modern art and literature. Whitman and Baudelaire were intense original observers of the city around them and so was Cornell in his own special way. I don't believe that he would have become an artist had he spent his life cooped up in some small town in Maine or Kansas. He couldn't draw, paint, or sculpt, so what would he have done with himself there? In New York, he did what the city already does anyway: make impromptu assemblages out of many different kinds of realities. An image hunter is how he described himself. He had no clear idea what he was looking for or what he would find. For years, before he made any art, he roamed the streets in a state of expectancy. In that respect, he was not unlike thousands of other unknowns, then and now, who in certain inspired moments experience their own solitude and unhappiness as a kind of poetry.

Cornell said that when he studied astronomy in school, he was frightened by the concept of infinity. Imaginary travels were his lifelong occupation, but he made sure that he slept in his own bed every night. Except for the four years he spent as a student at the Phillips Academy in Massachusetts, he never set foot outside the New York City area. He was born in 1903 in Nyack to parents who were both descendants of old Dutch families in the region. His mother's grandfather owned schooners and prize-winning yachts. Cornell had two younger sisters, and a brother who suffered from cerebral palsy. His parents were ostensibly a happy, cheerful couple. They loved acting and performed at an amateur arts club. His mother, who had been a classmate of Edward Hopper, played the piano and his father sang. His father made his living as a salesman and then eventually as a textile designer for a manufacturer of fine woolen goods. Cornell was thirteen years old when his father died of leukemia, leaving behind enormous debts. The family had to move from the large Victorian house they occupied to smaller houses in Queens and then in 1929 his mother bought the house on Utopia Parkway where she and her two sons lived for the rest of their lives.

Cornell left school in 1921 and, following his father's example, went to work as a textile salesman. He never married. Women both obsessed and terrified him. A true loner, shy, self-absorbed, feeding himself mostly on cakes and ice tea, he nonetheless immersed himself in the culture of the city, taking in opera, classical music, theater, and ballet, and regularly visiting art galleries. He was also by now a compulsive collector. Walter Benjamin in his encyclopedic, unfinished study of Paris arcades has a number of interesting things to say about that compulsion:

> Perhaps the most deeply hidden motive of the person who collects can be described this way: he takes up the struggle against dispersion. Right from the start, the great collector is struck by the confusion, by the scatter, in which the things of the world are found. . . . The collector . . . brings together what belongs together . . . by keeping in mind their affinities.[1]

In every collector hides an allegorist and in every allegorist a collector, Benjamin goes on to say. For a true collector, the collection is never complete for as soon as he discovers an item missing his collection seems to him reduced to patchwork. On the other hand, there is the allegorist, for whom the universe is already fragmented and for whom individual objects are words in a secret dictionary that come to make their meanings known in certain heightened states of perception. Which type of collector was Cornell? He believed in chance, in lucky finds, so it's not easy to classify him. According to Diane Waldman's new book, *Joseph Cornell: Master of Dreams*, here is where he poked around:

> He frequented The Metropolitan Museum of Art, the Brooklyn Museum, the Morgan Library, the Museum of Natural History, and the Hayden Planetarium. He made photostats of his favorite images from the Public Library Pictures Collec-

tion and the Bettman Archives. He scoured the Asian shops between 25th and 32nd Streets, where he found Japanese prints and the first small boxes for his objects, and he frequented a taxidermy shop in the Village and a pet store near Radio City Music Hall. Many of his favorite objects came from Woolworth's, the five-and-dime store from which he purchased stamps, wine glasses, marbles, gold-colored bracelets, and painted wooden birds. He hunted down clay pipes, specifically those that were Dutch in origin. What began as a pastime became an obsession that fed his everyday life and his creative imagination.

Some of the other places he haunted were Washington Square Park, Brentano's Bookstore, John Wanamaker stores, the Old Print Shop on Lexington Avenue, Renwick C. Hurry's Antiques, the F. A. O. Schwartz toy store, Bigelow's Pharmacy on Sixth Avenue in the Village, the Fourth Avenue used bookstores, and the Christian Science Reading Room on Macdougal Street. He had converted to Christian Science at the age of twenty-two and remained a lifelong member of the church, attending meetings several times each week. Waldman argues convincingly that Christian Science provided him with a metaphysical frame for understanding Surrealism. Both believed that spirit is the foundation of matter and that knowledge lies within us. Improbable as this may sound, in the work of Joseph Cornell, Mary Baker Eddy meets André Breton. Had she read this passage from Breton's *Second Surrealist Manifesto* (1929), I suspect, she would have agreed:

> Everything leads us to believe that there is a certain point in the spirit from which life and death, real and imaginary, past and future, communicable and incommunicable are no longer perceived as contradictories. It would be vain to look for any other motivation in surrealist activity than the hope of determining this point.[2]

In his years of roving around the city, Cornell assembled a vast collection of what he called ephemera and what most of us would regard by and large as trivia. If he had not eventually figured how to make original twentieth-century art out of his stashes of old movie magazines, moldy engravings, yellowed postcards, maps, guidebooks, film strips, photographs of ballet dancers, and hundreds of other items stored in shoe boxes and scrapbooks in his basement, they would have ended up at a dump or in a flea market. Creative filing, he called it. Each file was an arcane compilation, the result of a complex chain of private associations. He had no other use for them in mind; but unknown to him at the time, his archives supplied him with the material and even more importantly with the technique for how to go about making art.

The story of how he became an artist is by now familiar and Waldman tells it succinctly and well. In November 1931, Cornell strayed into the Julian Levy Gallery at 602 Madison Avenue and watched Levy himself unpack Surrealist artworks intended for an exhibition. The gallery had recently opened and was soon to become the place where American artists could keep abreast of the European avant-garde. The art he saw that day, despite its unfamiliarity and oddity, gave him an idea of what to do with the stuff he'd been piling up in his basement. As his diaries show, Cornell may not have paid much attention to theoretical controversies, but he certainly knew how to look at art.

Shortly after seeing some of Max Ernst's collages in which nineteenth-century illustrations from scientific, commercial, and popular magazine stories were cut up and combined into startling new images, he returned to the gallery with his first modest efforts. Levy made them part of a group show, Surréalisme, in January 1932. Levy also asked Cornell to design the cover for the catalog. The show included paintings and photographs by Dalí, Ernst, Picasso, Man Ray, Eugène Atget, László Moholy-Nagy, and Marcel Duchamp's ready-made *Why Not Sneeze Rose Sélavy?* (1921), which consisted of a painted birdcage filled with marble cubes, wood, cuttlebone, and a thermometer. Cornell's own contribution was a glass bell with a mannequin's hand inside it holding a collage of a rose. Glass bells became popular in the Victorian period for displaying clocks, model ships, dried flowers, stuffed birds, and other valuables.

What he quickly learned from the Surrealists is that just about anything from a medicine chest or a pill box to a coin-operated contraption with a peephole in a penny arcade can be used as a setting for a work of art. Perhaps getting down on all fours and peeking into some dark corner under one's bed is a good introduction to his shadow boxes. If a small hoard of lost items happens to be there—so much the better. Who hasn't made believe in one's own childhood that a small pebble that fell out of a shoe was an animal or a human being? Cornell's constructions recall for us a time when we had a few imaginary friends and some favorite broken toy as secret playmates. That's not the whole story of their appeal, of course, but that's surely where it all begins.

Here—just so the reader knows what is involved in such constructions—is a shortened inventory of the items Monique Beudert found in his early masterpiece *L'Égypte de Mlle Cléo de Mérode*, his homage to the famous courtesan and ballerina of the 1890s which Cornell made in 1940:

> Hinged casket; lid lined with marbleized paper, cutouts of printed phrases *L'EGYPTE / de Mlle de Cléo Mérode / COURS ELEMENTAIRE / D'HISTOIRE NATURELLE* and picture of seated Egyptian female; box divided by sheet of glass into 2 horizontal levels. Contents of sealed lower level: loose red sand, doll's forearm, wood ball, German coin, several glass and mirror fragments. Contents of upper level: 12 removable cork-stopped bottles (tops of corks covered with marbleized paper, most bottles labeled with cutout printed words), in 4 rows of 3 set in holes in sheet of wood covered with marbleized paper; strips of glass forming 2 rows of glass-covered compartments (3 each) at sides of bottles. Contents of each bottle (and labels): (1) cutout sphinx head, loose red sand; (2) numerous short yellow filaments with glitter adhered to one end . . . ; (3) 2 intertwined paper spirals . . . ; (4) cutout of woman's head . . . ; (5) cutout of camels and men, loose yellow sand, ball . . . ; (6) pearl beads . . . ; (7) glass tube with bulge in center, residue of dried green liquid . . . ; (8) crumpled tulle, rhinestones, pearl beads, sequins, metal chain, metal, and glass fragments . . . ; (9) red paint, shell or bone fragments . . . ; (10) threaded needle pierced through red wood disc . . . ; (11) bone and frosted-glass fragments . . . ; (12) blue celluloid liner, clear glass crystals.[3]

If this was not already crazy enough, the individual bottles have labels with names like *Le Mille et une Nuits, Temps fabuleux,*

Cleopatra's Needle to make our imagination run wild. By what inner logic, chain of chance associations, or esoteric principles were all these things arranged here? one wonders. Cornell learned from Duchamp and the Surrealists about the poetic qualities an object acquires once it is removed from its habitual context and given a new name calling into question its identity. Only what is useless is beautiful. Objects are more interesting when we overlook their function and their latent symbolism and admire them solely for their appearance. Cornell had an exquisite sense of design and he put things next to each other in his boxes as much for their private, emblematic qualities as for the visual pleasure they gave him. He wanted to create a new visual experience without worrying very much what it all means in the end. In other words, aesthetic considerations for him prevailed over specific meaning, but to what degree we cannot be sure. Many of his constructions leave us uncertain whether to regard them as allegories or as abstract art.

Waldman's study proceeds chronologically from Cornell's earliest assemblages to his box constructions of the 1940s and 1950s, his homages to Romantic ballet and portraits of women, and finally to his late collages. There are separate chapters on the *Medici* series and his *Aviary* boxes, and one devoted to his *Observatories, Night Skies,* and *Hotels.* The illustrations are good and plentiful. Although her book covers mostly familiar ground, as an introduction to the artist and his work, it is first-rate. Any study of Cornell is an effort to trace and understand the many influences on him. The art, literature, films, and books he loved come in for close scrutiny and the results of that inquiry are at first surprising and then seem inevitable. For example, Waldman discusses the influence of Vermeer on the *Medici* boxes:

> Cornell understood the fundamentals of Vermeer's art, especially the rigor with which the Dutch master structured his images, his interest in perspective, color, and light, and his painstaking attention to detail. Vermeer created domestic interiors in which the everyday and the commonplace take on the aura of the transcendental and the sublime.

For his *Medici* boxes, Cornell used photostats of Renaissance paintings of young boys and girls. In *Untitled (Pinturiccio Boy)* (1942–52), as in other works in the series, Waldman writes,

> space is fragmented into small rectangles and bisected by black lines crossing the surface. The inner sides and the bottom of the box are covered with Baedeker maps of Venice and augmented by the ubiquitous spiral and two freestanding "toy blocks."

Like its companion, *Untitled (Medici Princess)* (1948), "these boxes are notable for their tinted glass: brown for the young boy, blue for the young girl. The colors contribute to the tone of solemnity and purity." In his diaries, Cornell records seeing faces in poorly lit subway stations, little tableaux that, he writes, could have been magical on film. He describes what he saw as a kind of purgatorio climate of light. The ever-maddening elusiveness of such experiences is a constant worry for Cornell, for they were something that no words could hold. "Expressivity of eyes music of language," he writes elsewhere in his diaries.[4]

Then there is Mondrian and his grid paintings. Cornell moved in the same circles as the Dutch painter and he not only knew his work but was also aware of his interest in theosophy. Waldman makes the point that Mondrian's paintings were influenced by the buildings he saw in Manhattan. Not only entire buildings, I would surmise, but particular windows too. Cornell, in a diary entry for October 17, 1956, confesses that the original inspiration for his *Aviary* series was "the magic simplicity of store windows." Waldman observes that his boxes in the late 1940s begin to have an abstract, architectonic, gridlike appearance. Indeed, they make one think of vacated office buildings with their whitewashed interiors, bare floors, and rows of curtainless windows. It's a poetry of absences, of spacious, empty spaces swept clean except for some odd object left behind. "Great sense of everything white—but more than just physical ambience—a sense of illumination," Cornell writes.[5] "N.Y. City Metaphysics" is the name he gives to such almost mystical experiences.

For anyone familiar with Cornell's shadow boxes, it is hard

not to think of them now and then as one walks the streets of New York. "My work was a natural outcome of love for the city," he said to Jack Kroll of *Newsweek* magazine.[6] He also insisted that whatever he did sprang from real experiences, and I have no reason to doubt him. Along with this down-to-earth side, he saw himself as an explorer of spiritual mysteries. Both Duchamp and Mondrian thought of him as a poet. They did not say what kind, but I suspect they had in mind someone like Mallarmé, another Symbolist master famous for the ambiguity of his verses. Cornell did not regard any of his works as ever finished and no poet does either. Their meaning was as unresolved for him as it is for us. It is because what we see with our eyes can be a poem, too. The intersection I happen to be hurrying across today with its panorama of white clouds and dark buildings on a late summer dusk is unfathomable in its beauty. Cornell once had a vision of Fanny Cerrito, the famous dancer of the Romantic era, in the windows of the Manhattan Storage and Warehouse Company on West Fifty-second Street. Undoubtedly, the reason we love cities is that they set the imagination free. Like a shadow discreetly following a lone pedestrian as he makes his slow way down a long block, we are drawn to Cornell's art because it holds us spellbound while continuing to keep its secret. Diane Waldman's book happily never loses sight of that.

NOTES

1. Walter Benjamin, *The Arcades Project,* ed Rolf Tiedemann, trans. Howard Eiland and Kevin McLoughlin (Belknap Press/Harvard University Press, 1999), p. 211.

2. Michel Carrouges, *André Breton and the Basic Concepts of Surrealism* (University of Alabama Press, 1974), p. 11.

3. *Joseph Cornell,* ed. Kynaston McShine (Museum of Modern Art, 1980), p. 282.

4. *Joseph Cornell's Theater of the Mind: Selected Diaries, Letters, and Files,* ed. Mary Ann Caws (Thames and Hudson, 1993), p. 201.

5. *Joseph Cornell's Theater of the Mind,* pp. 220, 303.

6. "Paradise Regained," *Newsweek,* June 5, 1967.

"The Water Hose Is on Fire"

1.

More than fifty years separate these two new collections of Kenneth Koch's poetry. While *Sun Out* gathers for the first time some of his earliest and most experimental poems, *A Possible World* is the work of the last years of his life. He died last July at the age of seventy-seven. In addition to eighteen books of poetry, which include *Selected Poems, 1950–1982,* he left behind two works of fiction, numerous short plays, and two books on teaching poetry to children.

As a poet he is grouped with John Ashbery, Frank O'Hara, and James Schuyler, as one of the founders of the so-called New York School. Their poems—or so the story goes—were inspired by Abstract Expressionist painting and modern French poetry. This may be difficult to believe today, but in the 1950s there was little knowledge in this country of the European literary avant-garde. Reading the literary magazines of the period one would not suspect that Breton, Mayakovsky, and Lorca ever wrote. As Koch joked years later, it was the time when T. S. Eliot was the Great Dictator of literature. One was not supposed to fool around in poems. The critics praised *irony, ambiguity,* and *tension* while expecting young poets to sound more British than American.

Existentialism was all the rage in intellectual circles, but the movement had nothing to do with poetry. New York poets, with their cosmopolitan sophistication that included knowledge of modern music, dance, and theater, were an anomaly in a country whose poets have always found deeper satisfaction in nature.

Review of *Sun Out: Selected Poems, 1952–1954* and *A Possible World,* by Kenneth Koch. From the *New York Review of Books,* January 6, 2003.

As is frequently the case with staunch New Yorkers, these poets came from elsewhere. Koch was born in Cincinnati in 1925, was drafted into the army in the Second World War, and went to Harvard afterward, where he met Ashbery and O'Hara. Apart from travels abroad, he lived in New York for the rest of his life and for many years taught at Columbia.

Koch's poem "Fresh Air," written in 1956, reads like a manifesto of the new poetry. Its setting is a meeting of the "Poem Society" (a.k.a. Poetry Society of America). That evening's topic is poetry on the subject of love between swans. Some fellow in the audience, who has had enough of the discussion, gets up and starts shouting:

> "You make me sick with all your talk about restraint and
> mature talent!
> Haven't you ever looked out the window at a painting by
> Matisse,
> Or did you always stay in hotels where there were too many
> spiders crawling on your visages?
> Did you ever glance inside a bottle of sparkling pop,
> Or see a citizen split in two by the lightning?"
> . . . .
>
> Where are young poets in America, they are trembling in
> publishing houses and universities,
> Above all they are trembling in universities, they are bathing
> the library steps with their spit,
> They are gargling out innocuous (to whom?) poems about
> maple trees and their children,
> Sometimes they brave a subject like the Villa d'Este or a
> lighthouse in Rhode Island,
> Oh what worms they are! They wish to perfect their form.[1]

Later on in the same poem, Koch brings on a character dressed in a cowboy suit, called the Strangler, who goes around strangling bad poets. His ear is alert for the names of Orpheus, Cuchulain, Gawain, and Odysseus and for poems addressed to various personages no longer living in anyone's thoughts. A kingdom of dullness ruled with the scepter of the dumb, the deaf, and the creepy is how Koch sees American poetry. What misfortune, he says, to walk out into the air of a beautiful spring day and happen to read an article on modern poetry or see examples of it in magazines like the *Hudson Review* or *Encounter.* Suppose, he says, one goes and burns down the building where their offices are and ends up in prison with trial subscriptions to the *Partisan, Sewanee,* and *Kenyon Reviews*! What could be worse than that?

The inclination to say something new and in a new way is what Koch values. Poetry for him has to be constantly saved from itself. The idea is to do something with language that has never been done before. Newness may in fact be the main thing a poet sets out to achieve, he stated in an essay. "It's like searching for Shangri-la in a winged vehicle of your invention," he wrote. "Fortunately, there is a great deal of technology behind you: all the poetry other poets have written."[2] The new poem Koch is calling for—although influenced by Mallarmé, Shelley, Byron, and Whitman, plus a million other poets—will be entirely original, he claims. And it was.

What the New York poets learned from the painters, David Lehman points out in *The Last Avant-Garde,* is "that it was okay for a poem to chronicle the history of its own making—that the mind of the poet, rather than the world, could be the true subject of the poem."[3] Even more importantly, Lehman contends, they saw that a poem as much as a painting is a field of action where both real and imaginary things can be combined. While their contemporaries in poetry were confessing the secrets of their tormented inner lives or yearning for mystical visions, the New York poets made one feel like a first-time visitor set adrift in the streets of Manhattan.

For Koch, one's identity is not a stable property. He's a poet of metamorphosis. His imagination tempts him to enter every living and inanimate thing. He has the extraordinary gift of becoming someone else. It's the approach he used in teaching children poetry. "I'm the floor of a house. Everytime someone steps on me I laugh," wrote one four-year-old.[4] Koch likes that aspect of poetry too much to restrict himself to any one type of poem. Poetic truth, he wrote, is not a general truth that can be separated from its expression in a particular poem. Single meanings have no interest for him.

Introducing the poet at a reading in the 1960s, John Ashbery said:

> Koch's poetry gives you the impression that you are leading
> an interesting life: going to parties and meeting interesting
> people, falling in love, going for rides in the country and to
> public swimming pools, eating in the best restaurants and
> going to movies and the theater in the afternoons. By com-
> parison, most other modern poetry makes me feel as if I were
> living in a small midwestern university town.

This was not a universal opinion, of course. There are still critics
who maintain that the New York poets were a talentless bunch
who never wrote anything that could even remotely be described
as a poem. Koch's gift for mockery made him even more irritat-
ing. Mind-numbing verse that sounds respectful of great verities
is less of an offense than one that thumbs its nose at them. Light
verse is acceptable and so are irony and wit, but a poem that
ridicules the very idea of poetry is a scandal. One of Koch's
lengthy poems, "The Pleasures of Peace," even includes a list of
possible critical reactions: "A wonder!" "No need now for any
further poems!" "He can speak for us all!" "A real Epic!" "The
worst poem I have ever read!" "Abominably tasteless!"

"When they ask for apples, give them pears," the Chilean poet
Nicanor Parra advised me once. This is the spirit of much of
Koch's work. He takes tremendous risks in his poems, seemingly
unafraid to make a fool of himself. The similes and metaphors he
uses are far-fetched and outrageous. Koch routinely takes things
that resemble one another very little and presents them as comparable. "I love you as a sheriff searches for a walnut / That will
solve a murder case unsolved for years," he says in a poem. The
speakers in his poems are at the mercy of their imaginations.
Wherever fancy takes them—or rather, wherever a particular
word takes them, since poetic imagination needs language to
travel—the poem goes. "One's words, though, once excited,
mate and marry / Incessantly, incestuously, like patients / Gone
mad with love," he says in "The Duplications."

Of course, to change the rules for how comparison operates
is to change how the world appears to the reader. "It is possible
to think that if poetry remains faithful to what is rational and
clear, then it will also remain a prisoner of what is already
known: it will say, no matter what the poet intends, essentially

the same old things," he writes. The point is to stretch comparisons as far as they will go, preferably farther, in the hope that a surprising likeness that has been locked with the key of the rational will be freed. This is more or less the theory that the French Surrealists peddled. Nevertheless, in comparison to Koch's work, which conveys what feels like total imaginative freedom, their poems sound contrived.

"Early oddities" is what Koch calls the poems in *Sun Out*, explaining that they never quite fit into his other books. They are, indeed, very different. In a short introductory note, this is his explanation of how the poems were written:

> I had just spent a year in France, immersed not only in French poetry but in the French language, which I understood and misunderstood at the same time. Words would have several meanings for me at once. *Blanc* (*white*) was also *blank* and, in the feminine, *Blanche,* the name of a woman. The pleasure—and the sense of new meanings—I got from this happy confusion was something I wanted to re-create in English.

Of course, there were also literary influences like Raymond Roussel's poems and novels, Gertrude Stein's "Tender Buttons," and I imagine Wallace Stevens too. In many ways the poems in *Sun Out* anticipate the experiments of the later avant-garde movements such as the Oulipo group in Paris in the 1970s and of the so-called Language Poets in United States. Stein said that poetry is all about vocabulary, and Koch takes her up on that. In "When the Sun Tries to Go On," a poem consisting of one hundred stanzas, each twenty-four lines long, a number of identical words reoccur in different contexts and are often used independently of their meaning. This can get pretty boring. There is no story, no progression, and no characters. Reading the poem is like walking through a library, taking books down from the shelves, quickly opening them, and reading a few lines. The shorter poems are similarly opaque, which is not the case with Koch's later poetry. The brief plays included in the book work better even at their silliest. "Guinevere or The Death of the Kangaroo" brings to mind *Ubu Roi*, Alfred Jarry's masterpiece of the absurd. Both in the plays and in the poems the fun comes from isolated phrases and images that make a kind of sense on their own regardless of the context:

> You would look nice in a wastebasket
> A nightingale leans over her ironing board
> Be merry as a phone
> Llama-periwinkle
> . . . .
> Crossword palaces blankets or bent crowds
> Of rats, like a billion speeding prescriptions
> For gout!
> Piano kimono. . . .
> These modern master chew up moths. . . .
> Daiquiris of blue knives
> . . . bakery
> Of distinguished sighs
> O mournful existence within a matchbox
> With a sullen cockatoo

A "China of sentences," a phrase from one of the poems, may be the perfect name for them. If one can keep oneself in a state of Keatsian negative capability while reading and not worry what it all means, then there are things here to enjoy. It may be that the love of language and the love of nonsense are the two most important prerequisites for appreciating poetry. If so, one comes to a scandalous conclusion: What if realism impoverishes life? What if poetry is at its nicest when it keeps its distance from sense? "Dusk moved silently, like pine-needle mice," he writes in one of the poems, and I for one am enchanted.

2.

I said that the poems in *Sun Out* are not typical. Koch is still funny and wildly inventive in his later poetry, but there's usually no problem understanding him. *On the Great Atlantic Rainway: Selected Poems, 1950–1988* is the book anyone interested in contemporary American poetry ought to own. There's simply nothing like it. The poems in it are so varied, so different from one

another, that the volume reads like an anthology. There are didactic poems, prosy narratives, poems that sound like philosophical musings; others that sound like comic books, adolescent adventure stories, satires, true confessions, Dadaist plays,
and romantic lyrics. The effect is a carnival of styles. Diverse
kinds of verbal clowning and slapstick take place.

Koch's poems are performances, magic acts in which wild
imaginings are converted into realities. Laughter for him is an
aesthetic, and humor the greatest homage one can pay to language. Imagination used so freely at times arouses indignation.
This is just plain stupid, one says, reading him, only to be thoroughly delighted in the very next moment. As any reader of
Koch soon realizes, he didn't care to be pinned down to a particular style, nor did he accept the false antithesis between traditional and modern verse:

> They say Prince Hamlet's found a Southern island
> Where he lies happy on the baking sand
> A lovely girl beside him and his hand
> Upon her waist and is completely silent;
> When interviewed, he sighs, and makes a grand
> Gesture toward the troubled Northern places.
> I know them not, he cries, and love them less.
> Then he is once more lost in loveliness.
> They say King Lear, recovered in his mind
> From all those horrors, teaches now at some
> Great university. His course—Cordelia—
> Has students by thousands every term.
> At course's end, he takes his students out,
> Points to the clouds and says You see, you see her!
> And every one, unable not to cry,
> Cries and agrees with him, and he is solaced.
> O King, you should retire and drink your beer!
> And Hamlet you should leave your happy island
> And wear, with fair Ophelia, Denmark's crown.

Koch is a master of the long poem, which makes him extremely difficult to quote. "I like to write things that go on forever," he said in an interview.[5] He once wrote a mock epic, *Ko,
or A Season on Earth,* in Byronic *ottava rima* about a Japanese

baseball player and a score of other amusing characters. His inspiration was Ariosto's *Orlando Furioso*. He also has a thirty-page poem modeled on Ovid called "The Art of Love." It draws equally on contemporary dating and sex manuals. Accordingly, it contains instructions on how to perform in bed; cause all the women eating in a given restaurant to fall in love with you at the same time; build a house ideally suited for love; prepare Greek aphrodisiac foods; make love on the bridge of a ship in twenty-five different positions; construct mazes in which to hide naked women and chase them; plus hundreds of other pieces of advice. Koch loved catalogs as much as Whitman did. Here, for instance, is the beginning of another long poem, "Sleeping with Women":

> Caruso: a voice.
> Naples: sleeping with women.
> Women: sleeping in the dark.
> Voices: a music.
> Pompeii: a ruin.
> Pompeii: sleeping with women.
> Men sleeping with women, women sleeping with women,
>   sheep sleeping with women, everything sleeping with
>   women.
> The guard: asking you for a light.
> Women: asleep.
> Yourself: asleep.
> Everything south of Naples: asleep and sleeping with them.
> Sleeping with women: as in the poems of Pascoli.
> Sleeping with women: as in the rain, as in the snow.
> Sleeping with women: by starlight, as if we were angels,
>   sleeping on the train,
> On the starry foam: asleep and sleeping with them—
>   sleeping with women.
> Mediterranean: a voice.
> Mediterranean: a sea. Asleep and sleeping.
> Streetcar in Oslo, sleeping with women, Toonerville Trolley
> In Stockholm asleep and sleeping with them, in Skansen
> Alone, alone with women,
> The rain sleeping with women, the brain of the dog-eyed
>   genius
> Alone, sleeping with women, all he has wanted,

The dog-eyed fearless man.
Sleeping with them: as in The Perils of Pauline
Asleep with them: as in Tosca
Sleeping with women and causing all that trouble. . . .

The poem continues in this manner for another 130 lines or so. I once heard him read it. The effect is cumulative. The repetition, the accumulation of exotic images, and the sheer excess of it all were spellbinding.

Koch is by and large a love poet. He hasn't had much competition since most of the time our poets are too wrapped up in themselves to notice anyone else. It's also unusual to have a contemporary poet follow in the footsteps of Byron and Ovid, and then again why not? Genuine novelty in any given literary period always includes the restoration of something old that has been either forgotten or dismissed as second-rate. Koch's preferred method is to take a word, a phrase, or an experience and then play with it, literally and figuratively, over and over again until different poetic possibilities and ideas arise from it. I'll quote a few passages from "The Boiling Water" which will give some idea of how this works:

A serious moment for the water is when it boils
And though one usually regards it merely as a convenience
To have the boiling water available for bath or table
Occasionally there is someone around who understands
The importance of this moment for the water—maybe a
    saint,
Maybe a poet, maybe a crazy man, or just someone
    temporarily disturbed
With his mind "floating," in a sense, away from his deepest
Personal concerns to more "unreal" things
. . . .
A serious moment for the island is when its trees
Begin to give it shade, and another is when the ocean
    washes
Big heavy things against its side. One walks around and
    looks at the island
But not really at it, at what is on it, and one thinks,
It must be serious, even, to be this island, at all, here,
Since it is lying here exposed to the whole sea. All its

Moments might be serious. It is serious, in such windy
     weather, to be a sail
Or an open window, or a feather flying in the street. . . .
Seriousness, how often I have thought of seriousness
And how little I have understood it, except this: serious is
     urgent
And it has to do with change. You say to the water,
It's not necessary to boil now, and you turn it off. It stops
Fidgeting. And starts to cool. You put your hand in it
And say, The water isn't serious any more. It has the
     potential,
However—that urgency to give off bubbles, to
Change itself to steam. And the wind,
When it becomes part of a hurricane, blowing up the beach
And the sand dunes can't keep it away.
Fainting is one sign of seriousness, crying is another.
Shuddering all over is another one.
A serious moment for the telephone is when it rings,
And a person answers, it is Angelica, or is it you. . . .
A serious moment for the fly is when its wings
Are moving, and a serious moment for the duck
Is when it swims, when it first touches water, then spreads
Its smile upon the water. . . .
A serious moment for the match is when it bursts into
     flame. . . .
Serious for me that I met you, and serious for you
That you met me, and that we do not know
If we will ever be close to anyone again. Serious the
     recognition of the probability
That we will, although time stretches terribly in between. . . .

One doesn't expect him to pull it off, but he does in the end,
finding never-suspected connections between seemingly remote
realities. Something as familiar as water coming to a boil is seen
as if for the first time by an observant and intelligent visitor
from Mars. Comedy, one realizes, reading him, casts its net
much wider than tragedy and melodrama, which tend to be
claustrophobic. It's a rich, multifaceted world, similar to what
we encounter in Cervantes and Rabelais. Very much in their
spirit, Koch carries out here a comic examination of seriousness
which after many unexpected twists and turns becomes a love

poem. Trying to imagine anything in the mystery of its being is like falling in love, he concludes. That's why his poem ends with an address to a woman he loves.

A Possible World is his last book of poems. As is to be expected, they are less playful and more melancholy. Koch had always been the poet of happiness. What he called his "real life" was some merry, never-to-be-forgotten occasion with friends or lovers on a particular day in a particular year. Brooding on mortality was not his thing. He sought an atmosphere of high spirits in his poems. "The very existence of poetry should make us laugh," he said. Being funny, of course, doesn't prevent one from being philosophical, and it didn't with Koch. In fact, the two are inseparable in much of his work. Nevertheless, this is a book of quiet, not-so-obvious farewells. He still fiddles around with language, does a few high jinks, fails a few times, and then turns around and writes a poem unlike any poem he has written before:

Mountain

Nothing's moving I don't see anybody
And I know that it's not a trick
There really is nothing moving there
And there aren't any people. It is the very utmost top
Where, as is not unusual,
There is snow, lying like the hair on a white-haired person's
    head
Combed sideways and backward and forward to cover as
    much of the top
As possible, for the snow is thinning, it's September
Although a few months from now there will be a new crop
Probably, though this no one KNOWS (so neither do we)
But every other year it has happened by November
Except for one year that's known about, nineteen twenty-
    three
When the top was more and more uncovered until
    December fifteenth
When finally it snowed and snowed.
I love seeing this mountain like a mouse
Attached to the tail of another mouse, and to another and
    to another

In total mountain silence.
There is no way to get up there, and no means to stay.
It is uninhabitable. No roads and no possibility
Of roads. You don't have a history
Do you, mountain top? This doesn't make you either a
    mystery
Or a dull person and you're certainly not a truck stop.
No industry can exploit you
No developer can divide you into estates and lots
No dazzling disquieting woman can tie your heart in knots.
I could never lead my life on one of those spots
You leave uncovered up there. No way to be there
But I'm moved.

There are several other moving poems in the book, the long
one called "Bel Canto" among them. On the whole, this is not
as strong a collection as *Straits* (1998) and *New Addresses* (2000),
which contain some of his most ingenious and accomplished
poems. Koch is overdue for an expanded edition of his selected
poems that would include work from the five collections that
he published in the last ten years. It would, I hope, correct a neglect and lack of understanding of the astonishing range of his
poetry, which comprised everything from comic epics to one-
line poems in both formal and free verse. I will go out on a limb
and say that some of the most original and satisfying poetry in
the last fifty years will be found in that ample selection. The
book might even include this short poem "Barking Dogs in the
Snow," from *A Possible World*, which despite its brevity sounds
like an elegy for the poet:

Barking dogs in the snow! Good weather is coming!
Good weather is coming to barking dogs in the snow.
A man changes only slowly. And winter is not yet past.
Bark, dogs, and fill the valleys
Of white with your awful laments.

NOTES

1. *On the Great Atlantic Rainway: Selected Poems, 1950–1988* (Knopf,
1994), pp. 70–72.

2. *Making Your Own Days: The Pleasures of Reading and Writing Poetry* (Scribner, 1998), p. 69.

3. *The Last Avant-Garde: The Making of the New York School of Poets* (Doubleday, 1998), p. 3.

4. *Wishes, Lies and Dreams: Teaching Children to Write Poetry* (Random House, 1970), p. 23.

5. Anne Waldman, "Excerpt from an Interview with Kenneth Koch, New York City, 1980," *Jacket*, December 15, 2001.

Tsvetaeva

The Tragic Life

When it comes to the Russian poetry of the last century, Osip Mandelstam, Anna Akhmatova, and Boris Pasternak are reasonably familiar names, but not Marina Tsvetaeva, who is their equal. Because she is extraordinarily difficult to translate, her work is almost unknown, and even when it becomes available it makes little impression. She seems foreign and beyond reach with her elliptical syntax and her unusually tangled metaphors. There's also the sheer volume and range of her writing. One of her long poems, for instance, celebrates Lindbergh's transatlantic flight, while others derive their plots from fairy tales. She has hundreds of poems, a number of near epic length in addition to a fair amount of prose, including memoirs, diaries, and letters, as well as several plays in verse. Not everything she wrote is, of course, first-rate, but a lot is. Is she as good as Eliot or Pound? one may ask for the sake of comparison. She is as good as they are and may have more tricks up her sleeve as a poet.

Her life makes for an unusually gripping story, which several fine biographies of the poet published in the last twenty years have recounted in great detail. Tragic lives, of course, cannot be compared in their degree of awfulness. Even in normal times one can't be sure how much the mess people make of their lives is due to failings of character and strings of bad luck, and how much to the circumstances in which they found themselves.

Review of *Earthly Signs: Moscow Diaries, 1917–1922,* by Marina Tsvetaeva, trans. Jamey Gambrell; and *Milestones,* trans. Robin Kemball. From the *New York Review of Books,* February 13, 2003.

When it comes to men and women who lived through decades of wars, revolutions, and exile, it gets harder to know whom or what to blame. As Tsvetaeva said in a poem, "I fear that for such misfortune the whole of / Racine and the whole of Shakespeare is not enough! . . ."[1]

Marina Tsvetaeva was born in 1892 in Moscow and grew up in an atmosphere of culture and refinement. Her father was a classical philologist who taught at Moscow University and was the founder of one of the city's important museums. Marina's mother was an accomplished pianist who wanted her daughter to be a musician. In 1902, on the advice of her doctors after being diagnosed with tuberculosis, she withdrew Marina and her younger sister from school and traveled to Italy in search of a cure. In 1905 the family returned to Russia, where the mother died a year later. Marina attended school in both Russia and Paris, where she started writing poetry and translating from French. A collection of her poems, *Evening Album,* was published in 1910 and well received. Her verses were romantic and sentimental, as was to be expected from an adolescent, but she also was said to have brought in this connection a new and bold intimacy to Russian poetry.

In 1912 Tsvetaeva married Sergei Efron, who came from a well-known family of encyclopedia publishers and political radicals. He was younger than she was. That same year she brought out her second book of poems, *The Magic Lantern,* and gave birth to a daughter, Ariadna (Alya). Money from her family made the newlyweds well-off. They bought a house in Moscow and spent their summers on the Crimean coast. The marriage, however, was not a success. Tsvetaeva had affairs with the poets Sofia Parnok and Osip Mandelstam. In April of 1917, her second daughter, Irina, was born and Efron, wanting most likely to get away from the awkward situation at home, volunteered for the Imperial Army. The October Revolution caught Tsvetaeva in the Crimea. She returned to revolutionary Moscow in late November, while her husband was joining the White Army to fight the Bolsheviks. For the next three years she had no word of him.

Tsvetaeva found herself alone at twenty-five, nearly destitute with no means to support herself and her two small children. She survived with the help of friendly neighbors and by selling her belongings. Here's a description from the prose collection *Earthly Signs* of her life in Moscow:

> I get up—the upper window is barely gray—cold—puddles—saw-dust—buckets—pitchers—rags—children's dresses and shirts everywhere. I split wood. Start the fire. In icy water I wash the potatoes, which I boil in the samovar. (For a long time I made soup in it, but I once got it so clogged up with millet that for months I had to take the cover off and spoon water from the top—it's an antique samovar, with an ornate spigot that wouldn't unscrew, wouldn't yield to knitting needles or nails. Finally, someone—somehow—blew it out.) I stoke the samovar with hot coals I take right from the stove. I live and sleep in one and the same frightfully shrunken, brown flannel dress, sewn in Alexandrov in the spring of 1917 when I wasn't there. It's all covered with burn holes from falling coals and cigarettes. The sleeves, once gathered with elastic, are rolled up and fastened with a safety pin.

A thief once broke into Tsvetaeva's flat and was horror-struck by the poverty he found. She asked him to sit down and talked to him. When he got up to leave he offered her money. Nevertheless, in her diary after one such dark moment, she makes a surprising remark:

> I didn't write down the most important thing: the gaiety, the keenness of thought, the bursts of joy at the slightest success, the passionate directedness of my entire being.

Despite the never-ending hardship, this was a productive period for her. She wrote long verse dramas and dozens of short lyrics. She also filled her notebooks with what she saw and heard as she took trips to the provinces in quest of food. Some of these comments are included in *Earthly Signs,* a marvelous selection from her diaries and essays in an exceptionally fine translation by Jamey Gambrell. They give us a view of the times not very different from that found in Isaac Babel's stories. Tsvetaeva is an excellent reporter. Despite what historians may pretend, in revolutionary times stealing is more important than ideas. While the leaders of the revolution promise the moon, murder and looting are the only reality the powerless know.

Tsvetaeva's autobiographical writings and her essays are filled with memorable descriptions and beautifully turned phrases. "The heart: it is a musical, rather than a physical organ," she says, for example. Or: "Death is frightening only to the body. The soul can't conceive of it. Therefore, in suicide, the body—is the only hero." Her views on everything from the behavior of human beings to the nature of poetry are shrewd and original. None of that sharpness of insight was much in evidence in her own life where she made one mistake after another. In the winter of 1919–20, unable to feed her children, she placed them in an orphanage. The older one, Alya, became ill, and Tsvetaeva brought her back home and nursed her to health. In February her younger daughter, who was not yet three years old, died of starvation in the same orphanage. Overcome by guilt for what amounted to her neglect of the child, she only very rarely mentioned her again.

"I am an inexhaustible source of heresy," Tsvetaeva declared. "Not *knowing* a single one, I profess all of them. Perhaps I even create them." She didn't like Chekhov with his sense of proportion; she always took sides. One of the funniest memoirs in *Earthly Signs* contains her description of a poetry reading with eight other women at which she read poems in praise of the White Army to an audience consisting mostly of Red Army soldiers. The duty of poetry, she believed, was to take the side of the defeated. She also found the word "poetess" applied to herself to be insulting. There are more essential distinctions in poetry, she said, than belonging to the male or female sex. Her courage and independence are remarkable when one remembers that other decent people had to grovel and that most of the other poets—even those who changed their minds later—were welcoming the Revolution. For a long time they could not accept that all that suffering was for nothing.

While Tsvetaeva's early poetry was admired by her contemporaries, the same cannot be said of her work in the 1920s. This is how her former lover Mandelstam described her poems: "The sorriest thing in Moscow is Marina Tsvetaeva's amateurish embroidery in praise of the Mother of God." Complaining about women's poetry in general and about her specifically, he went on to say that hers is a kind of verse that offends both ear and historical sense.[2] Leon Trotsky, in his once widely read and revered *Literature and Revolution* (1923), agreed, calling it a narrow poetry encompassing the poetess herself; a certain gentleman in a derby hat or military spurs; and finally God, who performs the duties of a doctor specializing in female complaints. In émigré literary circles, it was usually the same story. "She enters literature wearing curlers and a bathrobe as though she were headed for the bathroom," a critic wrote.[3]

Jamey Gambrell sums up well the difficulties of Tsvetaeva's work in her concise and extremely perceptive introduction to *Earthly Signs:*

> Tsvetaeva is not easy reading, even for educated native speakers of Russian. She confronts readers with a Joycean profusion of idioms and styles, ranging from the metaphorical speech of fairy tales and the circumlocutions of peasant dialect to a high literary diction steeped in Greek and Roman myths, the classics, and German Romanticism. She used almost all the classic Russian meters, adding her own innovations, and she made original use of Russian folk rhythms. Her subject matter draws on an equally diverse range of literary, historical, and folkloric sources. As Voloshin once said, ten poets coexisted in Tsvetaeva.

The linguistic density of her poems can be compared to that of Gerald Manley Hopkins, except that she has many more voices. In a letter to Rilke, with whom she had an epistolary romance, she writes:

> I am not a Russian poet and am always astonished to be taken for one and looked upon in this light. The reason one becomes a poet (if it were even possible to become one, if one were not one before all else!) is to avoid being French, Russian, etc., in order to be everything.

A bit later in that same letter, however, she says: "Yet every language has something that belongs to it alone, that *is* it."[4] Tsvetaeva is the poet of that *it*. "In an almost biblical sense," Gambrell writes, "the Word is the vehicle of creation; engendering both subject and emotion, it is the incarnation of the spirit."

To be a poet of the ear and make sound more important than sight is to make oneself virtually untranslatable. None of the translations of her poetry that I've read—and there are a great many of them—are able to convey her full verbal power, though some, like the ones by Nina Kossman and Michael M. Naydan, come close. In translation she is too often made to appear painfully awkward and dull when she is nothing of the sort. Here's how Robin Kemball renders one of her poems in *Milestones*:

Poem Number 31

A wild old hag told me plainly
Bent like a yoke in her frenzy:
—Not yours to lie idly dreaming,
Not yours to be bleaching linen,
Yours to reign—in some lost outstation,
Yours to kiss, my dearie—a raven.

I went white as a cloud as I listened:
Bring out the white burial vestment,
The black foal's no more for whipping,
The cathedral pope's no more for tippling,
Lay me peacefully under the apple tree,
With no prayers, no incense to cradle me.

A low bow is the thanks I say for
The advice and imperial favor,
For those pockets of yours, so empty,
For your prisoners' songs in plenty,
For the shame half-shared with sedition,—
For your love, for the fierce love you've given.

When the bell tolls from the cathedral—
I'll be dragged away by the devils.
As we sank our glasses together,
I was saying, and I'll tell the Creator—
That I loved you, my sturdy youngling,
Beyond fame and beyond the sunshine.

This doesn't sound like the great poet I've been praising. Unfortunately, this is the impression one gets from *Milestones,* a collection of mostly short lyric poems written in 1916. Many of the translations, even when they partially succeed, are marred by an unfortunate, unidiomatic choice of words and phrases. Tsvetaeva translating her poems into French herself did not do much better. She took greater liberties than Kemball does, transposing and changing the tonality of the poems, not only using different words but also changing images in the hope of preserving the essential, claiming that in another language one has to write something new. This seems like sensible advice, except the translations she made were no good. Still, in my view, taking freedoms now and then is the only way to proceed with translations of her poems and, with luck, pull off the impossible.

In May 1922, Tsvetaeva left Russia with her daughter to rejoin her husband, who was then living in Prague. She got as far as Berlin, where, while waiting to be reunited with Efron, she had an affair with her publisher. After two months in Berlin, the family moved to a village on the outskirts of Prague, where they lived for the next two and a half years. Her son, Georgy (known as Mur), was born in 1925. The years in Czechoslovakia were comparatively happy. There were stipends for Russian émigré students and intellectuals generously provided by the government. Tsvetaeva was also writing. Some of her long poems were written at this time, including *The Swain* and *The Pied Piper* (both of which are based on fairy tales), and two of the very best, *Poem of the Mountain* and *Poem of the End,* were both inspired by another infatuation. In a letter that her husband wrote at that time, he describes what it was like living with her:

> Marina is a woman of passions. . . . Plunging headfirst into her hurricanes has become essential for her, the breath of life. It no longer matters who it is that arouses these hurricanes. Nearly always (now as before)—or rather always—everything is based on self-deception. A man is invented and the hurricane begins. If the insignificance and narrowness of the hurricane's arouser is quickly revealed, then Marina gives way to a hurricane of despair. A state which facilitates the appearance of a new arouser. The important thing is not *what* but *how.* Not the essence or the source but the rhythm, the in-

sane rhythm. Today—despair; tomorrow—ecstasy, love, complete self-abandon; and the following day—despair once again. And all this with a penetrating, cold (maybe even cynically Voltairean) mind. Yesterday's arousers are wittily and cruelly ridiculed (nearly always justly). Everything is entered in the book. Everything is coolly and mathematically cast into a formula. A huge stove, whose fires need wood, wood, and more wood. Unwanted ashes are thrown out, and the quality of the wood is not so important. For the time being the stove draws well—everything is converted to flame. Poor wood is burnt up more quickly, good wood takes longer.

It goes without saying that it's a long time since I've been any use for the fire.

Her own explanation in a letter doesn't contradict her husband's:

I am not made for [this] life. With me, everything is a conflagration. I can be engaged in ten relationships at a time (fine "relationships," these!), and assure each one from the deepest depth that he is the only one. But I cannot tolerate the slightest turning of the head away from me. I HURT, do you understand? I am a person skinned alive, while all the rest of you have armor. You all have art, social issues, friendships, diversions, families, duty, while I, in the depth, have NOTHING. It all falls off like the skin and under the skin there is living flesh or fire—I'm Psyche. I do not fit into any form, not even the simplest form of my poems.[5]

Almost all of the poems that make up her greatest single collection, *After Russia*, were written at that time. Here is a poem from that book which is one of the first I ever read of hers and which I have never forgotten. It comes from *The Penguin Book of Russian Verse*, published in 1962 in what the editor calls "plain prose translation," which I still prefer to several other versions in verse:

An Attempt at Jealousy

What is your life like with another woman? Simpler, isn't it?
    A stroke of the oar! Did the memory of me,
a floating island (in the sky, not on the waters), soon re-
    cede, like a coastline? . . .
Souls, O Souls, you will be sisters, not lovers!

What is your life like with an *ordinary* woman? *Without* the
divine? Now that you have dethroned your queen and
have yourself renounced the throne,
what is your life like? How do you busy yourself? How are
you shivering? How do you get up [from your bed]? How
do you manage to pay the price for immortal triviality,
poor fellow?
"I've had enough of convulsions and palpitations—I'll rent a
house!" What is your life like with a woman like any
other, you, my chosen one?
Is the food more congenial and eatable? Don't complain
if you get sick of it! What is your life like with a
semblance—you who have trodden upon Sinai?
What is your life like with a stranger, a woman of this world?
Tell me point-blank: do you love her? Does shame, like
Zeus's reins, not lash your brow?
What is your life like? How is your health? How do you sing?
How do you cope with the festering wound of immortal
conscience, poor fellow?
What is your life like with a market commodity? The price is
steep, isn't it! After the marble of Carrara what is your
life like with a piece of crumbling plaster of Paris?
(God was hewn out of a block, and has been smashed to
bits!) What is your life like with one of a hundred thousand women—you who have known Lilith?
Have you satisfied your hunger with the new market
commodity? Now that magic has lost its power over
you, . . . what is your life like with a woman of this earth,
without either of you using a sixth sense?
Well, cross your heart: are you happy? No? In a pit without
depth what is your life like, my beloved? Harder than my
life with another man, or just the same?

In November 1925, the family moved to Paris in the hope
that Tsvetaeva would have more contact with writers. Her first
public reading was a triumph she never managed to repeat.
After being initially well received by the Russian community, relations eventually soured over the years for both literary and political reasons. Soviet literature was anathema to the émigrés,
but not to her. She praised Communist poets like Mayakovsky in
public. In the meantime, the family lived in poverty. Her hus-

band had no profession, no practical skill, and no wish to get a regular job. Only Russian politics interested him. In the 1930s he become involved with an organization called the Union for Returnees to the Soviet Union, which was widely and correctly believed to be a front for the Soviet secret service. After his political views took a Stalinist turn, Tsvetaeva, who had supported the family with her writing and with financial help from her rich friends, found herself more and more ostracized because of her husband's activities.

At home, the atmosphere was tense. Efron talked about going back to Russia and expiating his guilt for having fought with the Whites in the Civil War. The children took their father's side. Her daughter started working for a French Communist magazine and began moving in pro-Soviet circles. Tsvetaeva with her experience of communism had fewer illusions. It must be remembered that this was the time of Stalin's Great Terror. Going back was almost as crazy as for a Jew to return to Hitler's Germany. Efron, she told people, saw what he wanted to see and closed his eyes to what was really happening in Russia. Even after her daughter left for Moscow in 1937, she was reluctant to follow. Then, life became impossible for her in France. Her husband was interrogated by the French police in connection with the murder of a Soviet spy who had refused to return home.

In September of 1937, before they could ask him any more questions, Efron fled to the Soviet Union. Later investigations established that he worked for the NKVD and participated in several assassinations, including that of Trotsky's son. Not even Tsvetaeva's closest friends could believe that she knew nothing of her husband's intelligence work. People avoided her. She was excluded from literary gatherings and was no longer published. She survived with the help of a small stipend provided to her by the Soviet embassy while waiting to receive permission to return. Her loyalty to her husband and children, all of whom wanted to return, overrode any reservations she had. On June 12, 1939, she and her son finally departed. In her last letter before sailing from Le Havre, she wrote to a Czech friend: "Goodbye! What comes now is no longer difficult, what comes now is fate."

In Moscow she learned that her sister was in the camps. Barely two months after Tsvetaeva's return, her daughter was arrested and accused of spying for Western powers, and shortly after so was her husband. Efron was most likely shot soon after, while her daughter spent some seventeen years in the camps and in exile in Siberia. Tsvetaeva was never to see them again. She had no money and no place to live. Old friends were afraid to have anything to do with a wife of an "enemy of the people" and an ex-émigré. As a writer, for the Communists she did not exist. If she wasn't standing in some prison line to leave a parcel for her husband and daughter, she was looking for work. She did some translating which brought a little money, and even put together a collection of poems, but it was rejected by the publisher with the explanation that her poems had nothing to say to the Soviet people. Pasternak did what he could to help, but it wasn't much. When Germany invaded Russia in June 1941 and the bombing raids over Moscow increased, her panic grew. She managed to be evacuated to Elabuga, a small town on the Toima and Kama rivers. Tsvetaeva rented a room in Elabuga from a local couple, and went to a larger town nearby, where a number of writers had already been settled, and tried to get a permit to move there. She even applied for a job as a dishwasher in the writers' cafeteria.

There was reason to hope that she would get permission, but by this time she herself was beyond hope. On August 31, while her son and her landlords were out, she hanged herself in the entrance way of her room. She left three notes, two of them pleading to friends to take care of her son and the last one to him: "Forgive me," she wrote,

> but it would only have gotten worse. I am seriously ill, this is no longer me. I love you madly. Understand that I couldn't live any more. Tell Papa and Alya—if you see them—that I loved them to the last minute, and explain that I had reached a dead end.

Tsvetaeva was buried in an unmarked grave in Elabuga's cemetery. Mur was drafted into the army in 1943 and was killed in combat in July of 1944.

One of her biographers, Victoria Schweitzer, writes:

When she was removed from the noose and taken to the morgue, the undertaker found a tiny (1x2 cm) blue morocco-bound notebook in one of the pockets of her apron. There was a very slim pencil attached to the notebook, but to all intents and purposes the notebook was too small to write in. The undertaker kept this notebook, kept it for more than forty years and, on his deathbed asked for it to be given back to Tsvetaeva's relatives. In it, like a message from the other world, was one word in Tsvetaeva's handwriting: Mordovia.

This was the name of the Soviet republic in the Urals where her daughter Alya had been sent to a camp.

"God, do not judge! You were never a woman on this earth," she once wrote.

NOTES

1. Viktoria Schweitzer, *Tsvetaeva* (Farrar, Straus and Giroux, 1992), p. 275.

2. Simon Karlinsky, *Marina Tsvetaeva: The Woman, Her World, and Her Poetry* (Cambridge University Press, 1985), pp. 128–29.

3. Karlinsky, *Marina Tsvetaeva*, p. 157.

4. Boris Pasternak, Marina Tsvetaeva, and Rainer Maria Rilke, *Letters: Summer 1926* (New York Review Books, 2001), p. 221.

5. Karlinsky, *Marina Tsvetaeva*, p. 135.

Conspiracy of Silence

I first read W. G. Sebald's *The Emigrants* when it came out in English in 1996 and remember feeling that I had not read anything so captivating in a long time. The book is difficult to classify. Told in the first person by the author, it reads at times like a memoir, at others like a novel or a work of nonfiction about the lives of four emigrants. They come from Lithuania and Germany and end up in England and the United States. The book includes, and this is another peculiarity of his, blurry, black and white photographs with no captions and not-always-clear connections to people and places being talked about in its pages. As for the author, one knew next to nothing about him except what one deduced from autobiographical details in the book, most importantly that he was a German living in England. *The Emigrants* was widely praised and called a masterpiece by many eminent writers and critics. The reviewers noted the author's elegiac tone, his grasp of history, his extraordinary powers of observation, and the clarity of his writing. While stressing his originality, critics mentioned Kafka, Borges, Proust, Nabokov, Calvino, Primo Levi, Thomas Bernhard, and a few others as Sebald's likely influences. There were some complaints about the unrelenting pessimism of his account of thwarted lives and the occasional monotony of his meandering prose, but even those who had reservations acknowledged the power of his work.

The narrator of *The Emigrants* is a loner and so are the rest of the characters. The countless victims of last century's wars, revolutions, and mass terror are what interests Sebald. One may say that he sought a narrative style that would convey the state of

Review of *On the Natural History of Destruction*, by W. G. Sebald, trans. Anthea Bell. From the *New York Review of Books*, February 27, 2003.

mind of those set adrift by forces beyond their understanding and control. Unlike men and women who have never known exile, whose biography is shaped by and large by social class and environment, to be a refugee is to have sheer chance govern one's fate, which in the end guarantees a life so absurd in most cases that it defeats anyone's powers of comprehension. Sebald served as a kind of oral historian and unconventional biographer of such people, reconstructing their lives out of bits and pieces he was told by them and out of additional research he did himself into their backgrounds. If his book is melancholy, it is because the task he gives himself is all but hopeless.

Eventually, other works of Sebald's were translated, though not always in order of their composition. *The Rings of Saturn* (1998), which came next, is a record of a walking tour of the eastern coast of England with lengthy digressions on Thomas Browne, Roger Casement, Joseph Conrad, the Battle of Waterloo, the Taiping rebellion, Rembrandt's *Anatomy Lesson,* and at least a dozen other topics. Another oddity of Sebald's prose, which either delights or exasperates his readers, is his digressions. He never hesitates to interject some interesting anecdote or bit of factual information arrived at by some not-always-apparent process of association. He does this without forewarning, transition, or even paragraph break. Clearly, he intends the reader to draw together the various threads in the book, the way one would do with images and metaphors in a poem, and make something of them. Here is an example from *The Rings of Saturn,* which tells of an event from the 1860 British and French punitive military expedition into China and anticipates some of his concerns in the new book:

> In early October the allied troops, themselves now uncertain how to proceed, happened apparently by chance on the magic garden of Yuan Ming Yuan near Peking, with its countless palaces, pavilions, covered walks, fantastic arbours, temples and towers. On the slopes of man-made mountains, between banks and spinneys, deer with fabulous antlers grazed, and the whole incomprehensible glory of Nature and of the wonders placed in it by the hand of man was reflected in dark, unruffled waters. The destruction that was wrought in these legendary landscaped gardens over the next few days, which

made a mockery of military discipline or indeed of all reason, can only be understood as resulting from anger at the continued delay in achieving a resolution. Yet the true reason why Yuan Ming Yuan was laid waste may well have been that this earthly paradise—which immediately annihilated any notion of the Chinese as an inferior and uncivilized race—was an irresistible provocation in the eyes of soldiers who, a world away from their homeland, knew nothing but the rule of force, privation, and the abnegation of their own desires.

Although the accounts of what happened in those October days are not very reliable, the sheer fact that booty was later auctioned off in the British camp suggests that much of the removable ornaments and the jewelry left behind by the fleeing court, everything made of jade or gold, silver or silk, fell into the hands of the looters. When the summerhouses, hunting lodges, and sacred places in the extensive gardens and neighboring palace precincts, more than two hundred in number, were then burnt to the ground, it was on the orders of the commanding officers, ostensibly in reprisal for the mistreatment of the British emissaries Loch and Parkes, but in reality so that the devastation already wrought should no longer be apparent.

The temples, palaces, and hermitages, mostly built of cedarwood, went up in flames one after another with unbelievable speed, according to Charles George Gordon, a thirty-year-old captain in the Royal Engineers, the fire spreading through the green shrubs and woods, crackling and leaping. Apart from a few stone bridges and marble pagodas, all was destroyed. For a long time, swaths of smoke drifted over the entire area, and a great cloud of ash that obscured the sun was borne to Peking by the west wind, where after a time it settled on the heads and homes of those who, it was surmised, had been visited by the power of divine retribution.

The secret of Sebald's appeal is that he saw himself in what now seems almost an old-fashioned way as a voice of conscience, someone who remembers injustice, who speaks for those who can no longer speak. There was nothing programmatic about that. He wrote as if nothing else was worth a serious person's attention. Like any one of us who takes time to read history, both ancient and modern, he was dismayed. No explanations along the lines of "war is hell," "human beings everywhere are like that," and so forth could make him forget for a moment the cruelties committed against the innocent. He'd agree with the Dowager Empress of China, who said before she died that she finally understood that history consists of nothing but misfortune, so that in all our days on earth we never know one single moment that is genuinely free of fear. What is strange—and it's no doubt owing to the marvelous translation of Michael Hulse, who worked closely with Sebald—is that the effect of his tales of horror is lyrical.

Vertigo, the very first prose book he wrote, when he was forty-six years old, came next. It was published in Germany in 1990 and not translated into English until 1999. It is a story of a journey across Europe in the footsteps of Stendhal, Casanova, and Kafka which ends in the narrator's native Bavarian village. *Austerlitz,* which followed in 2001 in a translation by Anthea Bell, is his one true novel. It is a story of a small child brought to England in one of the children transports from Germany in the summer of 1939 and his subsequent effort to find out about the death of his Jewish parents and his origins in Prague. Sebald said that behind the hero of the book hide two or three, or perhaps three and a half, real persons. Some of the narrative feels contrived with realistic description alternating with segments that could have come out of magic-realist fiction, and yet the book contains some of his best and his most moving writing.

I recall him saying in an interview that there are questions a historian is not permitted to ask, because they are metaphysical. The truth for him always lies elsewhere, somewhere yet undiscovered in myriad overlooked details of some individual existence. "I think how little we can hold in mind," he writes after a visit to a Belgian prison used by the Nazis, "how everything is constantly lapsing into oblivion with every extinguished life, how the world is, as it were, draining itself, in that the history of countless places and objects which themselves have no power of memory is never heard, never described or passed on."

There's a spooky scene in *Austerlitz* in which the hero, walking the empty streets of Terezin in Czechoslovakia where his mother had died in a camp, comes upon a closed antique store window cluttered with various objects that in all probability belonged to the inmates. There they were, these ornaments, utensils, and mementos that had outlived their former owners together with his own faint shadow image barely perceptible among them. All that remained was a Japanese fan, a globe-shaped paperweight, and a miniature barrel organ that brought home the reality of some vanished life and the full magnitude of what had happened.

After Sebald's death in December 2001 in a car accident we learned more about his life. He was born in 1944 in a small village in the Bavarian Alps to a working-class family. He studied German literature in Fribourg, Switzerland, and Manchester and eventually settled in England permanently where he taught European literature for thirty years at the University of East Anglia in Norwich. His first literary work was a book of prose poems, *After Nature*, which was translated and published in 2002. He traveled a great deal. He told his last interviewer, "My ideal station is possibly a hotel in Switzerland."[1] His literary reputation seems to have been much greater in English-speaking countries than in his native Germany. Even though he was born in 1944, the Second World War cast a long shadow over his writing. As André Aciman said, "Sebald never brings up the Holocaust. The reader, meanwhile, thinks of nothing else."[2]

His posthumous book, *On the Natural History of Destruction*, again has four parts and reads this time like a straightforward collection of nonfiction pieces. The subject of the first is the destruction of German cities by Allied bombing. The other three, which were not included in the original German edition, deal with the postwar German novelist Alfred Andersch; the Austrian-Belgian writer Jean Améry, who survived Auschwitz; and the painter Peter Weiss. The chapters on air war were based on lectures he delivered in the autumn of 1997 in Zurich. His thesis, which provoked considerable controversy when the lectures were published in newspapers in Germany, is that the destruction of all the larger German cities and many smaller ones by the Allied air raids was never adequately discussed in literature after the war. There was a conspiracy of silence about it as there was about many other things that occurred during the Nazi years.

This is not exactly a new discovery. Hans Magnus Enzensberger essentially made the same point in an essay called "Europe in Ruins" that he wrote in 1990. In contrast to Heinrich Böll, Primo Levi, Hans Werner Richter, Louis-Ferdinand Céline, Curzio Malaparte, and a number of foreign journalists, practically all German storytellers avoided the subject. So why did Sebald bring it up again?

Some accused him of being motivated by a need to have the Germans perceived as victims and thus minimize the suffering of others by creating a moral equivalence. This is completely unfair to him. Sebald knew that Germans provoked the annihilation of their cities and that they would have done the same and worse to others had they been able to. His detractors seem to believe that there is a moral scale by which the suffering of the innocent among different ethnic groups can be calculated, with the most deserving at the top and those least deserving of pity at the bottom, and they are shocked that he lacked their faith. The issues he raises about the war against the civilians have no simple answers. They defy description:

> Today it is hard to form an even partly adequate idea of the extent of the devastation suffered by the cities of Germany in the last years of the Second World War, still harder to think about the horrors involved in that devastation. It is true that the strategic bombing surveys published by the Allies, together with the records of the Federal German Statistics Office and other official sources, show that the Royal Air Force alone dropped a million tons of bombs on enemy territory; it is true that of the 131 towns and cities attacked, some only once and some repeatedly, many were almost entirely flattened, that about 600,000 German civilians fell victim to the air raids, and that three and a half million homes were destroyed, while at the end of the war seven and a half million people were left homeless, and there were 31.1 cubic meters of rubble for every person in Cologne and 42.8 cubic meters for every inhabitant of Dresden—but we do not grasp what it all actually meant.

In view of the number of civilian casualties in bombings of urban areas in the last century, there are reasons to think it may be safer to be a soldier at the front than a mother with children sitting in a cellar during an air raid. The figures for deaths in individual German cities are staggering, but they are equally horrendous elsewhere. Forty-three thousand died in the London Blitz; 100,000 in Tokyo in 1945, plus Hiroshima and Nagasaki where over 200,000 perished; and the list goes on. More recently there is Vietnam, where an estimated 365,000 civilians died, and finally Baghdad in the Gulf War for which the figures are kept secret. In Japan, not counting the atom bombs, over 300,000 civilians perished just in 1945. Of course, these rounded-off figures are at best educated guesses. Bombing history plays games with numbers to conceal the individuals' fate. The deaths of the innocent are an embarrassment. All religious and secular theories of "just war" from Saint Augustine to the United Nations charter caution against their indiscriminate slaughter. The Geneva Convention warns the parties to the conflict again and again to distinguish between civilian populations and combatants, and between civilian objectives and military objectives.

Since civilians, by international agreement, are not supposed to be the object of attack, the numbers for what we today call euphemistically "collateral damage" tend to vary widely in retrospect depending on the political agenda of the writer. Even when they are plainly given, they sound as inconceivable as astronomical distances. A number like 100,000 conveys horror on an abstract level. A figure like 100,001, on the other hand, would be far more alarming in my view. That lone additional person would restore the reality to the thousands of other casualties. To thumb through a book of old news photos or watch documentary footage of an air raid in progress is a sobering experience. One of the most common sights of the last century is a row of burned and still-smoldering buildings of which only the outside walls remain. Rubble lies in the streets. The sky is black except for dragons of flames and swirling smoke. We know that there are people buried under the rubble. I remember a photo of a small naked girl running toward a camera in a bombed village somewhere in Vietnam. After almost a hundred years of this sort of thing, it takes a staggering insensitivity not to acknowledge what a bombing raid on a populated area does and who its true victims are.

I myself remember the firebomb from my childhood in Yugo-slavia. It carries sticks of explosive that burst into flames. The sticks scatter loosely like straws in a game of jackstraws, each one a fire-starter. If the weather is dry and there's a bit of wind, such bombs can start a firestorm that can wrap an entire city in a blanket of fire. The glow of such fires, pilots report, is visible a hundred miles away and even the smell of burning buildings and human beings ablaze like matches reaches the high-flying planes. I knew a boy who lost both arms attempting to dismantle such a bomb. In the Second World War, there was also the fa-mous bomb cocktail in which different incendiaries were used to start fires on the roof, bigger bombs to penetrate all the way down to the cellar, and the heaviest ones to blow in windows and doors and make huge craters in the streets, so the fire engines could not reach the fires. Dante's and Jonathan Edwards's ghastly descriptions of hell pale in comparison to airmen's de-scriptions of what it was like to conduct and witness the effects of these raids.

It's not just the droning planes, the blood-red skies, and the deafening explosions that are frightening. Even more scary is the power of those who give themselves the right to decide whom to obliterate, whom to spare. It cannot be helped, is their excuse. If they are right, and I'm not convinced they are, that may be the most terrifying thing of all. No matter what history books have told us, bombing is a form of collective punishment premised on collective guilt. Prominent theoreticians of air power have never concealed that. In a war, they argue, there cannot be a differentiation made between military personnel and civilians. Especially when it comes to a nation like Germany, whose leaders ordered that millions of people be murdered and worked to death, and many of whose citizens carried out the orders, it is hard to feel sorry. The firestorms were universally regarded as a just punishment even if they didn't have much military and political logic, as is now fairly clear from the docu-mentary evidence. I understand the emotion perfectly. I grew up hating Germans.

But—and this is the crux of the matter—can dropping bombs on densely populated residential areas really be justi-fied? Can one hold the view that women and children of the enemy are not blameless and still pretend to have an ethical position? Are deaths of noncombatants truly of so little consequence? The answer—judging by the long, cruel history of last century's bombings—is yes. Killing innocents is thought to be a necessary evil. To that I'd say—and I speak from experience— that for those who are bombed it feels like destruction for its own sake. Since the bombs can hardly ever get at the leaders wining and dining in their well-protected underground shelters, the innocent will always have to pay for their crimes.

"How ought such a natural history of destruction to begin?" Sebald asks. He wants us to ponder what it means to have an entire city with all its buildings, trees, inhabitants, domestic pets, fixtures, and fittings destroyed. The remains of human beings are everywhere, flies swarm around them, the floors and steps of the cellar are thick with slippery finger-length maggots, rats and flies rule the city. The few eyewitness accounts are ghastly. In the midst of rubble, out of sheer panic, the population tries to carry on as if nothing has happened. There's a woman, for instance, washing a window of a building that stands in a desert of ruins. No wonder survivors found it difficult to talk about it. Sebald's parents would not. He grew up, he says, with the feeling that something was being kept from him at home, at school, and by the German writers he read hoping to glean more information about these events.

Silence about what happened to their cities was not just a German reaction. Twenty years after the bomb fell on Hiroshima most of the survivors could not speak of what happened that day. My mother, who lay next to me in the cellar during many an air raid on Belgrade, wouldn't talk about it either. In his books Sebald has always been interested in the way in which individual, collective, and cultural memory deals with experiences that lie on the border of what language can convey. Bombing is part of that, but there are other, even more terrible things human beings have had to cope with. In what is in my view the best essay in *On the Natural History of Destruction,* he quotes Jean Améry's description of being tortured by Gestapo:

> In the bunker there hung from the vaulted ceiling a chain
> that above ran into a roll. At its bottom end it bore a heavy,

broadly curved iron hook. I was led to the instrument. The hook gripped into the shackle that held my hands together behind my back. Then I was raised with the chain until I hung about a metre above the floor. In such a position, or rather, when hanging this way, with your hands behind your back, for a short time you can hold at a half-oblique through muscular force. During these few minutes, when you are already expending your utmost strength, when sweat has already appeared on your forehead and lips, and you are breathing in gasps, you will not answer any questions. Accomplices? Addresses? Meeting places? You hardly hear it. All your life is gathered in a single, limited area of the body, the shoulder joints, and it does not react; for it exhausts itself completely in the expenditure of energy. But this cannot last long, even with people who have a strong physical constitution. As for me, I had to give up rather quickly. And now there was a cracking and splintering in my shoulders that my body has not forgotten to this hour. The balls sprang from their sockets. My own body weight caused luxation; I fell into a void and now hung by my dislocated arms which had been torn high from behind and were now twisted over my head. Torture, from Latin *torquere*, to twist. What a visual instruction in etymology!

Sebald admires the Belgian resistance fighter's detachment and understatement, which prohibits both pity and self-pity. Only at the very end of his account, in that one ironic phrase which concludes a "curiously objective passage," as Sebald says, is it clear that his composure has reached a breaking point. If someone wanted to convey truly what it was like, Améry went on to say, he would be forced to inflict pain and thereby become a torturer himself. The utter helplessness of human beings in such circumstances, deep pity and solidarity with victims of injustice, are the recurring themes for both of these men. Sebald quotes a diary entry of one Friedrich Reck who tells of a group of refugees from bombing trying to force their way into a train at a station in Upper Bavaria. As they do, a cardboard suitcase "falls on the platform, bursts open and spills its contents. Toys, a manicure case, singed underwear. And last of all the roasted corpse of a child, shrunk like a mummy, which its half-deranged mother has been carrying about with her."

It's all just too much, one says to oneself reading such a passage. What worries Sebald, as it should worry any thinking person, is our newfound capacity for total destruction. Is it ever morally justified to fight evil with evil? It continues to be a worry despite what our most passionate warmongers and strategists tell us almost daily about the so-called smart bombs and mininukes which will spare the innocent and target only the guilty. For instance, the Pentagon's current war plan for Iraq, according to CBS, calls for a launch of between three hundred and four hundred cruise missiles on the first day, which is more than were launched during the entire forty days of the Gulf War, with the same number to follow the next day and presumably the day after.

The battle plan is based on a concept developed at the National Defense University. It's called "Shock and Awe" and it focuses on the psychological destruction of the enemy's will to fight rather than the physical destruction of his military forces. "We want them to quit. We want them not to fight," says Harlan Ullman, one of the authors of the Shock and Awe concept which relies on large numbers of precision-guided weapons. "So that you have this simultaneous effect, rather like the nuclear weapons at Hiroshima, not taking days or weeks but in minutes," says Ullman. In the first Gulf War, 10 percent of the weapons were precision-guided. In this war 80 percent will be precision-guided.

I have my doubts and I imagine Sebald would have them too. So much intellect, capital, and labor go into planning destruction, one can count on excuses being found in the future for some inadvertent slaughter. The ones who survive will again be faced with the same problem: how to speak of the unspeakable and make sense of the senseless.

NOTES

1. Maya Jaggi, "The Last Word," *Guardian*, December 21, 2001.

2. "Out of Novemberland," *New York Review of Books*, December 3, 1998.

Archives of Horror

The clarity of everything is tragic.
—Witold Gombrowicz

I still have a memory of a stack of old magazines I used to thumb through at my grandmother's house almost sixty years ago. They must have dated from the early years of the century. There were no photographs in them, just engravings and drawings. I was especially enthralled by scenes of battles that were most likely depictions of past Balkan wars and rebellions. They were done in the heroic manner. The soldiers charged with grim determination through smoke and carnage; the wounded hero lay with his chest bared in the arms of his comrades seemingly happy as to how things turned out. It was the kind of stuff that made me want to play war immediately. I'd run around the house shooting an imaginary rifle, crashing down on the floor mortally wounded, then immediately jumping up again to fire at the enemy until my grandmother ordered me to stop. Her nerves were frayed enough already since there was plenty of real shooting to be heard all around us.

The year was 1944, the Russian Army was closing in on Belgrade, the Germans were digging in to fight, while the Americans and the English took turns bombing us. If one escaped the city, one was in even greater danger, since a civil war raged in the countryside among Communists, royalists, and several other factions, with civilians being killed indiscriminately. Like many others, my parents went back and forth. Even a six-year-old had numerous opportunities to see dead people and be frightened. Still, I made no connection then, that I recall, between what I

Review of *Regarding the Pain of Others,* by Susan Sontag. From the *New York Review of Books,* May 1, 2003.

saw in those magazines and the things I witnessed in the streets. That was not the kind of war I and my friends were playing. This may sound unbelievable, but it took war photographs and documentaries that I saw a few years later to impress upon me what I had actually lived through.

One day when I was in third or fourth grade our whole class was taken to a museum to see an exhibition of photographs of atrocities. The intention, I suppose, was to show the youth of a country whose official slogan now was "brotherhood and unity" what the fascists and their local collaborators had brought about. We, of course, had no idea what we were about to see, suspecting that it would be something boring, like paintings of our revolutionary heroes. What we saw instead were photographs of executions. Not just people hanged or being shot by a firing squad, but others whose throats were being cut. Ordinarily, we took the opportunity of these class trips to tease the girls and generally make a complete nuisance of ourselves, but that day we were mostly quiet. I recall a photograph of a man sitting on another man's chest with a knife in his hand, looking pleased to be photographed.

As terrifying as the scenes were, they tend to blur in my mind except for a few vivid details. A huge safety pin instead of a button on the overcoat of one of the victims; a shoe with a hole in its sole that had fallen off the foot of a man who lay in a pool of blood; a small white dog with black spots who stood in the distance, wary but watching. It was like seeing hard-core pornographic images for the first time and being astonished to learn that people did such things to one another. I could not talk about this to anybody afterward; neither did my schoolmates say anything to me. Our teachers probably lectured us afterward about what we saw, but I have no memory of what they said. All I know is that I never forgot that day.

I suspect Susan Sontag has written a book others thought of writing but chickened out of. The images of war atrocities may seem like a subject about which there'd be plenty to say, but somehow it turns out not to be the case. As with other all-powerful visual experiences, there's a chasm between what one sees and what one can articulate. For instance, I can recall down to its minutest details Ron Haviv's close-up photograph taken in

1992 of a Muslim man begging for his life on the streets of the town of Beljina in Bosnia. I feel the horror at what is about to take place, can even imagine what is being said, know well enough that these men with guns are without pity. And yet nothing that I can imagine or say equals the palpable reality of this terrified, pleading face on the verge of tears.

Who is this witness, I ask myself, this photographer who gives himself the godlike right to be there? Did he just happen to come along? What took place after the camera's click? How come the killers let him go with the evidence of their crime? Did they exchange any words before he went his way? Is it true then, as Sontag wrote in *On Photography* (1977), that the camera is a passport that annihilates moral boundaries, freeing the photographer from any responsibility toward the people photographed? If there's anyone capable of answering these thorny questions, it is she. As that early book demonstrated, she is a most probing critic, one of the very best writers on photography in its history.

Regarding the Pain of Others is a book about photographs without out a single illustration. It begins with a discussion of Virginia Woolf's *Three Guineas,* a book of reflections on the roots of war. In order to test our "difficulty of communication," Woolf proposes that we look together at images of Spanish Civil War atrocities. She wants to know whether when we look at the same photographs, we feel the same thing. Sontag tells us that Woolf professes to believe that the shock of such pictures cannot fail to unite people of goodwill:

> Not to be pained by these pictures, not to recoil from them, not to strive to abolish what causes this havoc, this carnage— these, for Woolf, would be the reactions of a moral monster. And, she is saying, we are not monsters, we members of the educated class. Our failure is one of imagination, of empathy: we have failed to hold this reality in mind.

Who are the "we" at whom shock-pictures such as these are aimed? Sontag wonders. In 1924, Ernst Friedrich published in Germany his *Krieg dem Kriege!* (*War Against War!*), an album of more than 180 photographs drawn from German military and medical archives, almost all of which were deemed unpalatable by government censors while the war was going on, thinking that circulating them widely would make a lasting impact. As Sontag describes it, the reader gets a photo tour of four years of slaughter and ruin: pages of wrecked and plundered churches, obliterated villages, torpedoed ships, hanged conscientious objectors, half-naked prostitutes in brothels, soldiers in death agonies, corpses putrefying in heaps, close-ups of soldiers with huge facial wounds, all of them meant to shock, horrify, and instruct. Look, the photographs say, *this* is what it is like. This is what war *does*. By 1930, *War Against War!* had gone through ten editions in Germany and had been translated into many languages. Judging by the refinements in cruelty in the next war, its effect was zero. Here's what Sontag has to say:

> The familiarity of certain photographs builds our sense of the present and immediate past. Photographs lay down routes of reference, and serve as totems of causes: sentiment is more likely to crystallize around a photograph than around a verbal slogan. And photographs help construct—and revise—our sense of a more distant past, with the posthumous shocks engineered by the circulation of hitherto unknown photographs. Photographs that everyone recognizes are now a constituent part of what a society chooses to think about, or declares that it has chosen to think about. It calls these ideas "memories," and that is, over the long run, a fiction. Strictly speaking, there is no such thing as *collective* memory—part of the same family of spurious notions as collective guilt. But there is collective instruction.
>
> All memory is individual, unreproducible—it dies with each person. What is called collective memory is not a remembering but a stipulating: that *this* is important, and this is the story about how it happened, with the pictures that lock the story in our minds. Ideologies create substantiating archives of images, representative images, which encapsulate common ideas of significance and trigger predictable thoughts, feelings.

I imagine most of the people carrying out the butchery in Croatia and Bosnia in the 1990s had already seen in previous photographs of war everything they were now doing. In the days of nationalist euphoria that preceded these crimes, television audiences all over Yugoslavia were being shown pictures of what one ethnic group did to the others in the past. Sontag is right when she points out that images of dead civilians serve mostly to quicken the hatred of your enemy. She writes:

> To an Israeli Jew, a photograph of a child torn apart in the attack on the Sbarro pizzeria in downtown Jerusalem is first of all a photograph of a Jewish child killed by a Palestinian suicide-bomber. To a Palestinian, a photograph of a child torn apart by a tank round in Gaza is first of all a photograph of a Palestinian child killed by Israeli ordnance.

Looking at pictures of Serbian atrocities in Croatia, it occurred to me that Serbs who saw them may have been envious. They yearned to do the same to Croats. Today, of course, Serbs find it difficult to look at photographs of what was done in their name. The usual response, as Sontag notes, is that these pictures must be fabrications since our brave fighting men are incapable of such barbarities. It seems that, for nationalists everywhere, feeling remorseful for the wrong one has done to others is a sign of weakness and nothing more.

Do photographs that permit one to linger over a single image make a greater impact on viewers than violence on television and in the movies? Sontag believes they do, and I agree. The collapse of the World Trade Center towers on September 11, 2001, was almost universally described as "unreal," "surreal," or "like a movie," and it was. The still images made by both professional and amateur photographers are at times more direct and thus more powerful, as anyone who has seen them will testify. Even the death and destruction in the Vietnam War, which was documented day after day by television cameras and brought to our homes, did not seem to make as much of an impression as a few famous photographs of that war did. "Memory freeze-frames; its basic unit is the single image," Sontag writes in *Regarding the Pain of Others*. Photographs, her argument runs, seem to have a more innocent and more accurate relation to reality, or so we tend to believe. They furnish concrete evidence, a way of certifying that such and such did actually happen.

We are more suspicious of movies and documentaries since

we know that they can be edited to make a particular aesthetic or political point. Even though the same can be done to a photograph, we rarely question what we are seeing. The most famous photograph of the Spanish Civil War is a blurred, black and white image of a Republican soldier shot by Robert Capa's camera at the same moment as he is struck by an enemy bullet. The photographer, we think, had the presence of mind to point his camera and bear witness and we admire him for it. "Everyone is a literalist when it comes to photographs," Sontag writes. It's disconcerting to learn from her book that this photo may have been staged, as were many other long-familiar war photographs of the past, for reasons of expediency and propaganda.

Is there a shame in finding oneself peering at a close-up of some unspeakable act of violence? Yes, there is. Can you bear to look at *this* without flinching? a photograph asks, and often we can barely find the strength to do so, as in the well-known Vietnam War photograph taken by Huynh Cong Ut, of children shrieking with pain and fear as they run away from a village that has just been doused with American napalm. What makes it shameful is that the photograph is not only shocking, it is also beautiful, the way a depiction of excruciating torments of some martyr can be in a painting. "The aesthetic is in reality itself," the photographer Helen Levitt once said. One ends up by complimenting the man with the camera who not only documents the horror but manages to take a good picture. Sontag writes:

> That a gory battlescape could be beautiful—in the sublime or awesome or tragic register of the beautiful—is a commonplace about images of war made by artists. The idea does not sit well when applied to images taken by cameras: to find beauty in war photographs seems heartless. But the landscape of devastation is still a landscape. There is beauty in ruins. . . . Photographs tend to transform, whatever their subject; and as an image something may be beautiful—or terrifying, or unbearable, or quite bearable—as it is not in real life.

"The photograph gives mixed signals," Sontag says. "Stop this, it urges. But it also exclaims, What a spectacle!" The Khmer Rouge took thousands of photographs between 1975 and 1979 of men and women just before they were to be executed. They stare straight at the camera, the number tags pinned to the top of their shirts. Their expressions are in turn serious, disbelieving, worn-out, and somehow still curious about what comes next. It's hard to meet their eyes, while at the same time one can't stop looking at them. We are all voyeurs, whether we like or not, Sontag writes, and who could pretend otherwise? "All suffering people look the same," a friend of mine likes to say. This is true up to a point, that is, before the camera makes them distinct. A little private light bulb that illuminates the life of each of us comes to be lit by the photograph. Our memories are dark, labyrinthine museums with an occasional properly illuminated image here and there.

"Is it correct to say that people get used to these?" Sontag asks. Are we better off for seeing images of atrocities? Do they make us better people by eliciting our compassion and indignation so we want to do something about injustice and suffering in the world? Finally, are we truly capable of assimilating what we see? She notes the mounting level of acceptable violence and sadism in mass culture, films, television, and video games. Scenes that would have had audiences cover their eyes and shrink back in disgust forty years ago are now watched without a blink by every teenager. The same is true of the world out there. People can get used to bombs, mass killings, and other horrors of warfare. Today I find it hard to believe that I once swiped a helmet off a dead German soldier, but I did. Despite what believers in long-repressed and buried memories may think, fear and shock unfortunately have expiration dates. For every dreadful image I recall, I have forgotten thousands of others. In *On Photography*, Sontag argued that an event known through photographs after repeated exposure becomes less real. As much as they create sympathy, she wrote then, photographs shrivel sympathy.

In her new book, she's no longer sure. "What is the evidence that photographs have a diminishing impact, that our culture of spectatorship neutralizes the moral force of photographs of atrocities?" she asks. Our military shares her uncertainty and has no intention of testing its truth by letting photographers roam freely on the battlefield. There are hardly any images of the dead in the first Gulf War, mainly stories of wild dogs tearing at the corpses of the Iraqi dead. A few pictures slipped past censorship of the war in Afghanistan, but the overall policy is to conceal the effects of warfare, especially on civilians. The military learned its lesson in Vietnam. "The war itself is waged," Sontag writes, "as much as possible at a distance, through bombing, whose targets can be chosen, on the basis of instantly relayed information and visualizing technology, from continents away." When local television stations begin showing images of civilian casualties we do not hesitate to bomb them into silence, as happened in the NATO bombing of Yugoslavia and with al-Jazeera in Kabul. "When there are photographs," Sontag writes, a war becomes "real." The revulsion at what the Serbs had done in Croatia, Bosnia, and Kosovo and the almost universal demand that something be done about it were mobilized by images. Unfortunately, as we've seen with Cambodia and Rwanda, photographs do not always guarantee accountability. Still, a war without pictures, or rather a war sanitized to a few propaganda images, is a frightening prospect.

Sontag is rightfully angry with certain French intellectuals fashionable in academic circles who speak of "the death of reality" and who assure us that "reality" is now a mere spectacle. "It suggests, perversely, unseriously," she writes, "that there is no real suffering in the world." And yet, there was a time when she was somewhat inclined toward that view, when she was tempted to say that it is images and not reality that photography makes accessible. She charged photography with doing as much to deaden conscience as to arouse it, and she was not wrong. "Photography implies," she wrote, "that we know about the world if we accept it as the camera records it. But this is the opposite of understanding, which starts from *not* accepting the world as it looks." Some reviews of the new book I have seen claim that she has now repudiated this view. This simplifies her ideas in the earlier book about the relationship of the image world to the real one which are not only more nuanced, but are also mindful of the long history of that question going back to Plato. By insisting that there is indeed such a thing as reality, it does not mean that she now embraces a reductive, either/or approach with truth and beauty as irreconcilable opposites. Lastly, it's not photographs of bell peppers, nudes, or the Grand Canyon that are her subject here, but rather what she once called "the slaughter-bench of history."

Timely as it is, Sontag's extended meditation on the imagery of war in *Regarding the Pain of Others* is guaranteed to make some readers uneasy. These are things they'd rather not dwell on. Consumers of daily violence, she knows, are schooled to be cynical about the temptation of strong feelings. Her book on the other hand bristles with indignation. She has no patience for those who are perennially surprised that depravity exists, who change the subject when confronted with evidence of cruelties humans inflict upon other humans. "No one after a certain age," she goes on to say, "has the right to this kind of innocence, of superficiality, to this degree of ignorance, and amnesia."

Sontag is a moralist, as anyone who thinks about violence against the innocent is liable to become. The time she spent in Sarajevo under fire gives her the authority. Most of us don't understand what people go through, she writes. True, we only have photographs. Even if they are only tokens, they still perform a vital function, Sontag insists. They certainly do for me. Like the one by Gilles Peress I saw some years ago of a child with eyes bandaged being led by his mother down a busy street in Sarajevo. Or another, by the same photographer, where we see a man in a morgue approach three stretchers with bodies lying on them and cover his face as he recognizes a friend or a relative. The morgue attendant is expressionless as he stands watching.

Men and women who find themselves in such circumstances, one says to oneself, do not have the luxury of patronizing reality. Such photographs preserve, however tenuously, the mark of some person's suffering in the great mass of faceless and anonymous victims. We ought to be grateful to Susan Sontag for reminding us of this. If photography is a form of knowledge, writing about it with critical discernment and passion, as she does, is bound to make trouble for every variety of intellectual and moral smugness.

Where the Fun Starts

Perhaps the ideal place to think about the literature of the last fifty years is in a library surrounded on all sides by rows of shelves well stacked with bound copies of old literary magazines. One can probably spend months there in some corner without being noticed, choking on dust, turning the yellowed, crumbling pages, lingering over some poem or story, and even sneak in Chinese food and an occasional bottle of wine to get rid of the blues. Time is cruel to all living things, but what it does to literary reputations is downright mean. Sometimes it takes no more than twenty years for someone thought of as a great writer by his or her contemporaries to be completely forgotten. Literary movements that were once a scandal now make one yawn. To read through decades of literary quarterlies and avant-garde magazines is to begin to feel a tinge of sympathy for Chairman Mao, who, when he grew tired of writers and poets, used to send them into the countryside to harvest rice and dig ditches.

So much of what one finds in old magazines is so incredibly boring and so obviously inconsequential; it is sometimes difficult to imagine why anyone ever took the slightest interest in publishing it. Poetry—and this may be my poet's bias—strikes me as far more unreadable than fiction or literary criticism. Fiction, no matter how artless it happens to be, has at least some tenuous relation to reality that can hold one's interest for a little while. Poems, one realizes, depend so much on whatever

Review of *The Paris Review Book of Heartbreak, Madness, Sex, Love, Betrayal, Outsiders, Intoxication, War, Whimsy, Horrors, God, Death, Dinner, Baseball, Travels, The Art of Writing, and Everything Else in the World Since 1953,* by the editors of the *Paris Review,* with an introduction by George Plimpton. From the *New York Review of Books,* July 3, 2003.

contemporary notion of the "poetic" was fashionable at the time that reading them years later one cannot escape being struck by how much they sound alike. Criticism, if it deigns to engage itself imaginatively with some literary work, can be wonderfully enlightening. Then, just as one thinks one has it all figured out, the miraculous occurs. One comes upon a piece of writing that doesn't seem to fit into any generalizations and that makes one feel like an idiot.

In 1953, when the *Paris Review* began publication in Paris, Stalin had just croaked, Julius and Ethel Rosenberg were electrocuted in Sing Sing, and Senator McCarthy claimed to have uncovered thirty thousand pro-Communist books in the State Department's overseas information libraries. In the United States, the leading literary magazines were the *Kenyon Review* and *Partisan Review*. In each issue they would publish a few poems, perhaps one short story, but they had other, bigger concerns. As a journal edited from an English department's point of view, the *Kenyon Review* was likely to contain a longish article on Donne's prosody, another on the theme of Ulysses in literature, in addition to several substantial reviews of academic books. *Partisan Review*'s interests were much broader. There were brilliant critical reflections on intellectual, political, and cultural topics from such writers as Hannah Arendt, Iris Murdoch, Elizabeth Hardwick, and F. W. Dupee as well as more academic pieces that bore titles like "Symbolism in the Novel" and "O'Neill and Irish Catholicism."

To be sure, many of the important fiction writers and poets of the time like Robert Lowell, Flannery O'Connor, Norman Mailer, Randall Jarrell, John Berryman, Mary McCarthy, Bernard Malamud, Saul Bellow, and James Baldwin did get published in these magazines. Even so, I think it's fair to say that they gave a rather narrow picture of the American literature of their day, with little interest in younger writers and poets. There were, of course, the other so-called little magazines like the *Black Mountain Review, Locus Solus,* and the *Fifties,* where one could see a much wider range of literary work, but they were mostly shoestring operations, poorly distributed and nearly impossible to get hold of if one lived outside New York, Boston, and San Francisco. Until the arrival of the *Paris Review,* there was not a single sizable publication in this country devoted almost entirely to new fiction and poetry with such wide taste in literature.

Today, looking at the early issues, I'm astonished to see how sophisticated its founding editors were in literary matters and conversely how provincial and ignorant their competition back home was. They had fiction by Samuel Beckett, Italo Calvino, Dino Buzzati, Terry Southern, William Styron, and Jean Genet; poems by Robert Bly, Geoffrey Hill, James Wright, Adrienne Rich, and W. S. Merwin (poets who were barely in their twenties then); portfolios of drawings by artists like Giacometti, Kokoschka, and Picasso. One of the best features of the *Paris Review,* then and now, is the interviews with writers and poets. Beginning with E. M. Forster in the first issue, there were interviews with Graham Greene, Alberto Moravia, William Faulkner, Dorothy Parker, Ralph Ellison, Georges Simenon, T. S. Eliot, Louis-Ferdinand Céline, Ezra Pound, and Hemingway. The idea was to give an opportunity to writers and poets to talk about their writing and their influences, explain the secrets of their craft, and also tell a few amusing stories. Most of the writers did just that, as one can see in this snippet from Dorothy Parker's interview:

> *Interviewer:* Did the lost generation attitude you speak of have a detrimental effect on your own work?
>
> *Parker:* Silly of me to blame it on dates, but so it happened to be. Dammit, it *was* the "twenties" and we had to be smarty. I *wanted* to be cute. That's the terrible thing. I should have had more sense.
>
> *Interviewer:* And during this time you were writing poems?
>
> *Parker:* My verses. I cannot say poems. Like everybody was then, I was following in the exquisite footsteps of Miss Millay, unhappily in my own horrible sneakers. My verses are no damn good. Let's face it, honey, my verse is terribly dated— as anything once fashionable is dreadful now. I gave it up knowing it wasn't getting any better, but nobody seemed to notice my magnificent gesture.

The interviews were expertly edited. The writers were not only made to sound like raconteurs, but they also managed to say many memorable things about literature. Not all of them, of course. Henry Miller comes across as a simpleton and Hemingway as annoyingly defensive and insecure. All this talking was done without any use of critical jargon, as if the interviewers had never heard, for instance, that the New Criticism had separated the author from his work. There was nothing about texture and structure of meaning, allusion and irony, symbolic imagination and disassociation of sensibility. It was more like overhearing an intelligent bartender on a slow night prod a lone customer to talk about himself. In the only editorial the magazine ever had (reprinted in this anthology from the first issue), William Styron explained the intentions of the editors:

> Literarily speaking, we live in what has been described as the Age of Criticism. Full of articles on Kafka and James, on Melville, or whatever writer is in momentary ascendancy; laden with terms like *architectonic, Zeitgeist,* and *dichotomous,* the literary magazines seem today on the verge of doing away with literature, not with any philistine bludgeon but by smothering it under the weight of learned chatter.

The result, he goes on to say, is that magazines were weighted in favor of critics, not creators. The new magazine's goal was

> to emphasize creative work—fiction and poetry—not to the exclusion of criticism, but with the aim in mind of merely removing criticism from the dominating place it holds in most literary magazines and putting it pretty much where it belongs, i.e., somewhere near the back of the book.

Even that practice didn't last very long. After a couple of years of half-hearted attempts to have "commentaries" on everything from ballet to Italian literature included in the magazine, the idea was abandoned, although not the portfolios of Parisian artists, some of whom were little known in the United States.

Styron also claimed in that same preface that the *Paris Review* had no axes to grind, nothing comparable to the "powerful blasts" in the first number of Pound's the *Exile.* That may have been true of these editors, but not, of course, of some other magazines in the 1950s and 1960s, which engaged in fierce polemic and made the American literary scene resemble warring mafia families with names like Academics, New York Poets, Beats, Black Mountain Poets, Deep Image Poets. Styron simply thought that if a magazine more or less ignored criticism but concentrated on finding good writers and good poets, it might possibly publish literature equal to that of any in the past.

As it turned out, this was a wise position to take. Against all odds, a good amount of the writing still seems fresh even after fifty years. That's not the way it is supposed to be, as I indicated earlier, but there it is. Did being in Europe cause the editors to be more cosmopolitan and thus more astute? The early issues are full of tantalizing ads that must have made readers back in Duluth or Tuscaloosa shut their eyes in reverie at what it must be like living there:

LES DEUX MAGOTS À ST.-GERMAIN-DES-PRÉS, RENDEZ-VOUS DE L'ÉLITE INTELLECTUELLE

Actually, Peter Matthiessen, the fiction editor, and Donald Hall, who was responsible for the poetry, were living mostly in the States, while Plimpton and later Robert Silvers put the actual magazine together in Paris. Notwithstanding, one can't help but be impressed by how shrewd the editors' choices were. In the 1950s few had heard of Philip Roth, Jack Kerouac, V. S. Naipaul, Mary Lee Settle, Gina Berriault, Richard Yates, Philip Larkin, James Merrill, Evan S. Connell, William Stafford, Philip Levine, Donald Justice, Ted Hughes, Louis Simpson, and a good many others when their work was published and yet eventually they all became major figures in American and British literature. Even making a selection from the first ten years of the *Review* would not be an easy thing to do with so much good work. Throw in another forty and the task becomes formidable. Of course, there are always obvious candidates for inclusion, memorable stories like Roth's "Conversion of the Jews," or a scandalous-sounding poem like John Updike's "Two Cunts in Paris," but, beyond that, how was one to decide? There was the additional problem of how to arrange the material. Should one proceed chronologically year by year, decade by decade, or follow some other organizing principle as if all the stories and poems were already immortal?

110

As one can see from the lengthy subtitle to the book, George Plimpton, who has been mainly responsible for keeping the magazine going, decided to subdivide the work by subject matter, namely: Heartbreak, Madness, Sex, Love, Betrayal, Outsiders, Intoxication, War, Whimsy, Horrors, God, Death, Dinner, Baseball, Travels. The reader can presumably pick and choose, begin, for instance, with Sex, check on Madness and God next, and conclude the evening with Dining and Death. I did something like that myself, comparing the thoughts of Nabokov, Mailer, and García Márquez, while worrying whether the editor had left out any important subject. Writers and poets like to imagine they are writing about the human condition or something equally vague, so it's shocking to see their work so clearly labeled. In reality, all one has to do is turn to the interviews with writers, whether in or out in the anthology, to realize that subject matter is very much on their mind. Here is John Cheever on sex:

It seems to me that one of the most critical problems faced today by a young writer of fiction is the emphasis on explicit descriptions of sexual intercourse. . . . The change, mutations and flow of literature, painting and music seem not to be organic. . . . For a writer of my generation to claim that explicit descriptions of fucking, etc. will reach saturation point and that readers will presently long for accounts of family life, storms at sea—the usual paraphernalia of fiction may be equally mistaken. One has two images. One of a lovely woman in a chair—perhaps a rocking chair—sewing blue cloth. The second is of the same woman, naked, with "fuck me" written on her back side. Both images are persuasive and full of meaning but it seems to me that the second is irresistible. My feeling is that one of your problems, perhaps your principal problem, is how to manage this irresistibility.

Under a different heading, each section of the anthology has two to three stories, a few poems, and short passages from interviews. These excerpts are perhaps the least successful aspect of the whole enterprise. Interesting as these fragments are, they are still fragments and seem like fillers. They should not have been interspersed throughout the book, but consigned to the final section entitled "The Art of Writing." Aside from that, the eccentric table of contents makes for lively reading. One simply has no clue what may come next. Here, for example, is a beautiful poem by Heather McHugh, whose verbally intricate poetry—and even this particular poem, for that matter—I would not immediately associate with heartbreak:

Intensive Care

*

As if intensity were a virtue we say
good and. Good and drunk. Good and dead.
What plural means is everything
that multiplying greatens, as if two
were more like ninetynine than one,
or one were more like zero than
like anything. As if
you loved me, you will leave me.
**
You (are the man who) made
roadmaps to the ovaries
upon his dinner napkin.
I('m the woman who) always forgot
where she was—in a state,
in a sentence. Absently stirring
my alphabet soup, I remember
childhood's clean white calendar
and blueprint of the heart.
***
As if friends were to be saved
we are friends. We talk to ourselves,
go home at the same time.
As if beds were to be made
not born in, as if love
were just heredity
we know the worst, we fear
the known. Today we were bad
and together; tonight
we'll be good and alone.

Heartbreak, indeed! That ending would fit fine in some country-and-western song. There are also drawbacks to grouping the material by subject matter. It tends to exclude poems and stories that are not easily classifiable. Without sitting down with a pencil and paper and doing the calculation, it appears to me there's scant evidence in the *Paris Review Book* of the avant-garde poetry that was published in the 1960s and 1970s. Except for a story by Donald Barthelme, the same is true of the more experimental fiction. Anything too literary, too self-consciously preoccupied with form at the expense of content is suspect. In that respect the taste of the editors has not changed in fifty years. They don't mind a light mix of surrealism and naturalism, but tend to be wary of works that have no interest in verisimilitude. If there's going to be any innovation, it will not be in style and form but in subject matter. The first-person point of view is still the most trusted one in both fiction and poetry. The interplay between autobiography and fiction is the norm. And yet, the moment I say that, I realize that there are plenty of exceptions to that view in the *Paris Review Book*.

This is especially true of short stories. Relying as they do on concision, nuance, and detail, even when they are the work of novelists whose manner we are familiar with, they tend to be less predictable than longer works of fiction. If novels could be compared to apartment houses, stories are more like single rooms somewhere in the back. They are interested in people who in novels may pass for minor characters not deserving a full treatment, as it were. It makes me think that part of our national genius in literature lies in this underrated art form. In stories and poems we are most original, most unlike anyone else. The mystery of character is one of the main preoccupations of many of these writers. Melville's Bartleby had a whole lot of children, it seems. Judging by the *Paris Review Book,* and the stories by such writers as Raymond Carver, Joyce Carol Oates, and David Foster Wallace, this is a country of loners, secret rebels, and misfits.

Edgar Allan Poe, speculating on the art of the short story in a review of Hawthorne's *Twice-Told Tales,* argued that a successful tale ought to be short enough to be read in one sitting so that the reader leaves the story with a single, vivid impression. That still tends to be our expectation. One can be browsing in a bookstore or lying in bed at home and reaching for something to read before turning off the lights, when one suddenly forgets whatever one was planning to do next because the opening of some story has captivated one's attention. If the trap has been properly baited by the writer, we are hooked for good and either buy the book or prop up the pillows and read to the end. Here, for instance, is how Larry Brown's "A Roadside Resurrection" starts:

> Story opens, Mr. Redding is coughing in a cafe by the Yocona River, really whamming it out between his knees. He's got on penny loafers with pennies in them, yellow socks, madras shorts, a reversible hat and a shirt that's faded, from being washed too many times. His wife, Flenco, or Flenc, as he calls her, is slapping him on the back and alternately sucking her chocolate milk shake through a straw and looking around to see who's watching. She's got a big fat face, rollers in her hair, and she's wearing what may well be her nightgown and robe. Fingernails: bright red.

And this is the opening of Michael Cunningham's "Pearls":

> Angela. I love what you left behind. Your scent, melony, yet sharp and immaculate as yogurt. Your diaphragm, placed, according to the promise, in my nightstand drawer as a token of fidelity. And the pearls. The pearls.
> I started finding them this evening, just after I got home. I'd expected a note. To be frank, I'd expected a present. You are such a maniac for gifts. So I entered the apartment in double-edged anticipation: dreading your absence, but looking forward to the surprise you'd planned, the particular way you had chosen to make yourself remembered. Of course, I found nothing at first, and read it symbolically. Leaving no remembrances was a way of saying "forget me." I felt greedy, and abashed. If I didn't deserve nothing you wouldn't have left me nothing, right? Stomach creeping, I went to the bathroom to wash my face. And there found the first pearl.

It's for that kind of unanticipated pleasure that we buy literary magazines. This anthology, spanning as it does decades and genres, is full of writing that ought to please the most discerning reader. There are stories by Lorrie Moore, Bobbie Ann Mason, Donald Barthelme, Stanley Elkin, Jonathan Franzen, Denis Johnson, Philip Roth, Grace Paley, Joyce Carol Oates, and several others; fine poems by Anthony Hecht, Kenneth Koch, Adrienne Rich, John Ashbery, Richard Howard, Robyn Selman, Nicholas Christopher, Donald Hall, Galway Kinnell, and Allen Ginsberg; plus articles on travel, sports, excerpts from novels, memoirs, and a few whimsical pieces. For example, James Merrill and David Jackson employ the Ouija board to conduct a posthumous interview with Gertrude Stein. Then there's a whole section of poems written to order by a group of poets who were given a series of titles and asked to supply a poem. The results were a surprise. Poets ordinarily not known for their wit wrote some pretty funny poems. Finally, as in any anthology this big, there is plenty more for anyone to enjoy:

> *Interviewer:* You haven't been to America, have you?
>
> *Larkin:* Oh no, I've never been to America, nor to anywhere else. . . . A writer once said to me, If you ever go to America, go either to the East Coast or the West Coast: the rest is a desert full of bigots. That's what I think I'd like: where if you help a girl trim the Christmas tree you're regarded as engaged, and her brothers start oiling their shotguns if you don't call on the minister.

Had Philip Larkin lived longer and eventually broken his rule about traveling and come to see us, he would have been amazed to hear that there are approximately six hundred active literary magazines in the United States. Some are older than the *Paris Review,* some are almost as venerable, while others come out irregularly and vanish after a few years to be replenished by new ones. How many people who profess an interest in literature and buy books have even heard of or have actually read an issue of *Agni Review, Boulevard,* the *Gettysburg Review, Tri-Quarterly,* the *Yale Review, Ploughshares, Salmagundi,* or *Tin House?* Not many, I suspect. Young writers and poets, of course, pay attention to them, since that's where they hope to publish their work, but I have no clear sense who their readers might be beyond that, or how these magazines and others I have not mentioned manage financially. Whatever one thinks of the state of American letters, their existence and survival in a country not known for its love of books is nothing short of heroic.

If they have learned anything from the *Paris Review,* and I believe they have, it is to keep the literary scholars out and stick to the original writing. And that, as anyone who goes out and buys this anthology is bound to discover, is when the fun starts.

Poetry in Unlikely Places

1.

The book that came to mean a lot to me as a young poet was an anthology of Latin American poetry that I discovered in a used bookstore in New York in 1959. Originally published in 1942 by New Directions, it had long been out of print, so neither I nor any of my poet friends had an inkling of its existence. It introduced me to the poetry of Pablo Neruda, Jorge Luis Borges, Jorge Carrera Andrade, Carlos Drummond de Andrade, Vicente Huidobro, Nicolás Guillén, César Vallejo, and dozens of other wonderful poets I had never heard of until that moment. I remember turning its pages in the store, realizing what a valuable book it was, paying for it quickly, and rushing home to read all of its 666 pages that very night. It was like reading Eliot's "Love Song of J. Alfred Prufrock" for the first time, seeing a Buster Keaton movie, hearing Thelonious Monk, and making other such exhilarating discoveries. I knew French Surrealist poetry, had already read Lorca, Mayakovsky, and Brecht, but I had never before encountered anything quite like this poem of Neruda's:

Walking Around

It so happens I am tired of being a man.
It so happens, going into tailorshops and movies,
I am withered, impervious, like a swan of felt
navigating a water of beginning and ashes.

The smell of barbershops makes me weep aloud.
All I want is a rest from stones or wool,

Review of *The Poetry of Pablo Neruda,* ed. Ilan Stavans. From the *New York Review of Books,* September 25, 2003.

all I want is to see no establishments or gardens,
no merchandise or goggles or elevators.

It so happens I am tired of my feet and my nails
and my hair and my shadow.
It so happens I am tired of being a man.

Yet it would be delicious
to frighten a notary with a cut lily
or do a nun to death with a box on the ear.
It would be fine
to go through the streets with a green knife,
letting out yells until I died of cold.

I do not want to go on being a root in the darkness,
vacillating, spread out, shivering with sleep,
downwards, in the drenched guts of the earth,
absorbing and thinking, eating every day.

I do not want so many afflictions,
I do not want to go on being root and tomb,
being alone underground, being a vault for dead men,
numb with cold, dying of anguish.

That is why Monday blazes like petroleum
when it sees me coming with my jailbird face,
and it howls like a wounded wheel as it passes,
and takes hot-blooded steps towards night.

And it shoves me into certain corners, certain damp houses,
into hospitals where bones fly out of the window,
into certain shoeshops with a stench of vinegar,
into streets as frightful as chasms.

There are sulphur-coloured birds and horrible intestines
hanging from the doors of the houses that I hate,
there are false teeth forgotten in a coffeepot,
there are mirrors
that ought to have wept for shame and fear,
there are umbrellas all over, and poisons, and navels.

I walk with composure, with eyes, with shoes on,
with fury, with forgetfulness,
I pass, I cross by offices and orthopedic shoeshops
and patios with the washing hanging from wires:
underdrawers, towels and shirts that weep
slow filthy tears.[1]

There were four other poems by Neruda in the anthology. Like "Walking Around," all but one of them came from *Residence on Earth*, the book that had made him famous in Spain and Latin America when it was published in 1935. The hero of the poems was a familiar figure—at least since the time of Whitman and Baudelaire, who invented the modern poem while walking in a city and recounting the marvelous and terrible things they encountered there. What astonished me about Neruda's poems were the images. Wildly inventive, they came in quick succession so that a poem of his was primarily a narrative made up of startling comparisons. "Natural surrealism" is what the American poet David St. John called it in an essay on this same poem.

Neruda had a fearless disregard for logical continuity and conventional notions of propriety. He was like a man showing up at a funeral wearing a somber suit and a loud tie. While Breton and the Surrealists sought poetry in the unconscious, Neruda was after a style. The manner of these poems resembled what was years later to be called "magic realism" in South American prose. Its chief trait was a rejection of any distinction between what is imaginary and what is real. Consequently an image like bones flying out of hospital windows was to be taken in stride, as if the poet had said there are some pigeons on the roof.

I was, of course, anxious to read more of Neruda. It turned out there were other, older translations by Angel Flores, H. R. Hays, and Samuel Sillen, all out of print and difficult to locate even in libraries. Finally, in 1961, Grove Press published his *Selected Poems* translated by Ben Belitt. Since then, there have been fifty-one books of translations, the work of almost a hundred translators. This information undoubtedly belongs in the *Guinness Book of World Records*. Is there another foreign poet who has been as much translated into English? Perhaps Rilke or Lorca— but no! They don't come close. So, what is the explanation? Is it that Neruda is a poet who is easy to read in a century in which some of the greatest poets are nearly impenetrable? The widely seen 1995 movie *Il Postino,* about Neruda befriending a village postman during his stay in Italy, may have also tempted the publishers, who usually expect to lose their shirts when it comes to poetry in translation.

Neruda was born Neftalí Ricardo Reyes Basoalto on July 12,

1904, in the village of Parral in southern Chile. His father worked for the railroad and his mother, who was a school-teacher, died of tuberculosis shortly after he was born. They were poor. The father remarried so they moved to a small town, Temuco, where Neruda spent his childhood and youth and got to know the poet Gabriela Mistral, who encouraged him to write. He started using the pen name Pablo Neruda in memory of the nineteenth-century Czech poet Jan Neruda to avoid conflict with his family who, like all parents, objected to their son's becoming a poet. While still a student studying French at the University of Chile in Santiago, he published his first book of poems, *Crepusculario,* in 1923. Next came *Twenty Love Poems and a Song of Despair* (1923–24), which gained him fame beyond the borders of Chile. In 1927, at the age of twenty-three, Neruda entered the diplomatic corps and was sent to Burma to be a consul in Rangoon. That assignment was followed by posts in Ceylon, Java, Singapore, Buenos Aires, Barcelona, and finally, in 1935, Madrid, where he met García Lorca, Rafael Alberti, Jorge Guillén, and the other Spanish poets who had already hailed his poetry.

The Spanish Civil War and the murder of Lorca radicalized his political views. "Come and see the blood in the streets," he wrote in a poem. He sided with the Spanish Republicans and quit his post. Increasingly, the poetry he was writing concerned itself with issues of the day. After a change of government at home, he resumed his diplomatic career in Paris and Mexico City. In 1945, he joined the Communist Party and was elected to the Chilean Senate. Soon after, he got in trouble. In an article published in a newspaper in Caracas because of censorship at home, he attacked President Gonzáles Videla for his repressive policies, which included the outlawing of the Communist Party. Neruda had to go into hiding and eventually into exile. He traveled to the Soviet Union and other Communist countries where he was received as an honored guest by their governments. In his articles he spoke of the truth and justice he found there, of the unparalleled triumphs and achievements of the Soviet people, and while seemingly forgetting that the soul of poetry is rebellion, praised Mayakovsky for being the first one to incorporate the views of the Party into his poems.

Neruda's travels beyond the Iron Curtain resulted in a book of poetic narratives, *Grapes of the Wind,* for which he was awarded the first Stalin Prize for Peace in 1953. I recall mentioning his name to Eastern European poets in the 1960s and being surprised by the violence of their reaction. They regarded him as another shameless opportunist and refused to entertain the possibility that he was also a great poet. As foolish and dishonest as Neruda was about Russia, his numerous pronouncements on the struggle for social justice in Chile and the rest of Latin America, of which he had firsthand experience, are an entirely different story. Here is what he wrote in 1952:

> With few exceptions, those who govern have cruelly treated the people of Chile and have ferociously repressed popular movements. They have followed the decrees of caste or the mandates of foreign interests. From the slaughter of Iquique to the death camp Gonzáles Videla erected in Pisagua, ours is a long and cruel history. Continuous war has been waged against the people, that is to say, against our country. Police torture, the club and the sword, siege, the marines, the army, ships of war, planes and tanks: the leaders of Chile do not use these weapons to defend our nitrate and our copper against foreign pirates, no, these are the instruments of their bloody assault against Chile itself. Prison, exile, and death are measures used to maintain "order," and the leaders who execute bloody acts against their countrymen are rewarded with trips to Washington, are honored in North American universities. This is in fact the politics of colonialism.[2]

Neruda was awarded the Nobel Prize for Literature in 1971. He established a permanent home on the Isla Negra in Chile, but continued to travel widely. I went to a reading of his at the Poetry Center of the Ninety-second Street Y in New York in June of 1966. The auditorium was packed. Neruda came onstage and read a poem by Whitman. The audience liked that very much, as I recall. His four American translators took turns reading his poems in English and he would follow in Spanish. Unlike the Russian poets who either shouted or chanted their verses, he had a sleepy way of saying his poems. My knowledge of the Spanish language is negligible, but since I knew in translation the poems he read, I found myself immensely moved. The next day I tagged along with some older poets who had a lunch date with him in the garden of a pizzeria in the Village. He charmed us all. Again the talk was of Whitman and how much he meant to him. Neruda died of leukemia in Santiago on September 23, 1973. They say that his death was very likely accelerated by the murder of President Salvador Allende and the terror that followed the military coup under General Pinochet. He left behind almost four thousand pages of poetry. He once said that he wanted a "poetry as impure as a suit or a body, a poetry stained by food and shame, a poetry with wrinkles, observations, dreams, waking, prophesies, declarations of love and hatred, beasts, blows, idylls, manifestos, denials, doubts, affirmations, taxes."[3] He certainly did that. In his fine little book on the poet, René de Costa writes:

> Neruda was a poet of many styles and many voices, one whose multitudinous work is central to almost every important development in twentieth-century Spanish and Spanish American poetry. He was once referred to as the Picasso of poetry, alluding to his protean ability to be always in the vanguard of change.[4]

Neruda recognized this himself, saying that he was the foremost adversary of Nerudism. Now that so much of his poetry is available in translation, it is possible to give the American reader a pretty good idea of what a major figure he was.

2.

The Poetry of Pablo Neruda advertises itself as "the most comprehensive single volume available in English"—and it is certainly that. Nearly one thousand pages long, edited with an introduction and an ample bibliography and notes to individual volumes by Ilan Stavans, it contains some six hundred poems selected from almost all of his books in new and old translations by thirty-seven translators, some of whom are well-known American poets. A number of the poems are also given in the original, and in some instances the editor has presented more than one version of the same poem. Finally, in the last section of the book, the editor has invited fourteen poets to pick out one or more of their favorite poems and bring them afresh into English. Here then are two poems that illustrate the vast range of his work. The first one comes from *Twenty Love Poems and a Song of Despair* and is translated by W. S. Merwin:

XX

Tonight I can write the saddest lines.

Write, for example, "The night is starry
and the stars are blue and shiver in the distance."

The night wind revolves in the sky and sings.

Tonight I can write the saddest lines.
I loved her, and sometimes she loved me too.

Through nights like this one I held her in my arms.
I kissed her again and again under the endless sky.

She loved me, sometimes I loved her too.
How could one not have loved her great still eyes.

Tonight I can write the saddest lines.
To think that I do not have her. To feel that I have lost her.

To hear the immense night, still more immense without her.
And the verse falls to the soul like dew to the pasture.

What does it matter that my love could not keep her.
The night is starry and she is not with me.

This is all. In the distance someone is singing. In the distance.
My soul is not satisfied that it has lost her.

My sight tries to find her as though to bring her closer.
My heart looks for her, and she is not with me.

The same night whitening the same trees.
We, of that time, are no longer the same.

I no longer love her, that's certain, but how I loved her.
My voice tried to find the wind to touch her hearing.

Another's. She will be another's. As she was before my kisses.
Her voice, her bright body. Her infinite eyes.

I no longer love her, that's certain, but maybe I love her.
Love is so short, forgetting is so long.

Because through nights like this one I held her in my arms
my soul is not satisfied that it has lost her.
Though this be the last pain that she makes me suffer
and these the last verses that I write for her.

In the eighty years since its publication, *Twenty Love Poems and a Song of Despair* has been translated into a great many languages and has sold millions of copies. At first, readers and critics were scandalized. There was too much raw sex in the poems. Being sentimental about love, extolling it as an ideal was okay; there was ample precedent for that, but not glorifying what lovers did in bed. For Neruda—as for Octavio Paz—the poetic act and the sexual act are intertwined. There can be no erotic feeling without the participation of the imagination. Poetry and eroticism both make the phantoms of our desire palpable. In 1959, Neruda brought out the book *One Hundred Love Sonnets.* He may not have believed in God, but he was an expert blasphemer in his poems. He spoke of the body of his beloved as if it were a soul and of her soul as if it were her body. A friend of his once said, "He could not conceive of human existence without the permanent state of being in love. Solitary people worried him; he found them incomprehensible."[5]

This next poem comes from *Canto General* (1950), the epic cycle of 320 poems which through multiple narrators and a variety of poetic styles from lyrical to dramatic retells the history of the conquest of South America, its liberators, dictators, oppressors, and betrayers. The heroes are ordinary men and women. As René da Costa shrewdly observes, this is a peculiarly American poem infused with messianic optimism in which the New World ends up by triumphing over the Old. Neruda, as he often did, has shed his previous poetic persona. He is now the poet of a larger community and the new consciousness that comes with the feeling of solidarity with all those who cannot speak:

What did you do, you Gideans,
intellectualizers, Rilkeans,
mystifiers, false existential
sorcerers, surrealist
butterflies, incandescent
in the tomb, Europhile
cadavers in fashion,
pale worms in the capitalist
cheese, what did you do
confronted with the reign of anguish,
in the face of this dark human being,
this kicked-around dignity,
this head immersed
in manure, this essence
of coarse and trampled lives?
You did nothing but take flight:
sold a stack of debris,
searched for celestial hair,
cowardly plants, fingernail clippings,
"Pure Beauty," "spells,"
works of the timid
good for averting the eyes,
for the confusion of delicate
pupils, surviving
on a plate of dirty leftovers
tossed at you by the masters,
not seeing the stone in agony,
no defense, no conquest,
more blind than wreaths
at the cemetery, when rain
falls on the flowers still
and rotten among the tombs.[6]

"I have assumed the poet's time-honored obligation to defend the people, the poor and the exploited," he wrote in a preface to a Portuguese edition of his work. However admirable this may sound to our ears, historically there's hardly any truth in what Neruda says. Still, this was undoubtedly the passion that drove many of his poems. On the other hand, the brooding poems of the first two sections of *Residence on Earth,* which he denounced after becoming a Party member and even prevented from being reprinted and translated, make it still one the most original collections of poems published in the last century. I would give the same unconditional praise to the twelve mystical poems "The Heights of Macchu Picchu," from *Canto General,* to the three books of *Elemental Odes* (1952–57), and to poems in *Extravagaria* (1957–58).

Neruda started writing odes for a daily newspaper, having in mind readers who ordinarily do not read or like poetry. Accordingly, the language is simple and so is the subject matter. There are odes to laziness, wine, an onion, salt, a tomato, a watermelon, a fallen chestnut, a hummingbird, a seagull, a bicycle, a wristwatch at night, a pair of wool socks, and many other items one would not expect to have poems written about. Each ode is an immersion in the present moment, a lighthearted dialogue between what the poet sees and what he imagines. There's even a moral at the end, a tongue-in-cheek piece of advice about the practical uses of the item being praised and a reminder of its beauty. *Extravagaria,* too, is a book of whimsical, occasional poems on every conceivable subject from watching a cat sleep to being told to exercise. In this book, Neruda broke his own rule that poetry must have a social function and instead left an intimate record of the events of his life.

As one would expect from an undertaking aiming to be so comprehensive in scope, *The Poetry of Pablo Neruda* is an uneven book. There are first-rate translations by John Felstiner, Margaret Sayers Peden, Jack Schmitt, Greg Simon, Alastair Reid, and a dozen others alongside many mediocre ones. I'm not competent to judge the accuracy of individual translations, but I can compare their quality as poems since there are previous renderings of the same poems which seem to me far superior to the ones we have here. For instance, neither of the two versions of "Walking Around" in this book are as good as the one I quoted by H. R. Hays, or the one W. S. Merwin did years ago. At their worst, the translations do not convey the stylistic range and verbal ingenuity of the original, making Neruda sound instead like a Chilean Carl Sandburg.

The choice of poems is also at times debatable. In order to

make the book representative of all of Neruda's work, Stavans has left out some well-known poems and included plenty of questionable ones. For example, the poems about the siege of Stalingrad and the arrival of the Red Army at the gates of Prussia may have documentary value, but they are otherwise worthless. The same is true of a number of poems in the cycle "Let the Woodcutter Awaken." Reading lines like the following, one begins to understand why he was not universally loved:

> In three rooms of the old Kremlin
> lives a man named Joseph Stalin.
> His bedroom light is turned off late.
> The world and his country allow him no rest.

The problem with Neruda's Communist poems is that they are nearly identical to countless other Communist poems that were written from China to Patagonia in those years. Rebellion may be one of poetry's traditions, but so is eulogizing the goodwill and godlike wisdom of some murderer. At the same time, I don't wish to leave the impression that I'm condemning all of his political poems. When he mocked and thundered against tyranny and injustice, he was a magnificent poet. While earlier editors rightly sought to include only his best work and ignored the rest, *The Poetry of Pablo Neruda* takes a different approach. Over three hundred pages in it, for instance, are devoted to the poems he wrote in the last decade of his life, when fifty pages would have been more than enough. I can imagine even the most devoted fan of the poet growing weary. The later poems are often repetitive and feel contrived as Neruda recycles the rhetoric and the imagery of his earlier poems. Understandably, no poet, no matter how great he or she is, can have a book this thick without a loss of quality. My problem is that I don't see how doing it this way serves the poet.

Neruda had an extraordinary ability to write about almost any subject. For a variety of reasons, political or programmatic, he frequently persuaded himself that it was necessary to do so. Nevertheless, he is a far more original poet in my view when he had no plans in mind, when a poem came to him in the fish soup he was eating, as it were. Something close at hand, perfectly familiar, and yet somehow never fully noticed in its peculiarity set his imagination going. Can't you see how interesting artichokes are? the poem about them says. For Neruda almost everything that exists deserves equal reverence and can become a subject of poetry. Many poets—including Whitman—have believed something like that. Ronsard wrote an ode to his bed and William Carlos Williams to a red wheelbarrow and some chickens. Still, I can't think of another poet who consistently found poetry in so many unlikely places as Neruda did. This is what makes any book of his unpredictable. Just as one comes to think one has him pegged, he springs a surprise. Here, for example, is the opening of a poem entitled "Ode to a Village Movie Theater" in a translation by Margaret Sayers Peden:

> Come, my love,
> let's go to the movies
> in the village.
>
> Transparent night
> turns
> like a silent
> mill, grinding out
> stars.
> We enter the
> tiny theater, you and I,
> a ferment of children
> and the strong smell of apples.
> Old movies
> are
> secondhand dreams.
> The screen is the color
> of stone, or rain.
> The beautiful victim
> of the villain
> has eyes like pools
> and a voice like a swan;
> the fleetest
> horses in the world
> careen
> at breakneck speed

Cowboys
make
Swiss cheese of
the dangerous Arizona
moon. . . .

If you find this as delightful as I do and want to read more, then perhaps *The Poetry of Pablo Neruda* is the book for you.

NOTES

1. *Anthology of Contemporary Latin-American Poetry,* ed. Dudley Fitts (New Directions, 1942), pp. 303–5.

2. *Passions and Impressions,* ed. Matilde Neruda and Miguel Otero Silva, trans. Margaret Sayers Peden (Farrar, Straus and Giroux, 1983), pp. 78–79.

3. *Passions and Impressions,* p. 128.

4. René de Costa, *The Poetry of Pablo Neruda* (Harvard University Press, 1979), p. 1.

5. *Pablo Neruda: Absence and Presence,* photographs by Luis Poirot, with translations by Alastair Reid (Norton, 1990), p. 134.

6. Translated by Martin Espada.

The Golden Age of Hatred

I first came across Norman Manea's name in 1991 when I read an essay of his in the *New Republic* on the concealed fascist past of Mircea Eliade, the widely known Romanian scholar of comparative religion and the author of such authoritative works as *Shamanism* and *A History of Religious Ideas: From the Stone Age to the Eleusinian Mysteries.* The revelation was not exactly news to me. In 1972, with my friend Vasko Popa, a Serbian poet of Romanian origin, I met the philosopher Émile Cioran in Paris. We spent the afternoon chatting in his attic apartment and walking in the Luxembourg Gardens. In the evening we were joined by Mircea Eliade and all four of us went to dinner. The conversation was partly in Romanian, partly in English for my benefit, so I have hardly any idea what all their talk was about. Afterward, I was astonished to learn from Popa that both Cioran and Eliade had been fascists in their youth.

Vasko was a lifelong Communist, a true believer, so I must have looked surprised. He went on to explain that Cioran had repudiated his fascist past while Eliade was in all probability still a secret sympathizer.[1] I remember asking him why he was friendly with people like that, whereupon, visibly miffed, he told me that even if he were to give me an answer, I would not understand it. I let it go at that and would not learn the seamy details of Eliade's past until I read Manea's article in the *New Republic.*

Manea wrote it five years after going into exile. He received a scholarship in West Berlin in 1986 that allowed him to go abroad, and he decided not to return to Romania. He made his way to the United States in 1988. A widely translated and pub-

---

Review of *The Hooligan's Return,* by Norman Manea, trans. Angela Jianu. From the *New York Review of Books,* October 23, 2003.

lished writer of fiction and an essayist, he was neither an active dissident at home nor one of the regime's officially approved authors. After his article appeared, he was attacked in Romania for denigrating the image of his native country, where, after the overthrow of Ceauşescu, Eliade and Cioran had become anti-Communist heroes. An equally absurd attack in the *Los Angeles Times* accused him of being sympathetic to Eliade and the fascist Romanian intellectuals of the 1930s.

The main point of his piece, that a critical examination of the past is the best defense against any totalitarian ideology, was simply ignored. No ethnic group in the world wants to hear about its evil deeds, and Romanians are no exception. In the Balkans, people inclined to criticize local behavior are routinely thought of as renegades in the pay of some foreign power. Ten years ago an aunt of mine in Belgrade went around saying that she had heard from a reliable source that Charlie was getting huge amounts of money in America to write anti-Serbian poems. It's considered the height of bad manners to remind one's compatriots of moral cowardice. Especially scandalized are those who pretended not to notice anything unusual at the time and who bravely kept quiet when they saw some injustice being committed.

When it comes to killing and uprooting innocent people, the twentieth century makes the efforts of previous centuries appear halfhearted. Never before have so many classes of human beings been regarded as having no intrinsic value and therefore having no right to exist. These ambitious projects for depopulating the planet of some national, ethnic, racial, or religious group would have been impossible without the accompanying idea that bloodshed is permissible for the sake of some version of future happiness. To have a theory of history that will excuse any crime is a promising start, but it's never enough. What is required is a large number of people to convert ideas into practice, through either their active participation or their passivity.

There's no better critique of such ideas and people than the account of someone who had firsthand experience of what they mean in reality. If only these lucky survivors would keep their mouths shut, the pogroms of the past could be passed off as a bit of youthful folly, idealism gone wrong, a lone blemish in an otherwise illustrious career. *The Hooligan's Return* is Norman

Manea's memoir of such an evil time. He was born in 1936 in a small town in Bukovina, a region in the north of Romania which had been part of Austria-Hungary till 1919. A mixed population of Romanians, Ukrainians, Germans, and Jews lived alongside one another in relative peace until the onset of the Second World War.

In October 1941 the entire Jewish population of the province was deported to labor camps in Transnistria, a place that previously did not exist on any map or in any geography book. It was a newly carved region in Ukraine, north of the Black Sea and Odessa that extended as far as the rivers Dniester and Bug. The Romanian army of Marshal Ion Antonescu, which participated in the Nazi attack on Russia, was given the land as spoils of that campaign, and Antonescu soon after set aside the region to be the graveyard for Romanian Jews. The order for expulsion in 1941 required the Jews to hand in immediately to the National Bank all the gold, currency, shares, diamonds, and precious stones they owned and to report on the same day to the train station with their hand luggage. Everything else was to be left behind and was promptly pillaged.

Manea was five years old when he, his parents, and grandparents made the journey in sealed freight-train cars. Back in Romania, Premier Antonescu declared:

> Our nation has not known a more favorable moment in its history. . . . I am in favor of forced migration. I do not care whether we shall go down in history as barbarians. The Roman Empire committed many barbaric acts and yet it was the greatest political establishment the world has ever seen.

Two hundred thousand Romanian Jews were sent to Transnistria half perished, Manea's grandparents among them. There were no gas chambers and crematoria; people were either shot, hanged, slaughtered, burned, starved to death, or died as the consequence of infectious diseases and the weakening of the body. Nazis were not involved since Romania was not an occupied country. This was an operation carried out by the local Romanian police and gendarmerie. Antonescu was an ally of the Iron Guard, the extreme right-wing nationalist movement of the 1930s, whose ideological father was Nae Ionescu, a professor of philosophy at the University of Bucharest much admired by Eliade.

The movement blamed Jews for such ills as poverty, syphilis, alcoholism, communism, prostitution, abortion, homosexuality, and feminism. In place of democracy, they called for dictatorship, nationalism, the adulation of the Orthodox Church, and a repudiation of liberal values. Tolerance was regarded as impotence; acceptance of death and sacrifice as a regenerative force. A virulent nationalism of this kind, which we have seen rage elsewhere with predictable results, may in the end be better understood by psychiatrists with experience in institutions for the criminally insane than by historians and political scientists. Manea gives an example in his essay on Eliade:

> Among the many crimes arranged by the Legion, or Iron Guard, must be mentioned the barbarous ritual murder of two hundred Jews, including children, on January 22, 1941, at the Bucharest slaughterhouse (while the "mystical" murderers sang Christian hymns), an act of ferocity perhaps unique in the history of the Holocaust. Ion Antonescu, their former ally, later dissolved the Iron Guard, but anti-Semitic murders did not cease under his military dictatorship. There were, to name but two, the terrible pogrom in Iai in June 1941, when thousands of Jews were murdered and thousands more put on the "death trains" to die of asphyxiation."[2]

In Transnistria, the deportees lived outdoors in rain, mud, and cold. Many lost their minds, while others committed suicide. For Jews left in Bucharest and other parts of Romania there were never-ending restrictions, expropriations of property, and humiliations to contend with. Their citizenship was revoked, their bicycles and household goods confiscated, their children expelled from school. They had to pay higher prices for bread and were forced to shovel snow and dig ditches while newspaper editorials demanded even harsher punishments for them. To give an idea of what the times were like, here is a ditty the Romanian Jewish writer Mihail Sebastian heard Gypsy children shout in the streets of Bucharest in 1941:

The train is leaving Chitila
Taking Stalin off to Palestine.
The train is pulling out of Galati
Full of hanged Jews.[3]

Elsewhere in his journal, Sebastian observes that practically everyone he meets disapproves of what is happening and feels indignant, while at the same time, as he says, being "a cog in the huge anti-Semitic factory that is the Romanian state." While saying they were "staggered" and "disgusted" with what was happening, these ordinary citizens, he tells us, acquiesced in the persecution of their neighbors and a good many were actually jubilant about it.

Once Antonescu realized that the Germans were going to lose the war, the treatment of the Jews improved. He calculated that their survival would provide him with an alibi after the war. The Russians retook Transnistria in 1943 and drafted some of the Jewish men into the Red Army. Manea and his parents had to wait until 1945 to be repatriated back to Romania. He was nine years old. He rediscovered food, clothes, school, furniture, books, and games. Like many others at the end of the war, his family assumed that the horrors of the past were behind them and that they would participate with their compatriots in righting the country's wrongs. The Communists, after all, had executed Antonescu and were gradually taking power with the help of the Red Army, which had liberated the Jews from camps and saved their lives. "From each according to work, to each according to his abilities" sounded like a pretty good slogan.

Manea's father joined the Party and was appointed to an important position in the local trade organization. Young Manea became the "commander" of the Pioneers, an organization for the students between nine and fourteen who had the best scholastic records. A "Red Commissar," as he calls himself in his memoir, he presided over a tribunal in high school which had the power to expel students on grounds of antisocialist behavior. The social class and family background of the accused students was exposed and discussed. Speeches were made about the need to be vigilant against deviationists, traitors, and agents of the bourgeoisie and American imperialism. Manea writes:

"If only 5 percent of the criticism leveled against you is correct, you have to internalize [all of] it" was the mantra repeated in the meetings of the early years of socialism. The rule had been enunciated by the great Stalin himself, and nobody would have mustered 5 percent of their courage to challenge it; implicitly, by accepting 95 percent to be untrue, the principle established the supremacy of imposture and false denunciation. It consecrated the intimidation of the individual and the exorcism of the community; it was distinguished by demagogy, routine, surveillance, intimidation, but also stage performance.

(One wonders here what Romanian expression is being translated as "internalize"; it is not a word that seems right for a "mantra.")

Then something happened to the young revolutionary. He began to sense in himself an unbridgeable gulf between the language he used in public with its canonic certainties and the words he kept to himself. This was a predicament familiar to millions who lived under communism. One either went along with the Party line and accepted the moral and intellectual compromises that this entailed or one refused in the name of one's conscience—a motive seemingly unknown to most of one's fellow citizens. With some difficulty, Manea disengaged himself from political militancy. He withdrew into himself. Although he was already drawn to literature, he studied engineering as the safest profession under the circumstances. As the result of what he calls "the wear and tear of everyday somnambulism," he even spent a brief time in a mental institution. His father was not doing well either. He lost his job and ended up in prison in 1958 for undermining the great socialist achievement, so the accusation went, by receiving meat from a butcher without paying. This ridiculous charge appears to have been the consequence of one of the tactical shifts that from time to time scrambled the ranks of the *nomenklatura*. While his father was in prison, his mother worked in a canning factory; she had to stoop all day over a huge trough of peppers, potatoes, and cucumbers that she was required to slice by hand.

The Hooligan's Return is a memoir of a troubled soul. It is fragmented and somewhat repetitive. Manea keeps digressing, circling around an incident as he tries to make sense of it. He scrambles the chronology as well as his narrative strategies and point of view as he tries to make sense of his life. There are passages of lyrical prose and even magic realism. He is most persuasive when he tells his story straight. Surprisingly, many periods of his life are given only hurried summaries. For example, he has little to say about how he became a writer or about Romanian literature and the literary milieu in which he grew up, so the reader is left in the dark about who influenced him and how. Although he argues that his true motherland is the Romanian language, he doesn't convey what that language is like and what may be lost in translation. He is also a bit skimpy in describing the Ceauşescu regime and the peculiar habits of a dictator who traveled through his starving country in a motorcade that included a limousine for his favorite dog. For a fuller account of daily life in Romania one has to turn to Manea's fiction and his fine book of essays, *On Clowns: The Dictator and the Artist*.

All this raises a question about the intended audience of *The Hooligan's Return*. Unlike Romanians, American readers need to know more than Manea tells us about the workings of a system in which for every police agent assigned to surveillance there were fifteen "volunteer" informers. "Suspicion and duplicity gradually infiltrated the kitchens and the bedrooms, insinuated themselves into sleep, language, and posture," he writes. When absolute obedience, self-abasement, and professions of loyalty were required of everyone and being a busybody became a civic duty, it was entirely normal to be paranoid and to strive to become invisible.

Manea broke that rule in 1981. He ceased to be a quiet, compliant citizen and officially became a troublemaker. In an interview published in a provincial literary magazine, he complained about resurgent nationalism and anti-Semitism in Romania. The smear campaign that followed was nasty. He was called "liberaloid," "Stalinist," "of another language and of another faith," "anti-Party," and so forth. It was frightening, infuriating, and exhausting. I recall being told in the 1990s by writers in Yugoslavia about the sheer weariness of having to listen to such moronic labels for more than fifty years. False denunciations are the grease that keeps the wheels of totalitarian societies rolling. When the system collapses and personal histories have to be speedily laundered, the man who opens his mouth and starts reminding people what someone said or did is in trouble. The message to Manea in 1981 was the same as in 1991, when he published his essay on Eliade. He was a traitor, an alien element, a public enemy.

The memoir begins with Manea's decision to make a long-postponed trip to Romania in 1997 and concludes with the description of his nine-day stay there. He agonizes about the journey. All the old fears he thought he had left behind return to torment him. His main purpose is to visit his mother's grave in the town where he was born. Otherwise he has no relatives left in the country; his father is in a nursing home in Jerusalem. He doesn't travel alone, but with an American friend, a renowned orchestra conductor who is to give a concert in Bucharest. He arrives without advance notice and once there refuses to give interviews. At the airport in Frankfurt before boarding the flight to Romania he wonders whether the ordinary-looking passengers are perhaps really agents of the new mafias or old secret service. Once he arrives, his torments continue. The atmosphere is alien, he's alien, the pedestrians are alien:

> I cross the boulevard over to the Scala cinema. Next to it is the Unic block of apartments where Cella's mother lived until her death. Everything is the same and yet not the same. Something indefinable but essential has skewed the stage set, something akin to an invisible cataclysm, a magnetic anomaly, the aftermath of an internal hemorrhage. Maybe it is the squalor, but if you look closer, it is not just that. There are signs of unfinished roadwork everywhere, but even this does not seem to point to real change. I stand and stare for much longer than I should. I gaze at the Unic store, then turn around to face the Scala cinema and the pastry shop of the same name, then the Lido Hotel, and the Ambassador Hotel. The estrangement is still incomplete, the wound still not healed, the rupture still active, although now somewhat muted. There is something else at work here, of an objective nature—the traumatizing, alienated reality itself. Gloomy immutability appears as permanence when, in fact, it is just a disease, a perverted wreck.

Death has passed this way, in the footsteps of the dead man now revisiting the landscape of his life in which he can no longer find a place or a sign of himself. After my death, Death visited this place, but was it not already here, was it not that from which I had fled? In 1986, the dictatorship had become Death, owning the landscape and the streets and the pedestrians, and all else besides.

I cross over quickly to the other side of the boulevard, where the former Cina restaurant used to be. I enter a narrow, deserted street. A thin rain begins to fall. I feel something unnatural surrounding me, some unnatural sense within myself. Could this moment and this no-man's-land be the time and place of an accident, a murder, a mysterious aggression?

This is a powerful description of the exile's estrangement. I felt the same way on my first visit to Belgrade after twenty years' absence. For the first couple of days I had no idea who I was. I reeled back and forth between several equally absurd identities, unprepared for a reunion with my childhood. Annoyingly, friends and complete strangers I met were certain they knew who I was. For some, I was unmistakably an American, for others I was still a Serb. Manea may have once regarded himself as a Romanian writer whose ethnicity was a strictly personal matter, but to his fellow countrymen he remained a Jew.

The Hooligan's Return is an angry book. Manea carries a deep feeling of injury from all the vicious things his compatriots said about him over the years. At times, he sounds as if twenty-two million Romanians think of nothing else but of his betrayal. Somewhat surprisingly, but understandably, he is more forgiving on a visit to his native province and his hometown than he is in Bucharest.

The fates of his mother and father still trouble him. They belonged, as he says movingly, to the vast category of innocents ignored by the chroniclers. Like millions of others, they did not deserve any of the sufferings inflicted on them. As a young man, Manea couldn't wait to get away from his mother. Her tearful stories, her exaggerations and fears, her claustrophobic world of suspicion and rumor, and their never-ending quarrels drove him from her. Now she haunts him like a ghost, catching up with him even on the streets of New York. She's old, frail, and blind, as she was in her last years. She walks by him without acknowledging him.

The memories of his father are equally poignant. Manea describes him as someone trapped in his own solitude, a man whose main defenses were silence and secrecy, who went through life unable to free himself from the conventions of dignity. "About suffering, as about joy, he would speak only rarely," he writes. Unlike his mother, he would never mention Transnistria or recall that he was beaten over the head with a bullwhip by a Romanian officer.

Manea's memoir ends up by being more powerful as a lament for his parents than as a narrative of Manea's own exile and quarrel with his compatriots. There was a time, he says, when his own people's suffering no longer interested him:

> After my juvenile fling with the Communist madness, I had come to hate anything that had to do with "we," with collective identity, which seemed to me suspect, and oppressive simplification. The chasm between "me" and "us" was one I was no longer disposed to cross.

No more. His memoir is a story of the gradual acceptance of that common fate. "Bring me a familiar and accessible God" must surely be every exile's prayer.

"A book should open old wounds, even inflict new ones. A book should be *a danger,*" Cioran counsels. *The Hooligan's Return,* ably translated from Romanian by Angela Jianu, fulfills that requirement. At the end of the memoir, Manea is like an insomniac who has gotten through a particularly bad night and who knows well there'll be many more nights like it. The trip home did not restore him. He has remained, as he says, "an embarrassed inhabitant of his own biography." Rather than a tragic figure, he sees himself as a clown. "Augustus the Fool is the pariah, the loser, the one who always gets kicked in the ass, to the audience's delight. Augustus the Fool is the exile," he writes. A friend of his once complained that he was too serious, too ethical, and not playful enough to fit that role. There's truth in what the friend says, but it doesn't take into account what makes Manea's writing powerful. This world of ours, in his view, is a place where the ridiculous reigns supreme over all human life and tortures everyone without respite, and therefore it cannot be ignored because it's not about to ignore any one of us. If that is so, fools are also martyrs. Words caused them to suffer and words are their salvation. Manea's strength as a writer comes from his deep solidarity with such people. He has in mind all those, including himself, who were left to play the fool in one of history's many traveling circuses.

NOTES

1. A recent book by Alexandra Laignel-Lavastine, *Cioran, Eliade, Ionesco: L'Oubli du Fascisme* (Presses Universitaires de France, 2002), provides the most extensive and perceptive account I have yet seen of Eliade's and Cioran's fascist and anti-Semitic writings in the 1930s and of their lifelong efforts to conceal that shameful past.

2. *On Clowns: The Dictator and the Artist* (Grove Weidenfeld, 1992), p. 92.

3. Mihail Sebastian, *Journal, 1935–1944* (Ivan R. Dee, 2000), p. 377.

What Ez Could Do

There's no great contemporary who is less read than Ezra Pound, I recall Hugh Kenner saying more than thirty years ago. If that was true then, it's certainly even truer today. How widely is Pound being taught in colleges and universities beyond the few poems included in anthologies? Are young American poets reading him and being influenced by him? I suspect not much. More than Eliot, Stevens, and Moore, Pound is looked upon as an impossibly difficult poet. Not many read his essays either, and yet when his subject was poetry, Pound was one of our most astute literary critics. His writings on religious, historical, economic, and political themes are another matter. He was wrong about a lot of things. After 1945, when his fascist sympathies and his broadcasts on Rome radio during the war became widely known and he was brought back to the United States to stand trial as a traitor and subsequently committed to a madhouse, there was even more reason to be wary of him. What does one do with a poet who compared Hitler to Jeanne d'Arc? These two new books with their magnificent poems and translations, meticulously annotated and edited by Richard Sieburth, remind us once again that the question will not go away.

With his stupefying contradictions, Pound is a kind of character, one is tempted to say, that only America can produce. Grandson of a congressman from Wisconsin and descendent of the poet Henry Wadsworth Longfellow on his mother's side, he was born in 1885 in Hailey, Idaho, where his father had gone to work for the Land Office. His parents moved back east shortly

Review of *Poems and Translations* and *The Pisan Cantos,* by Ezra Pound, ed. Richard Sieburth. From the *New York Review of Books,* December 18, 2003.

after, first to New York and then to a suburb of Philadelphia, where Pound grew up and published his first poem, a limerick on the defeat of William Jennings Bryant in the presidential election of 1896. He attended the University of Pennsylvania, where he met William Carlos Williams and Hilda Doolittle, and after graduation went to teach Romance languages at Wabash College in Crawfordsville, Indiana. His academic career ended abruptly in the very first semester of teaching. He was accused by his landladies of letting an actress spend the night in his rooms and swiftly sacked by the college. With nothing definite in view for the future, he sailed for Europe in March of 1908, going to Venice initially, where he published his first volume of verse, *A Lume Spento,* in 150 copies at his own expense and shortly after settling to work and live in London, where except for frequent trips to the Continent and one trip back to the States in 1910, he remained for the next twelve years. As for God's Own Country, there was no man living there whose art in letters was of the slightest interest to him, he said, no living American, with the sole exception of Bliss Carman, who will not improve by drowning.

This is how the novelist Ford Madox Hueffer (later Ford), who met him early on in London, described Pound:

> Ezra would approach with the steps of a dancer, making passes with a cane at an imaginary opponent. He would wear trousers made of green billiard cloth, a pink coat, a blue shirt, a tie hand-painted by a Japanese friend, an immense sombrero, a flaming beard cut to a point and a single, large blue ear-ring.[1]

The English appreciated eccentric behavior, he believed, and he obliged them by looking as if he had stepped out of an operetta by Offenbach. Amy Lowell, who met him then, spoke of his personal charm as well as of his thin-skinned, chip-on-the-shoulder personality. Pound always strove to call attention to himself. He challenged a minor Georgian poet to a duel for writing in favor of a return to Wordsworth as a source of inspiration. "Dear Mr Abercrombie," he wrote, "stupidity carried beyond a certain point becomes a public menace." The arts serve society best when they subvert its conventions and beliefs, he thought.

He seemed to know everybody. Not just established names like Henry James and Yeats, but all the best up-and-coming writers and poets in London and elsewhere. The publishing careers of Joyce, Eliot, Frost, William Carlos Williams, Hemingway, and several other major figures would not have been the same without his enormous efforts on their behalf. Time, that most reliable adjudicator of literary reputations, has proved Pound right. He had impeccable taste. The writers and poets he championed were completely unknown when he started badgering editors in England and this country to publish them. Not only that. Though penniless himself, at one point even fantasizing about writing ghost stories for the *Ladies' Home Journal,* he turned himself into a one-man Guggenheim Foundation, managing to find people willing to give money to writers. This is amazing considering how young Pound was. Like Emerson and Whitman, both of whom he tended to ridicule at times, he was a man with a mission who hoped to bring about a new intellectual awakening in America which would have an effect not only on the arts, but in politics and economics as well.

"To talk over a poem with him," Yeats said, "is like getting you to put a sentence into dialect. All becomes clear and natural." While he was being helpful to others, his own poetry for a long time did not sound modern at all. "A collection of stale cream-puffs" is how he described his early poems when they were re-published in 1965. Swinburne, Rossetti, Browning, and the so-called Decadent poets of the 1890s were his models. He mimics them:

> Aye! I am a poet and upon my tomb
> Shall maidens scatter rose leaves
> And men myrtles, ere the night
> Slays day with her dark sword.

Pound had also made the discovery of medieval Provençal poetry and that of the Italian Renaissance and had attempted to imitate their diction and versification in English. There's hardly any hint of Pound's own experience in these poems, little living language and nothing vurry Amur'kn, as he would put it. What makes him stand out from among his contemporaries is his uncompromising devotion to the art, his sense that a great lyric tradition has been lost sight of and needs to be recovered. Except for a few poems, like "Villonaud for This Yule," "The Tree," "Sestina: Altaforte," and others with moments of genuine poetry, there are just too many conventional and forgettable poems in *A Lume Spento* (1908), *A Quinzaine for This Yule* (1908), *Personae* (1909), and *Exultations* (1909).

Pound credits Ford Madox Ford for making him see the light one day. The novelist, who fought for Flaubert's precision and economy in English prose, collapsed on the floor laughing after hearing the stilted language of one of his poems. That roll, Pound said afterward, saved him two years. *Ripostes* (1912) is a much better book with truly fine poems like "Portrait d'une Femme," "The Seafarer," and the strange, visionary poem "The Return," in which the old Greek gods come back to earth in a language stripped of superfluous verbiage and in uneven lines of free verse:

> See, they return; ah, see the tentative
> Movements, and the slow feet,
> The trouble in the pace and the uncertain
> Wavering!
>
> See, they return, one, and by one,
> With fear, as half-awakened;
> As if the snow should hesitate
> And murmur in the wind,
> and half turn back;
> These were the "Wing'd-with-Awe,"
> Inviolable.
>
> Gods of the wingèd shoe!
> With them the silver hounds,
> sniffing the trace of air!
>
> Haie! Haie!
> These were the swift to harry;
> These the keen-scented;
> These were the souls of blood.
> Slow on the leash,
> pallid the leash-men!

In the meantime, there was the Imagist movement. It was invented by Pound in October 1912 in London and dead by 1914 when it was appropriated by Amy Lowell and others and became something totally different, short poems about nature with an Oriental flavor and a moral that could have come out of a fortune cookie. For Pound, however, its minimalist aesthetic became the foundation of his later style. Here's how he explained the tenets of Imagism for *Poetry* magazine in 1913:

1. Direct treatment of the "thing" whether subjective or objective.
2. To use absolutely no word that does not contribute to the presentation.
3. As regarding rhythm: to compose in the sequence of the musical phrase, not in sequence of a metronome.

One doesn't have to tamper with something to make it poetic, Pound is now saying. "Go in fear of abstractions," he advises. "Don't use such an expression as 'dim lands *of peace.*' It dulls the image. It mixes an abstraction with the concrete. It comes from the writer's not realizing that the natural object is always the *adequate* symbol."[2] An Imagist poem so conceived is an illustration of our wonder, a recognition of something that was always there in front of us, a homage to the pleasures of clear sight. "For it is not until poetry lives again 'close to the thing,'" he wrote, "that it will be a vital part of contemporary life."[3]

Yeats's comment after he read "The Return" was that it sounded to him as if Pound was translating at sight from an unknown Greek masterpiece. Certainly, not in the way Yeats meant it but in another, less obvious way, Pound was at his most ingenious when he pretended to be someone else. A good translator is an impersonator, someone who can play many roles and employ a variety of accents. His early translations of Provençal and Italian poetry lack that verbal range. His first genuine success came with Chinese, a language he did not even know. He not only invented a new kind of poem in English, but he changed how we think of Chinese literature. No one reading the earlier translations would have suspected that these poets were so fine. The original volume of *Cathay* (1915) contains fifteen poems of which only ten are included in the present volume. This is odd, because they are all worth preserving. The most famous poem in the book, "The River-Merchant's Wife: A Letter" is regularly included in anthologies as if it were an original poem of Pound's and not a translation. I imagine this is due to the controversies regarding the status of all the poems in *Cathay*. When they appeared, the Sinologists were scandalized and rushed to point out the numerous errors Pound had made. There's no question that he took liberties with the poems but he had a good excuse. He used the cribs, glosses, comments, and translations made by an American scholar, Ernest Fenollosa, who while living in Japan studied classic Chinese poets with Japanese tutors. Pound relied on his own literary savvy and very little else. Here's a poem, "The Beautiful Toilet" by Mei Sheng (140 B.C.), in Pound's version:

> Blue, blue is the grass about the river
> And the willows have overfilled the close garden.
> And within, the mistress, in the midmost of her youth,
> White, white of face, hesitates, passing the door.
> Slender, she puts forth a slender hand,
> And she was a courtezan in the old days,
> And she has married a sot,
> Who now goes drunkenly out
> And leaves her too much alone.

And here is the same poem by Arthur Waley, the most famous translator from Chinese, who published his own version three years after Pound's to correct his inaccuracies:

> Green, green,
> The grass by the river bank,
> Thick, thick,
> The willow trees in the garden.
> Sad, sad,
> The lady in the tower
> . . . .
> Now she is a wandering man's wife
> The wandering man went, but did not return.
> It is hard alone to keep an empty bed.

Pound's Chinese poems, Hugh Kenner points out, incorporate

> the *vers-libre* principle, that the single line is the unit of composition; the Imagist principle, that a poem may build its effects out of things it sets before the mind's eye by naming them; and the lyrical principle, that words or names, being ordered in time, are bound together and recalled into each other's presence by recurrent sounds.[4]

As for the subject matter, the poems with their war widows, disgruntled soldiers, fallen empires, and melancholy exiles had obvious contemporary parallels. The First World War was in full swing with all of its disruptions of normal life and its horrendous slaughter of an entire generation of young men on the battlefield.

There's a curious poem in his next book, *Lustra* (1916–17), called "Commission" that makes Pound sound like a revolutionary poet. Go my song, he says in it, to those enslaved by convention and bear to them my contempt for their oppressors. Even more than his other collections of poetry, *Lustra* is an anthology of styles, as if Pound was more interested in different ways of writing a poem than in developing a consistent voice and vision. There are satires and epigrams that echo Greek and Roman poets, Imagist poems about a cake of soap and a bathtub, others that show the influence of Chinese and Provençal poetry. Pound can be anecdotal, ribald, lyrical, and didactic. The quality, however, is uneven. Slight, occasional poems and imitations alternate with more successful ones and some that are truly memorable like "Provincia Deserta," "Near Perigord," and this little spoof of an anonymous Middle English lyric that his London publisher thought was too blasphemous and indecent to include in the volume:

Ancient Music

Winter is icummen in,
Lhude sing Goddamm,
Raineth drop and staineth slop,
And how the wind doth ramm!
Sing: Goddamm.
Skiddeth bus and sloppeth us,

An ague hath my ham.
Freezeth river, turneth liver,
Damn you, sing: Goddamm.
Goddamm, Goddamm, 'tis why I am, Goddamm,
So 'gainst the winter's balm.
Sing goddamm, damm, sing Goddamm,
Sing goddamm, sing goddamm, DAMM.

Once he got over the inhibition of mixing high and low diction and subject matter, Pound became a different poet. His three greatest poems, *The Cantos,* "Homage to Sextus Propertius" (1919), and the nineteen-part poem *Hugh Selwyn Mauberley* (1920), are each in their own way a grand collage. As much as the painters who drew with scissors by cutting headlines, words, and images from newspapers, he practiced the art of assemblage in his poetry. For his "Homage to Sextus Propertius" he went through the collected works of the Roman poet in their original Latin and underlined lines and sections in the poems that he wanted to translate and then made a series of poems out of these fragments. When it was published in *Poetry,* it aroused the ire of a classical scholar from the University of Chicago who was shocked to find mention of refrigerators and Wordsworth in a translation of a poet born in 50 B.C. For Pound it was a poem recalling the manner of Propertius, a record of his own mood while facing the infinite and ineffable imbecility of the British Empire as the old poet had to face the infinite and ineffable imbecility of the Roman Empire. It was also a love poem. Here's a sample of it:

Light, light of my eyes, at an exceeding late hour I was
    wandering,
And intoxicated,
and no servant was leading me,
And a minute crowd of small boys came from opposite,
I do not know what boys,
And I am afraid of numerical estimate,
And some of them shook little torches,
and others held onto arrows,
And the rest laid their chains upon me,
and they were naked, the lot of them,
And one of the lot was given to lust.

"That incensed female has consigned him to our pleasure."
So spoke. And the noose was over my neck.
And another said "Get him plumb in the middle!
"Shove along there, shove along!"
And another broke in upon this:
"He thinks that we are not gods."
"And she has been waiting for the scoundrel,
and in a new Sidonian night cap,
And with more than Arabian odours,
god knows where he has been,
She could scarcely keep her eyes open
enter that much for his bail.
Get along now!"

We were coming near to the house,
and they gave another yank to my cloak,
And it was morning, and I wanted to see if she was alone,
    and resting,
And Cynthia was alone in her bed.
I was stupefied.
I had never seen her looking so beautiful
No, not when she was tunick'd in purple.

Such aspect was presented to me, me recently emerged
    from my visions,
You will observe that pure form has its value.

"You are a very early inspector of mistresses.
"Do you think I have adopted your habits?"
There were upon the bed no signs of a voluptuous
    encounter,
No signs of a second incumbent.

She continued:
"No incubus has crushed his body against me,
"Though spirits are celebrated for adultery.
"And I am going to the temple of Vesta . . ."
and so on.

Since that day I have had no pleasant nights.

Hugh Selwyn Mauberley is a depiction of the English literary
milieu before the war and a lament for a generation that died
"believing in old men's lies." It is his last major shorter poem.

For the rest of his life, he devoted all of his efforts to *The Cantos* and to his numerous translations from Chinese, Japanese, Greek, and other languages. Increasingly unhappy in London and somewhat isolated, he began spending more and more time in France and Italy, and finally moved to Paris in 1921, where for a while he seemed to be again in the center of things. He befriended Cocteau, Picabia, the Dadaist Tristan Tzara, and the musicians Ravel and Stravinsky. There were also many Americans coming for shorter or longer stays, including Eliot, whose rough manuscript of *The Waste Land* he revised into the poem we read today.

The most famous expatriate in Paris was Gertrude Stein. Pound paid her a visit but the two egomaniacs did not hit it off. She called him "a village explainer" and she was not wrong. Pound combined in himself the incompatible temperaments of an aesthete and a rabble-rouser. He never passed up an opportunity to condescend to his compatriots. "Any country which is afraid of thought in whatever form it may be expressed is not a habitable country," he told an interviewer in Paris who had asked what his opinion of America was. He lectured everyone he corresponded with and everyone he ever met, not just Gertrude Stein who, as he said in a letter to William Carlos Williams, "wdn't empty a piss pot to save the bleedin world."[5]

Like many of his contemporaries in the 1930s, Pound was tempted by radical political cures. He thought he knew what needed to be done to fix things in Europe and America. Much of his cultural and political criticism of the United States is still on the mark and is no harsher than Mark Twain's or Dreiser's. He saw American history as one long struggle between the people and the financiers. The usurers, now called financiers, plotted against abundance while the press misled and distracted the people. The aim of finance, he wrote, is to profit by others' labor. He predicted that this greed for lucre, a greed that abandons all common sense and every sense of proportion, will blindly create its own undoing. He'd make a shrewd observation about the American tendency to mess in other people's affairs before establishing order in their own affairs and thoughts; he would then argue implausibly that the only cure for the nation was to adopt Confucian ethics, which recommends putting one's own house in order first. Hundreds of newspaper articles and essays and over eight hundred pages of his poem *The Cantos* endlessly reiterate these points, fulminate, and shout down all those who doubt his remedies.

Pound left Paris in 1924 and settled in Rapallo, a small seaside town near Genoa where, except for a short visit to the United States, he lived, until his arrest in 1945, in a kind of ménage à trois with his wife and his mistress of many years. Despite his vast interest in the subject, he was out of touch with political realities of the day. He now felt that sweeping economic reforms could only be carried out by strong leaders like Mussolini. "Usury is the cancer of the world which only the surgeon's knife of Fascism can cut out of the life of the nations," he wrote.

Some of the admirers of Pound's poetry still play down his anti-Semitism. There's no point in fooling oneself. It wasn't just his writing about Christianity being tainted by Semitic insanity, or his calling for a truly European religion unpolluted by Semitic influences; there was another, even crazier side to his obsession. For instance, he liked to speculate about the effects circumcision had on the mind of a Jew. "It must do something, after all these years and years, where the most sensitive nerves in the body are, rubbing them off, over and over again," he told Charles Olson.[6] After the disappointment of his 1939 trip to the United States, when he failed to persuade the senators and government officials he met in Washington of the wisdom of his economic and political ideas, he went back to Italy even more embittered. By then even his oldest pal, William Carlos Williams, had had enough of him. Here's a part of his reply to one of Pound's rants. It's dated November 26, 1941:

Dear Eazy:
Your brutal and sufficiently stupid reference to meat lying around on the steppes at this moment is quite an unnecessary flight of fancy, you'll find far more of it solidly encased in your own head. I used to think you had a brain, no more. . . .
You ask me what I know about doctrines that I do *not* read. What in hell do you know about the doctrines you *do* read? The presumptive effects of them never for one moment seem to dent your skull—or you wouldn't write such trivial wash. You have, I presume, read all the outpourings of your imbecillic

[*sic*] leaders and have swallowed everything they say, spittle and all. Is this or is this not true? Come on, let's have specific statements of just what and whom you are backing. Is it Hitler or Moussie [Mussolini]? Or both? I want facts. . . .

Barnum missed something when he missed you.[7]

Pound is like Céline, a monster who was a great writer. He is never going to be widely read and esteemed by his compatriots and yet American poetry of the last century is inconceivable without his contribution and his vast influence. What makes Pound unlike any other poet we have is that the voice of his poetry is American, but his landscape seldom is. There's far more of Britain, Europe, and ancient China in his poetry than the country where he was born. And yet no one heard our language and displayed its riches and nuances with such sure touch and with such brio.

When Joyce's *Dubliners* came out, Pound praised the book for being careful to avoid "telling a lot of things that the reader didn't want to know." One wishes he took that advice himself, instead of writing what ended up being one of the longest poems in world literature. Even a reader with a fair amount of knowledge of ancient and modern culture and history has a hard time with *The Cantos*. Nearly thirty years in the making, it is both an extraordinary and exasperating poem. The constant shifting of themes and contexts, the dipping into a multitude of cultural traditions, the long and short passages in Italian, Greek, Chinese, Latin, German, and a few other languages, were to serve as a demonstration of what he called *paideuma*—the tangle or complex of the inrooted ideas of any period.

Pound wanted to show through examples what had gone wrong in the past and what cultural values ought to be preserved. His expectation was for an all-knowing reader who would see the connection among the pieces. What his epic in fact requires is disciples, the few true believers willing to sit at the feet of the master. The problem with *The Cantos* is that the poem combines two conflicting strategies, a didactic view of literature with that of lyric poetry. With his ear for language Pound could make the poem flow, but with his inability to stick to one subject, he could not make its meanings clear. There's no credible overall structure. *The Cantos* only makes sense if seen as consisting of thematically related, but separate, groups of poems.

The eleven *Pisan Cantos* (1948), written while he was interred in an army prison camp near Pisa and now published in a separate volume by New Directions, are regarded by many critics as the finest section of the long poem. "A man on whom the sun has gone down" is how Pound describes himself. He is humbler, more introspective, and gives the impression of being embarrassed by his old hatreds and by his vanity. Even there, it's hard to be sure about the author's intent. At times, these cantos sound to me like the confession of a bad man; at other times like an elegy for Italian Fascism. When Pound is not caught up in his inner turmoil, when he looks around and pricks his ears, he is still the unsurpassed poet that he was, letting the eye and the ear work together as one and making that moment luminous:

> and there was a smell of mint under the tent flaps
> especially after the rain
> and a white ox on the road toward Pisa
> as if facing the tower,
> dark sheep in the drill field and wet days were clouds
> in the mountain as if under the guard roosts.
> A lizard upheld me
> the wild birds wd not eat the white bread
> . . . .
> . . . Sunset grand couturier.

NOTES

1. Peter Ackroyd, *Ezra Pound and His World* (Scribner, 1980), p. 21.

2. *Poetics of the New American Poetry*, ed. Donald Allen and Warren Tallman (Grove, 1973), pp. 36–38.

3. Ezra Pound, *Selected Prose 1909–1965* (New Directions, 1973), p. 41.

4. Hugh Kenner, *The Pound Era* (University of California Press, 1971), p. 199.

5. *Pound/Williams: Selected Letters of Ezra Pound and William Carlos Williams*, ed. Hugh Witemeyer (New Directions, 1996), p. 169.

6. Charles Olson, *Charles Olson and Ezra Pound: An Encounter at St. Elizabeths*, ed. Catherine Seeley (Grossman, 1975), p. 55.

7. *Pound/Williams*, pp. 209–10.

Adam's Umbrella

The first visual record of police interrogation we have comes from a Seventh Dynasty tomb in Egypt, two thousand years before Christ. The image shows a man being held by three others while the fourth one beats him with a bamboo stick and the fifth, who appears to be the one in charge, supervises the procedure. The sight is disheartening, Borislav Pekić comments. In four thousand years not much has changed. Prisoners still get beaten. And that's not the worst that happens to them, of course. There have been many refinements since the pharaohs in methods of inducing physical and mental pain. We must give credit to the Holy Inquisition, which contributed more than any other institution to the development of the role of the interrogator. The inquisitors' techniques of persuasion were especially admired by modern totalitarian states where ideological heresy likewise came to be regarded as a capital crime.

Only educated people conversant with nuances of doctrine and with a talent for abstract speculation could count on becoming inquisitors. Their task was no longer to bash heads and extract fingernails but to have the prisoner comprehend the nature of his transgression and make a public confession. Today, in the name of the war on terror, ill-treatment and torture in all their ancient and modern varieties are again being used more or less openly by some countries, including the United States. These practices, surprisingly, have the approval of a number of distinguished law professors and opinion makers who argue that to defeat evil we may have to do the unthinkable now and then.

Review of *How to Quiet a Vampire,* by Borislav Pekić, trans. Stephen M. Dickey and Bogdan Rakic. From the *New York Review of Books,* June 24, 2004.

Were he alive today, Borislav Pekić would not have been persuaded. His interest in the abuse and torture of prisoners comes from firsthand experience. Unlike his better-known Serbian contemporaries, the novelists Danilo Kis and Aleksandar Tisma, who also wrote extensively about imprisonment, Pekić actually spent time in jail as a political prisoner under the Communists. Born in 1930, he was arrested in 1948 in Belgrade while still in high school, and accused of organizing a conspiracy against the state. He did not deny his guilt. The secret student organization of which he was one of the founders planned to engage in sabotage in addition to proselytizing for democratic reforms.

This was an act of bravery akin to starting in Nazi Germany an association to combat the spread of anti-Semitism. He was interrogated, treated roughly, and made to sign a statement in which he admitted plotting against the state because, supposedly, he and his friends could not bear the freedom and happiness his fellow citizens now enjoyed. In other words, he was made to realize that rather than having fought for liberty as he had previously told himself, he had been a mortal enemy of that liberty. He served five years out of a fifteen-year sentence.

Exactly how he was made to confess the opposite of what he believed, Pekić describes in *Godine Koje su Pojeli Skakavci* (Years Eaten by Locusts), a three-volume memoir, still to be translated, of his time in prison, published in 1991, a year before his death. As much as he dwells on his own predicament, he is even more interested in the stories of his fellow prisoners and his jailers. Prison turned out to be a pivotal experience in his life. When he was arrested, he was an upper-middle-class boy whose father, ironically, had been a high police official before the war. After his pardon in 1953, Pekić was an outcast in a state where one's political past and unquestioning loyalty to the Party were decisive factors in getting ahead. The best thing a man like him could do under the circumstances was to become invisible. That, however, was never to be Pekić's talent. The day he was to be set free, he refused to leave the prison until the fountain pen that was confiscated at his arrest six years before was returned to him. The officials showed him a large stash of fountain pens and implored him to select the one he liked best, but he continued to insist that his own be given back to him.

After his release, Pekić studied psychology in Belgrade, and then between 1958 and 1964, he worked in the film industry writing numerous screenplays and publishing a few literary works under a pseudonym. His novel *The Time of Miracles* (*Vreme Cuda*) came out in 1965 when he was already thirty-five years old.[1] It turned out to be a success with both the critics and the reading public. The book is made up of stories based on Christ's miracles in the New Testament. Pekić reimagines the events from the point of view of those on whom the miracles were performed by a passing stranger who did not ask for their consent or care much what happened to them afterward. In place of traditional narrative and theology, he offers his own counter-parables as a corrective. What interests him, as it does in his other books, is the gap between some religious or political doctrine and the actual outcome for a particular person.

The Time of Miracles is a blasphemous book with scenes and images that could have come from Gnostic gospels and the canvases of Hieronymus Bosch. The story of resurrection is also given a twist. A disciple, greedy for salvation, begs Jesus to let him carry the cross so that he may save his own soul. Jesus, who never refuses anyone in spiritual need, lets him take up the cross while he himself vanishes in the crowd. The Roman centurions in their drunkenness do not notice the switch and crucify the wrong man.

The Houses of Belgrade (*Hodocasce Arsenija Njegovana*, 1970), Pekić's next novel, has a far more conventional narrative.[2] It tells the story of a well-to-do house builder and landlord who shuts himself inside his apartment on March 27, 1941, the day street demonstrations in Belgrade overthrew the government, which had signed a nonaggression pact with Hitler, and who doesn't emerge from it until June 3, 1968, when once more he discovers that the streets are full of protesting students. As the novel opens, Pekić's hero, an elderly man in failing health, is composing a commentary on his life. He lives on memories of the houses he built, which he observes through binoculars from his top-floor window. During the Allied bombing in 1944, he at first refuses to go down into the cellar, insisting on remaining at his window and trying to ascertain if any of his houses are being hit.

"How does one tell a story that is outdated, pointless, incomprehensible, perhaps risky and yet touching?" Pekić asks himself in one of his essays.[3] Arsenie Negovan, his hero, is a member of what in Serbia turned out to be a quickly emerging and as quickly declining class of urban merchants and professionals whose fates were sealed by the Second World War and communism. *The Houses of Belgrade* is an elegy for that lost world, a world to which Pekić's own family belonged. Arsenie Negovan was a builder in a country in which cities are forever being reduced to ruins by some foreign invader or, as in the case of Sarajevo and Vukovar, by home-grown lunatics.

In 1971, Pekić moved with his family to London where, except for a few extended visits to his homeland, he lived in self-imposed exile until his death. These were extremely prolific years for him. In addition to the books already mentioned, he published novels, plays, books of science fiction, and several works of nonfiction. His novel in seven volumes, *Golden Fleece* (*Zlatno Runo,* 1978–86), is regarded as his masterpiece. In 1990, Pekić participated in the founding of the Democratic Party in Serbia, to which both the recently assassinated premier, Zoran Djindjic, and the present one, Vojislav Kostunica, also belonged, before they became enemies. He also took part in the first demonstrations against the Milosevic regime.

The last things he wrote were newspaper articles and speeches and their theme was the democratic future of Serbia. Rereading the pieces today, I'm struck by his willingness to forgive his old enemies and by his rosy outlook. Like other moderate nationalists, he did not foresee what tragedies lay ahead, since, more than the others, he believed in compromise. Serious consideration of other people's views and a genuine attempt to understand them was the essence of democracy for Pekić. Without compromise, he wrote, there can be no normal life for us. He knew how difficult finding the middle ground politically had always been for Serbs; nevertheless, he hoped that for once they might come to their senses, seize the opportunity, and act wisely.

How to Quiet a Vampire, well translated by Stephen M. Dickey and Bogdan Rakic, is a book without a trace of optimism. First published in 1977, it is the story of a former SS officer, Konrad Rutkowski, now a professor of medieval history at the University of Heidelberg, who like thousands of other Germans vacations on the Dalmatian coast, in his case in the town of D. where twenty-two years before, during the Second World War, he served as a Gestapo officer. His wife, whose idea it was to take the trip, has no knowledge that this is the place where he was briefly posted, and so remains oblivious of her husband's inner turmoil. Rutkowski's efforts to both renounce and justify his past are detailed in twenty-six letters which he writes to his brother-in-law back in Germany, who also happens to be a professor of history. Pekić, writing as the narrator, depicts himself as the scholarly editor of the letters who provides a preface, numerous footnotes, and several additional documents and commentaries at the end of the book. In his introduction, he characterizes the writing as a mixture of personal confession and a historico-philosophical essay. These elements, of course, are present in Pekić's other fiction. He was always as interested in ideas as in his characters and his plots.

The former Gestapo officer, Professor Rutkowski, uses the letters to conduct a bitter polemic with the European intellectual tradition of which he proudly considers himself to be a descendant. He ascribes to it the great share of the blame for his personal tragedy as well as the moral ruin of Germany. The content of each letter is consequently associated with a different European philosophical school and a work of a particular philosopher. *The Meditations* of letter 1 belong to Marcus Aurelius; *Matter and Memory* of letter 2 to Henri Bergson; *Thus Spake Zarathustra* of letter 3 to Nietzsche, and so forth. By the last letter, Leibniz, Descartes, Freud, Schopenhauer, Berdayaev, Hegel, Spengler, Husserl, Erasmus, Plato, Hume, Abelard, Heidegger, Jaspers, Sartre, Saint Augustine, Camus, Marx, and Wittgenstein have all been alluded to. In his view, these are the real culprits for the delusions and violence of the twentieth century. He writes to his brother-in-law:

Although you've never read Wittgenstein, you worship him. Although you didn't understand Hegel, you worship him, too. The same goes for Kant, Schopenhauer, and Nietzsche. You owe this not only to your status as an academic, but also to your conviction that Ideas, especially philosophical ones, are a necessary corrective to the disgusting lives we're sometimes forced to lead. The idea that philosophy could inspire one such life, organize it, and defend it as ideal seems blasphemous to you. I assure you, however, that something just like that is what's going on. Your naive conviction (we'll see how naive it really is) that thinking philosophically means secluding oneself from reality and absolving oneself of all responsibility in connection with it—and that such seclusion is the condition *sine qua non* of every unbiased philosophical view—stems from an insidious wish, camouflaged in a general independence of the intellect, to disavow any responsibility for this world, whereby your harmlessness acquires a completely different meaning. . . . The thought that logical speculations could be connected in any way with beatings and the mutilation of people's souls seems to you to be a monstrous injustice—not against the people but against the speculations.

On a mundane level, Rutkowski's story goes like this. He was born in 1916 in a region of Yugoslavia called Banat, formerly a part of the Austro-Hungarian Empire, where his German ancestors settled in the fifteenth century. His father was a moderately well-off farmer. Rutkowski studied medieval history at the University of Heidelberg between 1934 and 1938 and received his doctorate there in 1940. The subject of his thesis was German-Polish relations before the Reformation. He returned home and began teaching grammar school in a town near Belgrade. When the war came, he failed to respond to the mobilization call to the Yugoslav army and soon after the arrival of German troops in April of 1941, became a member of the SS and eventually a Gestapo officer.

He carried out his police duties in Belgrade, except for temporary assignments in D. on the Adriatic coast and later in a town in Slovenia. Following both of these periods of service, he spent time in military hospitals suffering from extreme nervous exhaustion. When the war ended, he was subject to criminal proceedings by the Allied military authorities and sentenced to what was then known as work rehabilitation, following which he spent two years without steady employment until his former professor at Heidelberg brought him as a lecturer to the university and his academic career flourished.

The special operation in D. with which his letters are concerned occurs in 1943, when, following the capitulation of Italy, which had been occupying the Dalmatian coast, the German army and police moved into the region. Rutkowski is a member of a small unit led by an old Nazi Party member and experienced Gestapo investigator, a certain Standartenführer Steinbrecher, whose mission is to take over the police station and the duties the Italians performed until recently. As they are moving into their new quarters, Steinbrecher lectures Rutkowski on the complexities of police work in an occupied state. His ideas are terrifying. He sounds to me like a brilliant follower of the philosopher Carl Schmitt, who took his antiliberal philosophy of the state to its logical conclusions. In Steinbrecher's view, as in Schmitt's, a strong, healthy state must have perpetual adversaries. Enemies are the bolts that hold the machinery of the state together. Mutual suspicion, the covert desire of human beings to snitch on each other, ought to be encouraged. Since universal spying and denunciation are going to be the rule in the future, there'll always be plenty of work for cops to do. Police will only become unnecessary if every human being on earth becomes a policeman.

Even the famous incident in the Garden of Eden ought to be studied for what it can teach us about running a state. Forbidding the fruit to be taken from one tree, fruit completely indistinguishable from the fruit in any other tree, could have had as its goal only the enthronement of prohibition as such to test its effects on people. Plucking fruit from that tree in particular proved that this was not a matter of an ordinary theft, but a premeditated act violating divine order and thus an act of rebellion. According to Steinbrecher, the original sin was the first political crime. The craving to violate the prohibition and to disturb the established order, the conspiracy of a particular man and woman with that as its goal (abetment and solicitation), the participation of the serpent as an agent provocateur and probable informer, make it so. Finally one person, God, appears in every legal guise—as legislator, investigator, prosecutor, judge, and even the one who administers punishment in the end. Vishinsky, Stalin's infamous prosecutor in the 1930s who argued that there is no difference between the intention and the crime, would have agreed with that view. Adam and Eve should have confessed and asked for forgiveness long before they reached for the apple in the tree.

A few days after they move to D., the Germans discover in the cellar of the police station a middle-aged prisoner left behind by the Italians. The file clerk Adam Trpković, they find, was arrested for failing to salute the flag while passing the town hall and was subsequently forgotten by the Italians, who left in a hurry. He has survived by eating tangerines intended for the black market that were also in the cellar. To the great astonishment of the Germans, he still has with him his umbrella. They don't know what to do with him. They want to let him go, but the presence of that umbrella puzzles them and creates bureaucratic difficulties when it comes to filling out the forms for his official release. How are they to account for it? They can't. As one would expect, once Steinbrecher learns of the situation, he has a different view. Why shouldn't we begin our police work with him? he asks, even though he is ready to agree that the file clerk is an insignificant nobody. Nonetheless, he's a member of an enemy nation, and that is a sufficient reason to take a further look into his background. Rutkowski has no comment, but he's horrified. Despite all evidence to the contrary, he still holds on to the belief that their duty is to learn the truth. His commanding officer sets him straight:

The truth? My foot! What are we, a bunch of goddamned philosophers or something? We make truths, Obersturm-führer Rutkowski! We don't learn them, we make them! That's a creative endeavor, not an investigative one. We're artists, my dear sir. . . . I'd say poets.

Rutkowski pretends to himself that he can find a way to help the clerk. For Pekić, he has the intellectual's special ability to ignore evil by explaining it away. His unhappiness comes from his dim awareness that he is a hypocrite. In the end, he does nothing to help the innocent man. He who acts, he consoles himself, has no time for balances and scales. Rutkowski needs his "although," "maybe," and "on the other hand" to conceal his cowardice from himself. Steinbrecher, suspecting his ambivalence, assigns him to be the one who questions the clerk. He even provides him with the transcript of one of his own prized interrogations for guidance. The full text, included in the appendix of the novel, is worth studying closely for the way in which an extraordinarily logical mind can be an instrument of iniquity.

"A man can dodge even bullets, but not logic," Pekić writes. The task of the interrogator is to make the prisoner accept reason in place of reality and assume full responsibility for probable events that in truth never happened. Reality is a sin against reason for which the prisoner has to pay with his life. Chance is illogical; therefore it cannot and must not exist. In principle, it is always possible to show that it is more logical for something to have happened than not. One may say that philosophically it is necessary that everything be intentional; otherwise there can be no meaning. Because no such thing as coincidence can exist, there are also no mitigating circumstances. All circumstances in which one finds oneself are by their very nature aggravating. When our mothers warned us that someone who lies will also steal, that a thief will also commit murder, and that a murderer will end up on the gallows, they were giving expression to a view that a policeman of Steinbrecher's school can only confirm from his practice.

The clerk he is questioning through the night is not cooperating with Rutkowski. He barely replies, doesn't appreciate that his interrogator is suffering morally for his sake, and appears resigned to his fate. Even more infuriatingly, he is still clutching his ridiculous umbrella which no one, for some unknown, superstitious reason, dares to take away from him. How the memory of the clerk, Adam Trpković, comes to haunt Rutkowski and becomes his vampire is the story of the letters. Writing to his brother-in-law in the hope that words can cancel deeds, he seeks a compromise between suicide and apathy. In truth, his letters for the most part are a labored attempt to dodge responsibility and give a different explanation for his gutlessness.

"Can you recognize in Steinbrecher's linguistic jeremiad the semantic longings of Rudolph Carnap?" he writes to his brother-in-law, who, unknown to him, hasn't even bothered to read the letters. Pekić calls *How to Quiet a Vampire* "a sotie," deriving the term from satirical popular plays in France in the fifteenth and sixteenth centuries, in which a company of *sots*, fools, exchanged badinage on contemporary persons and events. It is a grim comedy about what happens to philosophical ideas when they end up in a police cellar. "Knowledge is the prerequisite for all evil," Steinbrecher says. Ignorance can be wicked when it gets the chance, but crime on a large scale comes from the learned. Pekić reminds us that respected scientists were asked for technical assistance to solve the problem of how to burn the most human bodies in the shortest time with the lowest expenditure in death camps. Rutkowski, as much as he denies it, is an intellectual monster himself. Once he comes to that realization, his solution to how to get rid of his remorse is equally hideous. He writes in the next to the last letter:

> The problem wasn't finding the key to my past—which was what I was passionately trying to do in my letters—but to find the one to my future. Tomorrow is what makes me human; yesterday is what makes me a corpse. The mistake was reviving something I should have taken long ago and buried forever. Our problem is not how to revive, but how to quiet our vampires. The past is a vampire and the real question is how to quiet it forever. We don't have a third option. Either we drive a stake through the vampire's heart or our blood is soon completely sucked dry. In order to achieve the former, we must for once begin with the excretion of the poisonous spirit of intellectual analysis from our lives.

For a short book, *How to Quiet a Vampire* has a complicated plot which I've barely sketched out. On one level, it is a psychological study of a descent into madness of an intellectual who in his ideas gradually begins to turn into an apologist for a brutal authoritarian state with its martyrs of destruction and saints of demolition. The story of the file clerk also takes many unexpected turns. He appears to Rutkowski as a ghost and perhaps even as the devil himself; his execution by hanging turns out to be a kind of mock crucifixion and resurrection. In my opinion, the realistic and fantastic aspects of the narrative are not as well intermixed as they are in Bulgakov's *Master and Margarita*, which undoubtedly was one of Pekić's models. He strives to inflate the clerk and the guilt-ridden professor of history into even more universal symbols after it has become unnecessary to do so. Leaving some of the subplots and commentaries out—and that includes most of the appendix—would have made a brilliant novel into a great one.

For Pekić, history is not to be understood as created by Hitler, Stalin, and all the countless lesser-known executioners who do their killing. Rutkowski and Adam Trpković are more revealing of the history of our time: the one who supposedly knows better, but closes his eyes, and the one who pays with his life for that negligence. There was nothing suspicious about this wretch, nothing incomprehensible except his umbrella, Rutkowski writes. Nevertheless, Steinbrecher orders that the clerk be hung with it. "Do you sense the advantage of farce over all other forms of human humiliation?" he tells Rutkowski. "Farce kills truth, destroys faith, ridicules every feat of heroism. Can someone be a hero in his underwear while holding an umbrella?" Not even Achilles could have managed that, Steinbrecher says. The reader of *How to Quiet a Vampire* will disagree. The funny little man who carries an umbrella in one hand while holding on to his shorts with the other as he is being led to the gallows is the only true hero in a tragic farce.

Northwestern University Press should be commended for its series Writings from an Unbound Europe, in which Pekić's novels and dozens of other first-rate works of fiction in translation from the former Communist countries of Eastern Europe have appeared and continue to appear.

NOTES

1. Translated by Lovett F. Edwards (1976; Northwestern University Press, 1994).

2. Translated by Bernard Johnson (1978; Northwestern University Press, 1994).

3. *Odmor od Istorije* (BIGZ, 1993), p. 175.

Down There on a Visit

For years now I've been looking at a photograph Walker Evans took in the summer of 1936 in the South. I thought of it again while getting ready to travel to the South a few weeks ago. At the intersection of two dusty, unpaved roads stands a dilapidated building with a small porch and a single gas pump. There's no human being in sight. The intense heat and the bright sunlight must have made the locals, a few of whom can be seen standing on the very same porch on another occasion, seek shade. The shutters of the two upstairs windows are closed except for small openings where the slats are broken or have been removed. The postmaster and his wife, who run the pump and the store, are most likely napping, their heads covered with newspapers to protect them against the flies.

Downstairs, in the small side room with a scale and rows of bins for the mail, there are a few letters whose recipients live too far or receive mail too rarely to bother making the trip. With so little to see and so much to imagine, a photograph like this is an invitation to endless conjecture. There's nothing more ordinary, nothing more American than what it depicts: a small town one passes with barely a glance on the way to someplace else.

This June, driving around Mississippi, Alabama, and Georgia, I decided to pay a visit to Sprott and Hale County, where Walker Evans and James Agee collaborated on *Let Us Now Praise Famous Men*, their photographic and verbal record of the lives of three dirt-poor tenant farmer families in the region. I wanted to, as it were, poke around the photograph on my wall. I drove from Mobile past a series of tiny little towns with names like Sunflower, Wagarville, Sunny South, Catherine, and Marion. It was

From the *New York Review of Books*, August 12, 2004.

early Sunday morning so my daughter and I were a bit dressed up, hoping to find a church along the way and attend a service. We saw plenty of houses of worship, but oddly, not much activity around them yet. Driving through one of the bigger towns, we were surprised to find a huge Wal-Mart open at 9:20 with dozens of cars parked outside.

The other puzzle was a number of abandoned churches both in towns and in the countryside. I recall a small, unobtrusive, white wooden church sunk in the earth, the grass and weeds grown tall around it. It had a thick, squat steeple, a single door, two windows on each side covered up with boards. The sky over it was cloudless, the quiet so deep we could hear the crows flap their wings as they flew over our heads in alarm. The people who came to pray there must have died or moved away years ago, but the spirit they sought after lingered on. I wondered if there was anything left inside the church, a hard bench, a hymnal, a suspended oil lamp, a skeleton of a dead bird.

The landscape of central Alabama alternates between patches of woods and rolling fields of cultivated land that open onto long vistas before closing up again. We found the crossroads Evans photographed and a small shut-down country store where the old one most probably stood. It did not appear that much had changed in sixty-eight years. There was a large sign announcing a rodeo in nearby Marion, two half-collapsed barns across the road, and a cat that came out of the bushes hungry and lonely, but ran away every time my daughter tried to make friends with it. The population of Sprott today is reputed to be ten people and that sounds about right. Hale County has 17,185 inhabitants and the county seat, Greensboro, only 2,731. I have no idea how many people lived there in the 1930s, when the cotton plantations were in full operation, but there must have been more. The impression one gets is that there's not much work to be had on the farms that remain. Most of these are large and require a small number of people to work the machinery. Whoever can pick up and leave the county does so, or if they decide to stay, they commute great distances to their jobs. On weekdays, the traffic to Tuscaloosa, Birmingham, and Montgomery tends to be heavy. Most of these commuters are heading to low-paying retail and service jobs in numerous shopping malls at the outskirts of these cities.

We headed south to Selma. What we found there surprised us. Its spacious downtown, where some thirty thousand people once gathered with Martin Luther King to march to Montgomery, is badly run-down. It's a shell of the town it once was. Many of its beautiful turn-of-the-century buildings and storefronts appear in part vacated while others are completely closed. This I found almost everywhere to be the case. The heart of Montgomery has broad avenues, a restored Greek Revival state capitol atop a hill where Jefferson Davis took the oath of office on February 18, 1861, as the president of the Confederate States, and the famous civil rights landmarks, like the Baptist church where the bus boycott was organized in 1956, but there are few people there even on a Monday morning.

The capital of Mississippi, Jackson, is deserted on Friday afternoon. No one walks its streets. There are no restaurants or bars and no hint of where people who work in its many offices get fed. Old photographs of all these places show streets teeming with pedestrians, stores big and small, signs and marquees advertising cafés, drug stores, tobacco shops, and five-and-dime emporiums. The centers of many of the most interesting Southern cities, the neighborhoods that make them most distinct and attractive, have been forsaken for fast-food places, gas stations, and shopping centers at the outskirts, which resemble any other place in the United States.

The middle classes and the rich reside in well-maintained old and new suburbs and vote Republican, while their impoverished neighbors, who tend to be mostly African-American and who outnumber them in many counties, live in rural slums. While there's no official segregation between the races, there is a caste system with clear class distinctions and accompanying inequality that is apparent wherever one goes. There are towns like Jonestown, Mississippi, that in their shocking poverty make one gasp. Weathered, sagging, and unpainted houses, boarded-up windows, others covered with plastic, yards full of dismantled rusty cars, their parts scattered about amid all kinds of other junk and trash, are everywhere. Idle people of all ages lounge on collapsing porches or stand on street corners waiting for something to do. In the countryside with its fertile dark soil, soybeans have become the chief crop, poultry farms are a major business, and there are nine gambling casinos in the next county. All that has increased per capita income in the region, but there was no evidence of it among the blacks I saw.

In Clarksdale, the former capital of the cotton kingdom, which President Clinton visited during his 1999 tour focusing on the nation's poorest communities, I saw in a parking lot of a closed supermarket two ancient cars parked side by side with their four doors wide open. Over their hoods, roofs, and doors, spread out and draped, someone's once-pretty dresses and worn children's clothes were covering every available space. Two black women sat on low stools, one on each side, waiting for a customer. This is the town, they say, where the blues began. One of its legends, Robert Johnson, was reputed to have sold his soul to the devil at a crossroads nearby. There's a blues museum in town and an excellent restaurant and juke joint called Ground Zero owned in part by the actor Morgan Freeman, a part-time local resident. The downtown buildings of what was once clearly a flourishing city reminded me of towns in the Midwest and New England after their industries went broke in the late 1960s and their factories were shut down. Clarksdale has the despoiled look of a conquered and sacked city. Ranking conditions of poverty is a risky business, but what I encountered in Mississippi surpasses anything I've seen in a long time in this country. That the people here vote Democratic and have a liberal black Democratic congressman has not been of visible help to them.

When one enters the small store that also serves as a post office in nearby Belen, one first comes upon shelves cluttered with ancient TV parts. On one side, in the half-dark, an old black man sits poking his screwdriver into the back of a black and white set that must be at least forty years old. Beyond the TV repair section, there's a grocery store selling a few absolute necessities like canned beans and white bread, and finally in the back, the post office itself with its single oval and barred window where one can purchase a stamp. The old white storekeeper who shows me and my friend around could have walked out of one of Eudora Welty's Depression-era photographs. He is so pale; he probably rarely leaves the premises. In the meantime, he is happy to chat. It's not a cliché that people are courteous in the South. Many of them tell memorable stories, love words, and can make something unexpected out of the simplest verbal ingredients. No wonder so many great writers have come from Mississippi.

My first acquaintance with the South was in 1961, when I spent four months at Fort Gordon, Georgia, being trained by the U.S. Army to be a military policeman. On my weekly passes, I went into Augusta, where there was little to do beyond getting drunk in dives frequented by soldiers. With the news of men and women who protested segregation being beaten and occasionally murdered all over the South, it was not the most comfortable place for a Northerner to be. Without even trying, one inevitably got into arguments with the locals. The place seethed with hatred, I thought then. All that changed, of course, over the years, and so did my own understanding of the complexities. There were plenty of racists to be sure, but there were also people of conscience who did their best to alleviate the wrongs in their midst.

Fifty miles from Jonestown, Mississippi, is William Faulkner's Oxford. It has a pretty courthouse square, a bookstore that could match any in New York City or Boston, fine cafés and restaurants, most of which have second-story porches with tables and chairs overlooking the square. People laze there for hours sipping a drink and gabbing. One could live here—one thinks–in a kind of timeless present. Bank, church, a few elegant stores, a barbershop, and a hotel—what more does one need? In the afternoons, when the shadows lengthen and the heat subsides a bit, one has an overwhelming sense of well-being as if everything were just dandy everywhere and one really had no cause to make oneself a nuisance to strangers with whom one happened to strike a casual conversation.

Unfortunately, the local newspapers brought me out of my reverie. The *Clarksdale Press Register,* which I'd bought earlier that day, had the following letter:

Dear Editor:
I am a Jesus freak.

Jesus said that you can't serve two fathers. Either you serve God the Heavenly Father or you are damned and serve Satan. All true conservatives will be against homosexuality. It's not acceptable in God's house. I believe they can be saved and change this lifestyle. Anyone that says it is OK to kill babies is damned. God made human life in His own likeness. We as Christians expect Americans to be against us. They were against Jesus. God has blessed us, but for how long? For America's weakness is turning its back on God. We better not think that God won't put his wrath on America soon. America better thank God for Christians who are praying for this country. The rest of the people are not getting what they can get in riches. May God heal the churches and people. It's time Christians take a stand in voices and elections. Get these liberals out of government, and get conservative Christian leadership in government.[1]

During my trip, I was asked several times point-blank whether I was a Christian. The first time it happened, I was so surprised I didn't know what to reply. Finally, I mumbled that I was brought up in the Eastern Orthodox Church and to further buttress my credentials, I mentioned that I had priests in my family going back a couple of centuries. As far as I could tell, that didn't seem to make much impression. What people were eager to find out was whether I had accepted Jesus as my Savior. For the writer of this letter, and for others I met, Christians are to be distinguished from the rest of Americans, who are something else— liberals, secular humanists, Catholics, atheists, abortionists, etc. They all share one thing in common, however: they are all going to hell.

The absolute certainty of that outcome, I found, is a source of deep satisfaction to the believers. They enjoy hearing about the torments that await the damned. That must be the explanation for the great success of *Glorious Appearing* by Tim LaHaye and Jerry B. Jenkins, the twelfth and final book in a series that recounts the story of those left behind when the Apocalypse arrives and the Rapture gathers the elect into heaven. The first eleven novels have sold forty million copies and the new one is also a best seller.[2] The blood and gore of the final battle of the ages between Jesus and the legions of the Antichrist are described at great length and in loving detail:

> Tens of thousands of foot soldiers dropped their weapons, grabbed their heads or their chests, fell to their knees, and writhed as they were invisibly sliced asunder. Their innards and entrails gushed to the desert floor, and as those around them turned to run, they too were slain, their blood pooling and rising in the unforgiving brightness of the glory of Christ.
> "For My sword shall be bathed in heaven; indeed it shall come down on Edom, and on the people of My curse, for judgment.
> "The sword of the Lord is filled with blood. It is made overflowing with fatness. For the Lord has a sacrifice in Bozrah, and a great slaughter in the land of Edom.
> "Their land shall be soaked with blood, and their dust saturated with fatness."[3]

It was reported that President George W. Bush tried to enlist the Vatican for help in his reelection when he paid a visit to the Pope last month. He has no need to make a similar appeal to the churches in the South. During many hours of listening to Christian radio, I was assured again and again that the Bible is the best source of information on contemporary events and the only guide anybody needs on how to vote. When I watched religious talk shows on TV at night, I heard that the many wars that the president has promised us have happily been foretold in the Bible. "Let us restore to God the thunder," the poet John Crowe Ransom wrote in 1930,[4] and the people who called in would have readily agreed. Peace on earth went unmentioned. What excited the people I heard was the force of deadly weapons. I got the impression that it was a greater offense to believe in evolution than to bomb a city into rubble. As a letter to the *Mobile Register* signed "Addison DeBoi" put it:

> What the left has not come to realize is that most of today's suffering is the result of the left's continued efforts to remove horror and pain from war. . . . The point is, war is hell, and it should be. The more respectable we make war, the more we

make it less horrific, the more we seek to not harm civilians, then the greater the risk and frequency of war.[5]

Skepticism, empirical evidence, and book learning are in low esteem among the Protestant evangelicals. To ask about the laws of cause and effect would be a sin. They reject modern science and dream of a theocratic state where such blasphemous subject matter would be left out of the school curriculum. Their ideal, as a shrewd young fellow told me in Tuscaloosa, is unquestioning obedience and complete conformity in matters of religion and politics. The complaint about so-called secular humanism is that it permits teachers and students too much freedom of thought and opinion. If evangelicals haven't gone around smashing TV sets and computers, it is because they recognize their power to spread their message. Aside from that, they would like to secede intellectually from the rest of the world.

As if to alert me to the danger of such sweeping statements, I stumbled on a magnificent exhibition of Baroque art at the Mississippi Arts Pavilion in Jackson. It came from the State Arts Collections in Dresden and included porcelain, costumes, sculpture, armor, and paintings by Rembrandt, Rubens, Titian, Mantegna, Velázquez, Van Dyck, Lucas Cranach, Vermeer, and a few other Old Masters. It was fairly well attended. There were even families with kids. I've no idea what they thought of the sensual teenage Madonna holding a mischievous-looking two-year-old. The museum guides and attendants appeared to be volunteers. They stood at various points of the huge exhibition and kept asking each visitor if he or she were enjoying the show and were exceedingly pleased to hear that we were. It sounded as if there had been complaints and they needed confirmation that they were, indeed, taking part in something worthy.

At the Mississippi Museum of Art there was another imported show—Paris Moderne, art deco works from the 1920s and 1930s. Almost next door, Confederate flags were flying over the state buildings, often in close proximity to landmarks commemorating the civil rights struggle. A few well-known participants in the most gruesome events of its bloody history are still alive in nearby towns and remain unconvicted, as columns in newspapers on the anniversary of their crimes reminded their readers.

On another cloudless day, I drove south toward Hattiesburg and Mobile. The roadside fruit stands were overflowing with baskets of ripe peaches, tomatoes, and watermelons. There was also something called "boiled peanuts" which I was wary to try. On the radio, the burning issue was the new policy just passed by the Mississippi legislature that will drop from Medicaid eligibility sixty-five thousand of the neediest elderly citizens and chronically ill patients with severe disabilities, leaving them to rely solely on the federally funded Medicare for their drugs. The governor, Haley Barbour, the brains behind the rollback, is the former chairman of the national Republican Party. In his view, taxpayers ought not to have to pay for free health care for people who can work and take care of themselves and just choose not to.

Most callers to the show sounded scared. The host of the program maintained that their fears were exaggerated, that Medicare would help out; but they were not buying it. They griped about the difficulties they already had signing up for the federal government's new prescription drug discount cards. The host of the show blamed the fiscal crisis in the state on a teachers' pay raise and so did some of the other callers. He was willing to admit that there may be some inconvenience to the elderly, but he wanted them to realize that in the end nothing could be done. What came through were the inability and the reluctance of more than a few people to grasp the kind of hardship that faced their fellow citizens. The familiar Republican Party line—less government, no new taxes—eventually silenced the most stubborn of the complaining voices.

This lack of compassion for the less fortunate is also to be found in New Hampshire, where I live. Our politicians are as heartless as the ones in Mississippi and see themselves, despite their assurances otherwise, as being elected primarily to serve the well-to-do. Let the fittest survive is their attitude. However, they don't invoke God as they go about ensuring that the poor stay poor. As for the losers, both in the South and in the North, their outrage is not directed against the politicians. This is one of the great puzzles of recent American politics: voters who enthusiastically cast their vote against their self-interest, who care more about "family values," school prayer, guns, abortion, gay marriage, or the teaching of evolution than about having decent health care insurance and being paid a living wage. They squabble, as they did in Alabama recently, over whether the Ten Commandments ought to be posted in a courthouse while the education of their children continues to be underfunded and their overcrowded public schools are violent and dangerous places.

The result of these dogmatic inconsistencies of belief—which I found wherever I went—is fragmentation: "the growing social, physical, economic, and cultural separation of Americans from each other," as Sheldon Hackney puts it in a fine new collection of essays by thirteen different authors, *Where We Stand, Voices of the Southern Dissent.*[6] Even Pentecostals don't see eye to eye when it comes to theology. A town with no more than five hundred inhabitants has a dozen churches lining the highway. They stand barely fifty yards apart, all belonging to different schisms and factions. One of them is just a large trailer with the hand-painted name of the church tacked to its side. The door is open. Three old-model cars are parked in front.

A dozen miles down the highway is Mobile with its modern skyscrapers, and not too far beyond, the pretty little town of Fairhope on the eastern shore of the bay with its elegant boutiques, art galleries, and good restaurants. Fairhope was founded in 1884 as a model community, inspired by a belief in land as common inheritance, and as a cooperative commonwealth free from all forms of private monopoly and opportunities to prey upon one another. In his bittersweet reminiscence of growing up in Fairhope, included in *Where We Stand*, Paul M. Gaston, whose grandfather was one of the founders and guiding forces of the community, laments its transformation into what it is today, an upscale resort town where one of the shops for the well-heeled women is called Utopia without any irony. He writes of the morally benumbed citizenry unconcerned about disparities of wealth and the social apartheid such towns as Fairhope seem to serve.

It's easy to put all that out of one's mind as one cruises past the sandy beaches of Mobile Bay. The end of a long pier with a gazebo at Point Clear seems a good place for an afternoon siesta on a bench with the blue sky and sea birds for company. It's hot, but there's a breeze from the water. After a while, I hear the sound of chamber music. It's live, coming from the spacious lawn of the resort hotel next door where a wedding, it appears, is about to take place. There are some fifty chairs lined up in rows with a pulpit in front but no guests yet, only a string quartet playing Mozart. Eventually, as the guests begin to emerge from the hotel, I draw closer. They are a distinguished bunch, the men in tuxedos and the women in stylish, well-cut summer dresses. They come alone or in pairs strolling across the rich lawn to take their seats. With the quartet playing a lovely minuet the four bridesmaids, all wearing dark red dresses, come out one by one trailed by the groom and his parents. The bride, on the arm of her father, is the last to appear. She's a very pretty blonde.

I'm too far away to hear the minister, but I can see them exchange rings. On a platform by the edge of the water, I see people setting up tables, decorating them with flowers for what I assume will be the wedding feast. It's all very proper, very charming, and very inviting. The servers are mostly black and I realize that they are the first people of color I've seen since I drove into the Fairhope region. By now the wedding is over, the sun is setting over Mobile Bay, and the photographer is in a hurry to have the newlyweds pose against it. He wants them smooching and they oblige again and again, each kiss more lusty than the last one, to the joy of the younger members of the wedding party and the disapproving glances of the old. After that's over, they all file by me on the way to dinner, smiling and nodding in a most friendly way.

Yes, people told me on my trip, the American dream has been going wrong somewhere. I saw TV evangelists bring thousands of ecstatic believers to their feet. These programs were a mixture of old camp meetings, revivalist tents, rock concerts, and sales pitches on how to make millions in real estate "without spending a dime of your own money." The huge crowds were made up of well-dressed, middle-class people of all ages and races. Their piety was touching. Their eyes grew moist when Jesus was mentioned. God frets about them individually and they count on his guidance in practical matters. So many of the sermons I heard were about turning around one's life, overcoming financial worries, achieving worldly success. The men doing the preaching had made millions saving souls and had no qualms offering themselves as a model to emulate. Their lack of humility was astonishing. I'm flying high, the faces said, because God has time for me.

"There is going to be trouble in this country," a lawyer warned me. He wouldn't tell me from what direction. Like others I had met in the South, he kept a gun in his car; he had, he said, several more at home and worried that the government might take away his arsenal. What are they for? In one of his books, the Mississippi novelist and short story writer Barry Hannah suggests an answer:

> The gun lobby, oh my peaceful friends, you may hate, but first you had better understand that it is a religion, only secondarily connected to the Bill of Rights. The thick-headed, sometimes even close to tearful, gaze you get when chatting with one of its partisans emanates from the view that they're holding a piece of God. There is no persuading them otherwise, even by a genius, because a life without guns implies the end of the known world to them. Any connection they make to our "pioneer past" is also a fraud, a wistful apology. Folks love a gun for what it can do. A murderer always thinks it was an accident, he says, as if a religious episode had passed over him.[7]

There are fireworks for sale in almost every town in Alabama. Small rockets wrapped in red, white, and blue paper. People are all set, I was told, to celebrate George W. Bush's reelection in November. He is liked a lot in the South, especially when he speaks about American moral supremacy and our right to kick someone else's ass in the world. I did not encounter many people able to entertain the thought that we could ever be at fault as a nation or that our president could be a fool leading us into a mess. When I asked what Kerry's chances were, even friends looked at me as if I had three heads. Near Flatwood, Alabama, I almost ran off the road after seeing a small "Elect Kerry" sign. It's the only one I came across. In fact, I didn't see any Bush signs either—there's no need for them since he's following God's plan, as everybody there knows. We have always had professional true believers, but in the past their apocalyptic views were marginal and never had such strong support in Congress and the White House, where they are now regularly invited and consulted on matters of national interest. Nor did they ever before have fans even among Catholic and Jewish intellectuals on the right, who find them to be model citizens even with their fanaticism and their love of violence.

"The grungier the town, the better the music and the ribs are liable to be." So I heard. Unfortunately, as I discovered, this is not really true. Most poor people eat mostly poorly prepared food and the better musicians tend to gravitate to cities where customers have cash to spend. The best ribs I had on my trip were not in any of the smaller towns, but in Atlanta. Fat Matt's Rib Joint is a small, unassuming place that promises little from the outside. It serves slabs of pork ribs on paper plates with slices of white bread. There are also bags of potato chips, bowls of rum-soaked beans, and plenty of paper napkins to wipe one's fingers and lips. The crowd is socially and racially mixed. Sitting side by side at long communal tables, eating and drinking pitchers of beer, are well-dressed men and women who could be doctors, lawyers, truck drivers, gas station attendants, and undertakers. The ribs are delicious and cheap, and there's live music. A terrific band is playing a little blues, a little country.

The four white musicians look as if they have day jobs. Three of them are grizzled men in their early sixties who could have come out of an R. Crumb drawing and all of whom one would guess have had plenty of ups and downs in their lives. The songs they play are bawdy, funny, and have a tough realism about them that any serious writer would envy. "A woman gets tired of one man all the time," an old blues song says. Cheating wives and husbands, bad luck, and trouble are the themes. The musicians are enjoying themselves and so is everybody else. That's what our protectors of virtue find so scandalous about the cities. The way diverse classes of people and races get together, drink beer, dance, and make whoopee. But as one of my tablemates, a woman from south Georgia, told me, "Atlanta is not the South."

NOTES

1. *Clarksdale Press Register,* June 3, 2004.
2. See Joan Didion's essay on the Left Behind series, "Mr. Bush and the Divine," *New York Review of Books,* November 6, 2003.

3. *Glorious Appearing: The End of Days* (Tyndale House, 2004), p. 226.

4. *Religion in the American South* (University of Carolina Press, 2004), p. 167.

5. From the *Mobile Register,* Sunday, June 6, 2004.

6. NewSouth Books, 2004, p. 189. The title recalls that of *I'll Take My Stand,* the collection issued in 1930 by the Southern Agrarian writers, including John Crowe Ransom, Allen Tate, Robert Penn Warren, and Randall Jarrell.

7. *Bats out of Hell* (Houghton Mifflin, 1993), p. 83.

Rx for American Poets

What an ambitious project for a critic to undertake! It's usually the poets who are in the business of prophecy. Poets have always been introspective about their art and never more so than in these last two centuries when everything from religion, philosophy, morality, to the social order was constantly being questioned. It was not easy for some of them to continue writing the same old verses in the same old way while the world all around them was talking about revolution and freedom.

Since the Romantics, poetry has engaged in a critique of all of its past assumptions, in order not only to construct a new kind of poetry, but to question everything from morality to metaphysics. There was to be no longer one official truth impermeable to change, but many individual ones grounded in experience that each poet needs to examine for its authenticity, as if poems were a laboratory for all human endeavors. What is scandalous about the polemical pronouncements and manifestoes of poets since the end of the eighteenth century is their conviction that truth, which now eludes religion and philosophy, can still be found in poetry. "A poet participates in the eternal, the infinite, and the one," Shelley writes in *A Defense of Poetry*, and then defines a poem as "the very image of life expressed in its eternal truth." It's lucky that the Church no longer tortures and burns heretics, otherwise being a poet would be the world's most dangerous occupation.

Poets in the United States usually speak with more reverence for authentic experience than for the imagination. They cultivate

Review of *A New Theory for American Poetry: Democracy, the Environment, and the Future of Imagination,* by Angus Fletcher. From the *New York Review of Books,* May 12, 2005.

strategies to make themselves sound sincere, as if poems were eye-witness accounts of real events and not artistic creations. We forget that Homer was blind, and like every good poet who came after him, he saw more with his eyes closed than most others see with eyes wide open. Poetry is one activity in life where consummate liars are not only admired but completely trusted. Of course, the hope for any poem is that it will convince the reader that this is exactly what happened, even if it did not.

With the advent of realism in fiction in the last century it was inevitable that poets, too, would start fretting about verisimilitude. How does a poem go about representing reality? Can language be a mirror? Perhaps it can, but not an ordinary mirror. Walt Whitman, Ezra Pound, and William Carlos Williams are only a few of the American poets discussed by Angus Fletcher who thought they had answers to these questions. What makes it tough on critics is that theory and practice rarely form a continuum since the relationship between reality and imagination keeps changing from poet to poet, and even from poem to poem, so that what often seems to be one turns out to be the other, or even more confusingly, a mixture of the two.

Angus Fletcher has a reputation as one of our most insightful Renaissance scholars and most wide-ranging theorists of literature and the arts. Among his previous books, the best known are *The Prophetic Moment: An Essay on Spencer, Allegory: The Theory of a Symbolic Mode,* and *Colors of the Mind: Conjectures on Thinking in Literature.* The Old Testament, Herodotus, Vico, Coleridge, Calvino, Stevens, *Don Quixote,* Milton's Satan, and Visconti's *Death in Venice* all come up in *Colors of the Mind,* a loosely related collection of essays on the ways in which the experience of thinking is conveyed in literature. Fletcher can write perceptively about the language of prophecy in Renaissance poetics, literary transparency or obscurity, the gnomic sentence and phrase, and he reflects on the possibility of silent thought. He is a collage artist. He gives the impression of having read everything from philosophy to modern physics as he juxtaposes ideas from these seemingly unrelated disciplines to shed new light on literary works. He is a critic who seeks the epistemological foundation of literature with a daring and originality that one rarely encounters today.

Fletcher's new book boldly sets out to describe what is most American about American poetry and to envision the future of the poetic imagination in America. He wants to do for us today what Emerson did 150 years ago for his contemporaries, by writing a work that would have the same kind of broad cultural relevance. Whitman is correct, Fletcher says, in thinking that poetry is elemental for democracy and that our democracy implies an artistic revolution. He breaks with critics who see American poetry as being little more than an extension of the Romantic tradition and emphasizes what he calls our pragmatic tendencies, which beginning with Whitman have given us another poetics that in his view has not been fully acknowledged or extensively explored. What the early settlers found here as they stepped ashore was time removed from history, "a scene of unparalleled newness whose only signpost pointed to the unknown future." It caused them to gradually forsake faith in the intricacies of older faiths and to become empiricists:

> *Whatever works* has always been the American motto, as critical as *e pluribus unum*, although one wonders if they do not amount to the same sentiment, while before these slogans could take root, Americans experienced a long foreground of European natural history, and then the great intellectual divide, the publication in 1859 of *The Origin of Species*. Then at last an ancient poetic wisdom moved into communication with a profound and comprehensive scientific vision. This science continues to advance alongside the poetry we have seen anticipating it and to this day accompanying it. When it is working right, poetry is a kind of knowledge and always anticipates science in a free and imaginative fashion. Poetry has the advantage of being set free from assuming the burden of proof.

This sounds right, but can it be the whole truth in a country where the teaching of evolution is still a controversial issue? If it is, then our poets with their empiricism and their secularism are really at odds with the majority of their fellow citizens who are deeply religious and suspicious of scientific evidence. Leaving that aside for now, Fletcher is right; by considering the work of some poets he will see that something unprecedented has taken place in literary history. He proceeds to show what that is by examining the poetry of John Clare, Walt Whitman, and John Ashbery, whom he regards as key figures responsible for a revolution involving democracy, environment, and the imagination.

His first example is the English poet John Clare (1793–1864). A poor, land-laboring peasant who had little schooling and who still managed to accumulate a considerable library, he wrote many poems and essays on the natural world, politics, corruption, poverty, and rural folk life. In 1837, Clare had a mental breakdown and was admitted to an asylum. Four years later, we are told, he discharged himself and walked the eighty miles home in three and a half days, living on grass he ate along the way. Later that year, he was certified insane and was committed to an institution where he lived for the next twenty years until he died in 1864. For Fletcher, Clare was like a journalist whose native fields and woods were his beat. He took note of everything he came across, no matter how commonplace, delighting in what he saw:

> so I went on with my heart full of hopes pleasures and discoverys expecting when I got to the brink of the world that I coud look down like looking into a large pit and see into its secrets the same as I believd I could see heaven by looking into the water so I eagerly wandered on and rambled among the furze the whole day till I got out of my knowledge when the very wild flowers and birds seemd to forget me and I imagind they were the inhabitants of new countrys the very sun seemd to be a new one and shining in a different quarter of the sky still I felt no fear my wonder seeking happiness had no room for it I was finding new wonders every minute and was walking in a new world often wondering to my self that I had not found the end of the old one the sky still touched the ground in the distance as usual and my childish wisdoms was puzzled in perplexitys.

Like Thoreau, who connected walking and writing, Clare had a love affair with perception. What we simply see, in all its immediacy, is what interests him. In his ability to wonder, and to take up that wonder as his guiding light, he reminds Fletcher of Pre-Socratic philosophers, such as Heraclitus, who rejected the mythical and religious tradition of their ancestors for a view of the world in which natural processes were no longer the whim of the gods but something to be studied with thoughtful attention. They were the first empiricists who were not satisfied with mere assertions, but who tried to gain support for their theories from the direct study of nature. Fletcher is wise not to overstretch this alleged resemblance between the two. Anaximander, Heraclitus, Parmenides, and the rest of them were as fond of abstract speculation as they were of observation. Clare, on the other hand, has eyes firmly on the ground. He doesn't go around looking for surprises; he just finds them:

Mouse's Nest

> I found a ball of grass among the hay
> And proged it as I passed and went away
> And when I looked I fancied something stirred
> And turned agen and hoped to catch the bird
> When out an old mouse bolted in the wheat
> With all her young ones hanging at her teats
> She looked so odd and so grotesque to me
> I ran and wondered what the thing could be
> And pushed the knapweed bunches where I stood
> When the mouse hurried from the crawling brood
> The young ones squeaked and when I went away
> She found her nest again among the hay
> The water oer the pebbles scarce could run
> And broad old cesspools glittered in the sun.

The virtue of such poetry, according to Fletcher, is that it records without a need to pass final judgment on experience. In place of edifying thoughts on the miserable condition of the animal and its resemblance to our human predicament, the poem emphasizes the unplanned, the casual, the intensely and precisely observed. The mouse, who doesn't appear particularly perturbed, simply runs back to her nest at the end of the poem. In contrast to a Romantic like Wordsworth, Clare immerses himself in the world; he doesn't stand apart and hold forth. For him, perception comes before any other mental categories. Clare prefers to describe what he saw, Fletcher says, rather than build it into a rhapsody of Platonic themes. He resists allegory and takes the world as he finds it. What concerns Fletcher, especially, is the way the environment that surrounds the alert eye of the poet becomes a principle for organizing the poem.

As Fletcher readily acknowledges, he owes many of his ideas on Clare to John Ashbery, who spoke on the poet in the Norton Lectures he gave at Harvard some years back.[1] What the two poets share is a fascination with the mere fact that something can be, that it exists in its own right. The Romantics maintained a hierarchy among experiences that come our way with the highest form reserved for the sublime. They were like mountain climbers impatient to behold the grand view. Clare is not in a hurry. In fact, he doesn't mind wasting time, since he takes it in his stride that the uncanny can be encountered everywhere. In comparison, as Fletcher says, Wordsworth is virtually an ecotourist, prospecting for higher laws. The secret Clare knew is "that there is nothing but the day, which is always disappearing, reappearing, disappearing, reappearing again in a perpetual sequence."

This may sound unfair to Wordsworth and the Romantics, but Fletcher has a point. One can get weary of visionary poems; their rhetoric can become insufferable and make the poet sound like a TV evangelist. Besides, there are other ways to approach higher mysteries. Fletcher blames the Romantics, but it seems to me that when it comes to American literature, Emerson may be even more of a culprit. And yet, there are few among us who are completely immune to visionary rhetoric for the obvious reason that we do, on rare occasions, have an experience that lifts us out of the ordinary and leaves us baffled, deeply moved, and ready to believe things we hadn't dreamed of. One can feel that way while at the same time agreeing with Fletcher's reminder that we do not live most of the time in exalted states. The content of our stream of consciousness is usually not so lofty. Our psychic life is more like a squabbling theatrical company trying to rehearse some play we don't even know the name of. A poem ought to take the chaotic state of our minds and our constantly shifting viewpoints into account. Such a poem could begin anywhere and stop anywhere. There would be no closure, no summing up, only a temporary resolution of differences.

For Fletcher, Walt Whitman was the poet who invented that

kind of poem by employing a new kind of descriptive technique that enumerates without pressing toward a conclusion. Whitman's aim was the creation of a continuous present in which all the senses participate, a prolonged, open-eyed amazement at the world's existence that the reader is made to share. Like the authentic democrat that he was, he treats everything and everyone with equal consideration. Description may seem antithetical to poetic imagination, but not for Fletcher. He is not interested in descriptive poetry, which concerns itself with some stationary landscape, interior, or object, but a kind of poem that can represent movement in the city streets and breaks down the distinction between the poet's interior life and the world outside. It's a poem that has neither narrative nor dramatic progression, where emotion and even the first-person pronoun are subordinated to an immersion in the quotidian. Fletcher calls it the environment-poem, a poem not about the environment, whether natural or social, but one that, he writes, imitates the reader's own environment of living:

> The environment-poem seeks symbolic control over the drifting experience of being environed, and it introduces the experience of an outside that is developed for the reader inside the experience of the work. While this outside/inside game closely resembles a stream of consciousness technique intended to reveal elusive states of mind, the environment-poem converts natural surroundings and their common surrogates, like the furnishing of a house, for example, into a surrounding that actually has more presence than any state of mind. It is as if the dream had become real.

When one reads such a passage, the thought intrudes that literary theory is most seductive, perhaps, when it is short on proof. One of the problems with *A New Theory for American Poetry* is that it provides little supporting evidence from poetry for Fletcher's advocacy of the "environment-poem." Do we really experience Whitman's poems as enclosing us within an egoless environment? Is that how we read "Crossing Brooklyn Ferry"? Or even the entire "Song of Myself"? Fletcher quotes "Sparkles from the Wheel," a poem in which environment, as he says, is directly and thematically spelled out. Here's the poem:

Where the city's ceaseless crowd moves on the livelong day,
Withdrawn I join a group of children watching, I pause
    aside with them.
By the curb toward the edge of the flagging,
A knife-grinder works at his wheel sharpening a great knife,
Bending over he carefully holds it to the stone, by foot and
    knee,
With measur'd tread he turns rapidly, as he presses with
    light but firm hand,
Forth issue then in copious golden jets,
Sparkles from the wheel.
The scene and all its belongings, how they seize and
    affect me,
The sad sharp-chinn'd old man with worn clothes and
    broad shoulder-band of leather,
Myself effusing and fluid, a phantom curiously floating, now
    here absorb'd and arrested,
The group, (an unminded point set in a vast surrounding,)
The attentive, quiet children, the loud, proud, restive base
    of the streets,
The low hoarse purr of the whirling stone, the light-press'd
    blade,
Diffusing, dropping, sideways-darting, in tiny showers of
    gold,
Sparkles from the wheel.

Fletcher suggests that each spark is like each one of us, a very
puny object suggesting the immense form of society at large. He
says that Tocqueville

> had remarked that, faced with "the still more imposing aspect
> of mankind," democratic man is threatened by a deep empti-
> ness: hence "his ideas are all either extremely minute and
> clear, or extremely general and vague; what lies between is an
> open void."

All right, one says to oneself, but what happened to the poem
that surrounds us like an environment and the peculiar experience of identification with it that a reader is supposed to un-
dergo? Fletcher is much more persuasive when he speaks else-

where about the distinctive phrases in Whitman that suggest a wavelike motion as we feel carried along by them, and when he describes the manner in which these phrase "units" combine into a larger union without recourse to logical progression. When it comes to explicating "Sparkles from the Wheel," he really doesn't have much to say about the poem and whatever textual analysis he does offer seems beside the point.

His theory becomes far more plausible when he turns to John Ashbery's poetry. As a poet of fragmented consciousness, immersed in dailiness, for whom even his own identity is a perennial issue, Ashbery is the ideal subject for Fletcher:

> But since I don't understand myself, only segments
> of myself that misunderstand each other, there's no
> reason for you to want to, no way you could. . . .

As Fletcher says of Ashbery, "the lyric 'I' is forever being diffused into You, He, She, and We and They, and various kinds of It," so that a poem of his becomes a special kind of fragment—what is conventionally called the beginning and the ending has been removed. By frustrating all the usual expectations of coherence, the poem pushes the reader into the unknown. It's a poetry where the reader has to be ready for digressions, and whatever other surprise comes along. According to Fletcher, poems of this kind are dedicated to showing how we adapt to the environments into which we are thrown by life. If they work, the poems have a way of adapting themselves to meet communicative needs of the reader at many levels. This, of course, is true of poems in general, but never more so than in Ashbery. In any case, Fletcher's theory works better with Ashbery's long poems like "Flow Chart," "A Wave," and "Self-Portrait in a Convex Mirror" than with short ones, like this one from his new book:[2]

A Below-Par Star

After the shouting in the wilderness
and the colors that don't quite match, and shouldn't,
behold I handle you, mournful love,
like a scene in a cigarette pageant.
Your face is as white as linen on a board.

I pray that the skies will soak up your electricity,
the birds founder and come to heel,
the drive-by stabbings evaporate into friendly if
    noncommittal steam,
and tragedy draw his petticoat across your face
because it doesn't happen enough.
A lifeboat almost swamped by shrugs, your famous kisser
now floats over all American cities like a drapeau.
They said you'd be here sooner. It's still early, but I can wait
no longer. It's bed and the movies for me.
Tomorrow, exceptionally, there may be a flawed native pearl
    for breakfast,
and in October, lots of weather, much of it cruder.

Very nice, but what's all this about? Is it a lament for lost love? A tongue-in-cheek yearning for the Sublime? Or is it a poem about the inability to give up that longing—as Meghan O'Rourke said of Ashbery's poetry in general in her review of *Where Shall I Wander* in *Slate*? If she's right, what happened to Fletcher's environment-poem, which was supposed to undermine Romantic poetics? The "environment" may be still there, but only as a strategy to involve the reader. The only way to unravel the ambiguities in "A Below-Par Star" is for the reader to become a poet too. Ashbery knows that a lyric poem with its long history is already full of ghosts of meaning. All poems are one poem. Poetry is like a deck of greasy tarot cards the poet keeps reshuffling; but in the case of Ashbery, he lets the reader be the fortune-teller.

Despite its considerable learning, many fine insights, and some beautiful writing in its pages, *A New Theory for American Poetry* fails to make a persuasive argument since it makes no mention of most of our major poets and their own theories. Even when some are mentioned—as Dickinson, Pound, and Stevens briefly are—they do not add much to the argument. Where is Charles Olson with his "Projective Verse" and his idea of a poem as a field of action? Or Robert Creeley, who argues in his numerous essays that a poet can only write what is in front of his senses in the moment of writing? Where's A. R. Ammons, who said a poem was a walk, irreproducible, dependent on moods, thoughts that are never the same, an act of discovery, a chance taken? What happened to Williams, Ginsberg, Frank O'Hara, and dozens of others with their own ideas and poems? With his idea of the environment-poem Fletcher proposes a new knowledge of reality and new theory of the imagination, but he makes it easy on himself by not engaging with those who mulled over these same issues in the past.

Still, much of what he says is right. Some of our poets since Whitman have indeed moved beyond Romantic poetics toward a poetry that is more empirical. And yet, even that generalization is suspect since in the last hundred years there have been too many poets—Anthony Hecht, for example—who don't fit that description in the least and who wrote poems that are as American and as good as those of the poets Fletcher studies. Theory rarely approximates practice. Great recipes do not necessarily make great cooks. Some of the best ones don't even read recipes. Envisaging the future of the imagination is an impossible task because we cannot know what sort of world poets will find themselves in and how that will affect what they write. If the United States is still at war years from now, its citizens killing and being killed in return, it may make it hard to continue being wrapped up in oneself. "Only a poetry that resists its own transcendental impulses, as I show the environment-poem resists them," Fletcher writes, "will usefully address the most serious conditions of our time along with numerous global changes." Perhaps, but I wouldn't bet on it. Even if we no longer can bear to hear about the Sublime, my guess is that we won't be able to live without it either.

NOTES

1. *Other Traditions* (Harvard University Press, 2000); see the review in the *New York Review of Books,* November 30, 2000.

2. *Where Shall I Wander* (Ecco, 2005).

Saul Steinberg

He drew a labyrinth and himself in it.

He drew a left hand drawing the right hand while the right hand drew the left hand at the same time.

He drew a man crossing himself out with a pen.

He drew the letter *E* sitting at a table and eating the letter *A*.

He drew a fat baby about to smash the globe with a hammer.

He drew two rabbits embracing inside a dragon's mouth.

He drew a man drinking champagne out of a woman's high heel shoe with a straw.

He drew a crowd of question marks facing soldiers with their guns pointed at them.

He drew Sisyphus pushing a huge question mark up the hill.

He drew the line of the horizon to hang and dry a pair of mended socks, a shirt, and a dishrag.

A man removed his nose as if it were a pair of wire-rimmed eyeglasses.

A cat sipped a martini with a goldfish floating in it.

A woman came into the room wielding a fly swatter like an ax.

Don Quixote charged a large pineapple with his spear.

A large man with a bow and arrow shot at a speech balloon over his head full of ornate, illegible writing.

A man carried a huge heroic portrait of himself down the sidewalk.

A woman carried a vase in place of her head with a single red rose in it.

A small dog at the zoo pulled at the leash in order to bark at a lion's cage.

From *Journal of Poetry Society of America* 58 (spring/summer 2002).

An old man raised a doll-like little girl so she could get a closer look at the moon.

Another man took a stern look at a blank canvas in a museum.

At a county fair there were shooting galleries called: Mondrian, Rimbaud, Rasputin, Kierkegaard, Fear & Trembling, etc.

He made a thumbprint on a sheet of paper then drew a shirt and a tie to go along with it.

He drew sixteen identical landscapes stretching to the empty horizon. Small indistinct figures, identically dressed in black, stood in groups or apart from each other.

A man held at the end of a string a winged angel who looked like himself.

The sphinx in the desert resembled someone's mother-in-law.

A portly businessman rode a horse, carrying a sword and a shield. His wife tagged behind, mounted on a donkey and wearing a pillbox hat, clutching a purse. Up ahead, they could see the sign for a MOTEL.

A knight chased a dragon down a steep hill while a huge boulder rolled after him.

An old married couple: the husband was the Jack in the Box who popped up smiling while his wife stood contentedly by his side.

A portly lady dressed like Queen Victoria swung a cat-of-nine-tails.

When a certain man opened his mouth to speak, a huge scribble came out of his mouth.

In an old school picture, with all the faces equally blurred, a blue arrow pointed to one face.

A bust of a woman sat on a TV table with wheels. On her head she had rabbit ears and from her back one could see a long cord plugged into an electric outlet.

A small dog sat on a carpet on which a huge lion had been embroidered.

He drew a cat with a raised saber standing proudly over a big fish.

He drew an American toothpick, then a French toothpick, and finally a Greek toothpick.

He drew a dinner plate with a rubber ball on it and a hammer placed on one side and a pair of pliers and a screwdriver on the other.

Saint George riding on his horse attacked a dragon no bigger than a toad in the grass.

Blind Justice with a sword in one hand and the scale in the other met a veiled Bedouin woman in the desert.

Uncle Sam was a matador. He waved an American flag in front of a huge Thanksgiving turkey.

A boy was being scolded by his mother after having cut off a peacock's tail with scissors.

The Peace Dove flew over our heads with a carving knife in its beak.

Here was a street of snarling, barking dogs and beat-up old cars with their hoods raised and their trunks open.

A man carried his exact double over his shoulders.

A large man on wheels had an opening on his back and a ladder down which ten of his lookalikes were descending.

Two men dressed to look like Uncle Sam watched with surprise a third man passing on the street who also looked like Uncle Sam.

A little girl sat on a seesaw with a pot of flowers sitting opposite her.

Uncle Sam and the Statue of Liberty were street musicians. He played the violin and she a toy drum while two ants danced at their feet.

Hotel Emperor was nothing but an enlarged photograph of a chest of drawers with many windows and a door drawn on it.

Then there was something called the SHEPHERD FACTORY where Romanian, Irish, Calabrian, and Sardinian shepherds were being manufactured.

In all of the drawings he made of me, I looked like a provincial Eastern European intellectual. I worked in the town hall shuffling yellowed, ink-stained land deeds and birth certificates and in my free time composed political manifestos and love poems to the widow of the local funeral parlor director.

The Singing Simics

I once broke a blood vessel in my mouth singing opera. I had
had a huge molar extracted, had gone to work the following day,
and just as I was putting on my coat to go home, I heard that one
of my coworkers was going to hear *The Magic Flute* that night at
the Met. To give him a sample of the great music he was about
to hear, I started singing the big "Queen of the Night" aria. At
the end of a coloratura passage, I hit a note so high all the dogs
being walked in Washington Square Park two blocks away must
have jumped. All of a sudden, something popped like a bubble
gum where the tooth had been pulled out. My mouth was full of
blood. I ran into the bathroom and stuck some paper towel on
the wound thinking, no sweat, it'll stop. Since I lived only six
blocks from the office, I waited to get home before I checked my
mouth again. The moment I removed the wad of paper the
blood started gushing. Somewhat alarmed, I stuck more paper
towels between my teeth and went in search of a dentist in the
neighborhood. I rang a lot of bells, but since it was Friday night
no one came to my aid. Then I did something very peculiar. I
went to the movies with my mouth clenched hard, figuring, I'm
no bleeder, this is bound to stop sooner or later. I saw *High Sierra*
with Bogart and Ida Lupino, which I had never seen before. I always liked her soulful, intelligent acting and she had me captivated. After the show, I went home, removed the wad, and the
blood filled my mouth again. Now I was really scared. I put a
fresh wad in and caught a taxi. It took me to the New York University Hospital, but for some reason which I now forget, they
couldn't take me. With my mouth closed I could not argue, so I
took their advice and set off for the Bellevue Hospital, which was

From the *Harvard Review* 25 (2003).

only a few blocks away. However, I had forgotten to ask in which direction. First Avenue was dark and empty, so I could see myself being mugged to top off a perfect evening. Somehow I got to the emergency room where they took my name and told me to take a seat. The waiting room was packed with people stricken with various emergencies. There were at least two pregnant woman in labor pains, a young fellow with blood on his face, and dozens of others looking equally miserable. I was there for hours, or so it seemed, before I saw the doctor. He put in a couple of stitches and that was that. I was so overwhelmed with gratitude, and not knowing how to repay them at that moment, I grabbed and kissed the nurse's hand on the way out.

Come to think of it, in our family we were always getting in trouble on account of singing. In the late 1950s and early 1960s my uncle Boris and I went often to the opera. At the old Met on Fortieth Street standing room tickets were sold an hour before the performance. There'd be a long line because they cost only a dollar, but if you came early enough you usually got in. The amazing thing about it was that once you were inside you stood next to some of the best seats in the house, brushing shoulders with men in tuxedos and women in evening gowns. Boris was a tall, balding fellow, an aspiring tenor who had quit a high-paying job in a trucking company to take lessons from an ex–voice teacher from the Julliard School of Music. He was extremely opinionated about every aspect of the performance and put on quite a show himself. Like other standees, we tried to position ourselves as close as possible to the stage, then if someone did not turn up or left early we'd take their seats. The only problem was that every time the lead tenor struck up an aria, Boris sang along. Sotto voce, or so he imagined, but lots of people heard him and tried to quiet him down. He protested loudly. He was merely demonstrating to me how the role was supposed to be sung and he didn't care to be interrupted. A couple of times an usher was summoned. Once the wife of one of the tenors singing who happened to be sitting close by came over to argue with Boris about the merits of her husband's performance. The opera was in progress, the short, bowlegged tenor and the hefty diva were swearing eternal love on the stage, and that woman in the audience was about to punch Boris. On another occasion, he was so annoyed with the tenor in *Cavalleria Rusticana* that he made a move to climb on the stage and show the poor fool and the whole house what grand opera was supposed to be like. Boris had a voice to wake up the dead, everyone agreed. Unfortunately, he had a bad ear, which his friends and family kept secret from him. After the opera was over, he sang in the street and on the subway on the way home. I recall the astonished faces of sleepy passengers on some downtown local opening their eyes wide to find in their midst Andrea Chenier himself, the great French Romantic poet and innocent victim of revolutionary justice dying on the guillotine and singing with his last breath:

> Come un bel di di di maggio
> che con baccio di vento
> e carezza di raggio
> si spegne di firmamento,
> col bacio io d'una rima,
> carezza di poesia,
> salgo l'estrema cima
> del' ecistenza mia.

It didn't help that I kept laughing while Chenier told everyone between sobs how, kissed by rhyme and caressed by poetry, he climbed the final peak of his existence. Who let these two lunatics loose? the grumpy passengers asked themselves as they exchanged glances.

My mother, too, liked to give impromptu performances in public. She had studied singing in Paris with a famous voice teacher, had taught singing for many years in a Belgrade conservatory and then in Chicago. In her old age, she told every stranger she met the story of her life, interspersed with vocal accompaniment. Short and stocky, armed with an umbrella, she'd stand in line at the dry cleaners and belt out an aria. She would do the same in a supermarket or in a dentist's waiting room. It embarrassed the hell out of me. Like her father, the much-decorated First World War hero, she was a lifelong hypochondriac who made almost nightly trips in an ambulance to the hospital where she entertained the emergency room staff with her vast repetoire. She had a small, well-trained voice that stayed youthful even into her eighties. Finally, some tone-deaf doctor got fed up with her and sent her to a psychiatrist. She broke into song there too. Eventually, I received a phone call from the shrink who begged me to come by and give him some basic information about my mother because he couldn't make heads or tails of what she was saying when she was not singing. Mozart was the love of her life, so what she gave him were genuine bel canto renditions in original Italian with many hand-gestures and eye rolls. I'm Zerlina, she would say, batting her eyelashes. Don't waste your time, I told the psychiatrist when I saw him. He was a young fellow and determined to get to the bottom of her imaginary maladies, or so he assured me. No sooner had we started rummaging in her dark closets, than we heard my mother's voice in the waiting room. That afternoon she was the countess in *The Marriage of Figaro:*

> Porgi amor, qualche ristoro
> ai mio duolo, a'miel sospir!

"What is she saying?" the shrink pressed me.

"I think it means, Grant, O love, some sweet elixir to heal my pain, to soothe my sighs," I told him. And that was the last I ever saw or heard of him.

Did my mother like the way Boris sang? Of course not. Her favorite singer in the family was my father. The two of them had met in a music school when they were in their early twenties. After graduation, they gave a recital together, sang lieder, old Italian art songs, and operatic arias. My father never sang professionally, only when he had too much to drink. He'd sit with a wineglass in his hand and start off softly. He was a handsome man with a pretty tenor voice and he knew how to deliver a song and make the lyrics vivid and poignant. I never heard anybody complain about him. He had the most incredible musical ear I ever encountered. He could harmonize with the hum of the refrigerator. Give him Johnny Cash or Billie Holiday on the radio and he'd immediately find a way to fit in. Otherwise he didn't try to show off. Now and then, at the end of a fine meal in a restaurant, he couldn't resist it, but he'd make it intimate, just for you and him and perhaps for that beautiful woman sitting alone at the next table.

Given that kind of competition, I never opened my mouth in public except for that one time, although I know lots of songs and arias. Once in a while in the shower, I'll sing Otello's "Esultate" or Figaro's "Se vuol ballare, Signor Contino," and then I remember Boris and my parents and stop right there with the soap stinging my eyes.

The Wealth Poverty Buys

1.

They wrote over 450 letters to each other between 1953 and 1985, often twice or three times a week, exchanging poems and commenting on them, copying for each other long passages from books they were reading, gossiping about their contemporaries. When they began corresponding, and for many years after, they were two unknown poets, Denise Levertov in New York or Mexico and Robert Duncan in San Francisco, struggling to make ends meet and depending on a small circle of literary friends for moral support. "Poetry's the wealth poverty buys," A. R. Ammons says somewhere. They published their poems and essays in small magazines with tiny circulations that were nearly impossible to obtain outside a few bookstores scattered across the country.

Duncan and Levertov rarely met face to face and when they did it was usually for no more than a day or two, and yet they were extremely close for almost thirty years. Levertov shared many of her most intimate secrets with Duncan, who was less forthcoming about his own private life. As she said in an interview, "No matter what anybody else said and however much praise and approval I got from other quarters, if I didn't have his, it didn't mean much to me."[1] Their friendship was gradually broken up during the Vietnam War. They disagreed over how—if at all—poetry could be both politically useful and aesthetically sound. Duncan doubted it could. After a final angry

Review of *The Letters of Robert Duncan and Denise Levertov,* ed. Robert J. Bertholf and Albert Gelpi. From the *New York Review of Books,* November 4, 2004.

exchange of letters, they stopped corresponding regularly in 1972 and were in touch only on rare occasions until Duncan's death in 1988. In the richness of their prose and their knowledge and in their escalating drama, their letters read like an epistolary novel with an unhappy ending.

Robert Duncan was born in 1919 in Oakland, California, and adopted as an infant after his mother died in childbirth and his father, who worked as a day laborer, could not afford to keep him. His foster parents were devout theosophists who consulted horoscopes and astrological charts while picking out which child to adopt. He grew up amid séances and meetings of the Hermetic Brotherhood and recalls his elders speaking in hushed or deepened voices, or speaking in voices that were not their own. He was told at that early age that his forebears had witnessed the destruction of Atlantis and that he himself was fated to witness a second death of civilization by fire and holocaust.

Duncan went to high school in Bakersfield, and in 1936 enrolled at the University of California, Berkeley, where he traded the writings of Madame Blavatsky and other occult classics for leftist politics. He read Ezra Pound and Gertrude Stein, published his first poems on social issues and class conflict, and started his own magazine. He dropped out of school in 1938, briefly attended Black Mountain College in North Carolina, and moved on to Philadelphia to join a male lover who had been one of his instructors at Berkeley.

In 1941 he was drafted and sent to San Antonio for basic training but was discharged after declaring his homosexuality. "I am an officially certified fag now,"[2] he told friends. Two years later, tired of male lovers, he got married and got divorced several months afterward. As Duncan described it, he next became a gigolo in New York. In 1944, his article "The Homosexual Society," in which he compared the plight of the gays in contemporary society with that of the Negro and the Jew, appeared in Dwight Macdonald's journal *Politics*. Duncan had a poem accepted and then rejected by John Crowe Ransom at *Kenyon Review*, who decided on reflection that he saw veiled erotic content in the poem.

In 1945 Duncan was back in Berkeley studying medieval history at the university and befriending the poet Kenneth

Rexroth, who introduced him to the poetry of Hilda Doolittle. She became a lifelong influence and the subject of his vast critical study of her work, of which only sections have been published so far. His first book of poems, *Heavenly City, Earthly City,* came out in 1947, the year he met Charles Olson and visited Pound at St. Elizabeth's Hospital in Washington, D.C. His next collection, *Medieval Scenes,* came out in 1950. The following year, he met the painter and collagist Jess Collins, who would become his lifelong partner and the illustrator of many of his books. For the rest of his life, save for an extended stay in Europe, he lived in San Francisco.

Levertov, who died in 1997, was born in 1923 in Ilford, England. Her Russian-born father was a Hasidic Jew who had converted to Christianity, married a Welsh woman, and ended up being ordained an Anglican priest. Her mother was a singer, painter, and writer whose Welsh ancestors included several visionaries, the most famous of whom was the tailor-preacher Angel Jones of Mold. Levertov and her older sister, who was born in 1914, were both educated at home by their parents, who read to them from the works of such writers as Willa Cather, Joseph Conrad, Charles Dickens, and Leo Tolstoy. They never attended regular school. Levertov's parents were also politically active, protesting fascism in Spain and Germany and providing aid to political refugees from Europe. When she was twelve she sent off some poetry to T. S. Eliot, who kindly replied offering her advice and encouraging her to go on writing.

Her first published poem, "Listening to Distant Guns," came out in *Poetry Quarterly* in 1940. During the war, Levertov worked as a civilian nurse in London and had her first book, *The Double Image,* published in 1946. The following year, working as a nurse in Paris, she met the American novelist and ex-GI Mitchell Goodman. They were married in December and eventually settled in New York City, where their only child, a son, was born in 1949. While Levertov's older poems were being included in the anthology *New British Poets,* edited by Kenneth Rexroth, the poetry she was writing now was coming under the influence of American language and the work of William Carlos Williams. She met the poet Robert Creeley, a Harvard classmate of Goodman's, who introduced her to a number of younger poets and small literary magazines. She first came across Duncan's name and poetry in 1948 in an issue of the magazine *Poetry* that she found in the American Library in Florence. It was a review by Muriel Rukeyser of his book *Heavenly City, Earthly City*, which included these lines:

> There is an innocence in women
> that asks me, asks me;
> It is some hidden thing they are
> before which I am innocent.
> It is some knowledge of innocence.
> Their breasts lie undercover.
> Like deer in the shade of foliage,
> they breathe deeply and wait;
> and the hunter, innocent and terrible,
> enters love's forest.[3]

In her short memoir of their friendship, written in 1975, Levertov writes that Duncan's poem, with its archaic diction and romantic sensibility, reminded her of her own work. Here was an American poet unafraid of sentimentality, a link for her to an older tradition she grew up with. However, once she married American literature, as she put it, she understood that to survive as a poet she had to start using the language she heard around her. By 1951 she was already sending her work to Williams and receiving his advice on how to revise her poems. He liked the luminous simplicity of her style. The poems she wrote under his influence and that of her friend Robert Creeley, with their avoidance of poetic rhetoric, have little in common with the poems she wrote in England or the lush, ornate verses that Duncan continued to write for the rest of his life.

What they shared was a belief in dream and myth, what Albert Gelpi in his excellent introduction to their collected letters calls "the mystique and metaphysics of the visionary imagination." For Duncan, imagination is our supreme cognitive faculty, the only one able to take hold of the reality and the mystery of our inner experience. Levertov had no problem with that. "The poet—when he is writing—is a priest," she writes in an essay; "the poem is a temple; epiphanies and communion take place within it."[4]

Duncan agreed with Modernists that everything can be the stuff of poetry but he did not have Levertov's eye for detail and the interest she took in the physical world. He was a bookish poet. What he missed in modern poems was angels, gods, and abstract ideas. Time and time again, he says, men have chickened out in the fear of what the genius of poetry demands of them. Poetry was brought to heel and made obedient to the criteria of rational discourse and its old role as a vehicle of vision and prophesy suppressed. For Duncan, if a poet is not a seer, he or she is not a poet.

Their first exchange of letters occurred in 1953 when Duncan sent her a poem intended as homage to a poem of hers he had read and admired in a magazine. Levertov did not know what to make of it. There was no name or address, only the postmark San Francisco and the initials R.D. at the bottom of the poem. She found the poem, written in the style of Gertrude Stein, equally puzzling and was not sure whether she was being mocked. If R.D. was Robert Duncan, this did not sound like his poetry. She wrote to him, the misunderstanding was cleared up, apologies made, but it was really only two years later, after their first meeting in New York City, while he and his friend Jess were living in Spain, that their correspondence began in earnest:

> We are settled in, with more space than we have ever had before. It is the apartment which the Creeleys had here last year. Somewhat settled in that is, beds and mattresses do not arrive from Palma until Tuesday. And when in the world does the Spanish tongue arrive? Here I am an old gabbler in a town of continual gabble, about anything, and I can only really say goodday.

Levertov replies:

> My mother arrived 2 weeks ago and has been ill most of the time since so I've had no time or concentration for letters. But I do have 3 poems. Damn it, ever since you were here I've felt as if I cd. do so much with just a bit more time & quiet to get hold of things, & I've been snowed under with housewifery. Though sometimes I wonder if I don't tend to produce more under pressure. I am not sure.

In that same letter, Levertov confesses that she is not as enthusiastic about Paul Blackburn's poetry as Duncan is. Their letters are full of such frank exchanges. Duncan, for example, calls Ginsberg's *Howl* and *Kaddish* as close to poetry as Kipling's "If," which he disliked. He revised that view of Ginsberg, somewhat, over the years, but continued to be suspicious of the man, regarding him as a self-promoter who liked to shout like Hitler or an evangelist when he gave readings. Levertov, in turn, describes spending an evening with Robert Lowell and finding to her astonishment that, by her own standards, he did not have an accurate ear for poetry. "Imagine," she writes, "it *never occurred* to him to think of Emily Dickinson's dashes as aural notations, rests or rallentandos." Much of this back-and-forth is very entertaining, as when Duncan describes for her what to expect when she gives a reading in San Francisco:

> The audiences here are avid and toughend—they've survived top poetry read badly; ghastly poetry read ghastly; the mediocre read with theatrical flourish; poets in advanced stages of discomfort, ego-mania bumbling; grand style, relentless insistence, professional down-the-nosism, charm, calm, schizophrenic disorder, pious agony, auto-erotic hypnosis, bellowing, hatred, pity, snarl and snub.

Levertov's tastes in poetry were much broader than Duncan's. She has nice things to say about Hayden Carruth, W. S. Merwin, Jim Harrison, Richard Wilbur, and a number of other contemporaries, while Duncan can find little of value in the work of poets beyond his circle, which included Olson and Creeley. For him, there was one and only one true church. He looked upon the poets she recommended as unbelievers and blasphemers. Even a friendly critic and anthologist like Don Allen, whose *The New American Poetry* (1960) made Duncan's work widely known, was written off for showing as much interest in Ginsberg and Frank O'Hara as he did in Duncan.

This inflated view of his work should not come as a surprise. Poets can be opinionated and often downright stupid about their contemporaries. While being so, they are forced to define their ideas of poetry in interesting ways. Here's Duncan explaining to

Levertov the kinds of poems he sees their contemporaries are writing:

> the conventional poet = the universe and life are chaotic; the poet (the civilized or moral man) is given an order to keep against chaos. Every freedom is a breakdown of form.
> the free-verse poet = the universe and man are free only in nature which has been lost in civilized forms. The poet must express his feelings without the trammel of forms. Every formal element is a restraint of true natural feeling. O wild wild wind etc.
> the organic poet = the universe and man are members of a form. Our freedom lies in our apprehension of this underlying form, towards which poetic invention and free thought in sciences alike work.

His objection to formal verse and free verse is that they do not encourage innovation in poetic form. The first relies on established conventions and the latter believes in no rules. For Duncan and Levertov, every experience has its own inherent and unrepeatable form which lies there to be discovered. In other words, form is not something the poet gives to things, but something he receives from things. This idea of the primacy of the process of composition over the end product, which has its roots in Emerson's and Whitman's poetics, was further developed by Pound, Williams, and their followers. Many other poets and critics don't see it that way. They are suspicious of a theory and practice that can be primarily corroborated only by a discerning ear. It comes down to subjective judgment—as if there was any other. I can hear an original music in Levertov, but not as often in Duncan's poems, which for me carry too many reverberations of Romantic and Victorian poetry.

2.

The true test of all these poetic theories came with the war in Vietnam and the need to convey something of the helpless outrage and despair writers felt at the time. Explaining how one of her early war poems got written, Levertov writes:

Looking at the fragile beauty of human bodies I was struck afresh by the extreme *strangeness* of men actually *planning* violence upon each other—I mean, it is so *bizarre* when one stops to think about it, isn't it. That we can ever take it for granted.

As the war dragged on and more people were slaughtered, Duncan's and Levertov's lives were more and more taken over by the events. She marched in peace rallies and participated in group poetry readings to benefit the resistance movement and so did Duncan. He wore a peace button and a black armband in mourning for young Americans conscripted to kill, and he attended a number of demonstrations, including the rally for writers, artists, and intellectuals at the Justice Department and the big march on the Pentagon the following day. Still, when it came to poems reacting to the war, his letters are full of caution. He sees a conflict between Levertov's admirable desire to stop evil and a poet's true task, which is to understand the nature of that evil. A poem that forgets that task is either futile or belongs to a political meaning that has *no truth in itself.* "Give over trying to win thru the poem," he advises her.

Anybody like me who went to dozens of antiwar poetry readings during those years would have to agree. Most of the poems one heard were like political speeches or editorials one readily agreed with and then quickly forgot. Among the hundreds of antiwar poems by known and unknown poets, one image sticks in my mind after forty years, from a poem about President Johnson sitting late at night in the kitchen of the White House with a pencil and paper trying to write a poem that will explain to the antiwar poets the kind of political mess he finds himself in. He wants to say that he's not such a bad guy, but has a tough time finding the right words. I thought it was marvelous. What we usually tend to recall in poetry is a voice that says the unexpected.

On the other hand, when Levertov writes, "I stand fast by what has caused me to feel," I can comprehend that too. It's not easy to preserve an aesthetic distance while watching, on the late evening news, villages being burned, men, women, and children being hunted down in their fields. Notwithstanding his cautionary letters, Duncan himself wrote many angry war poems, in one

of them going so far as to perceive Satan's features in Eisen-
hower's idiot grin, Nixon's black jaw, and the sly glare in Gold-
water's eye:

> Now Johnson would go up to join the great simulacra of
>   men,
> Hitler and Stalin, to work his fame
> with planes roaring out from Guam over Asia,
> all America become a sea of toiling men
> stirred at his will, which would be a bloated thing,
> drawing from the underbelly of the nation
> such blood and dreams as swell the idiot psyche
> out of its courses into an elemental thing
> until his name stinks with burning meat and heapt honors
> And men wake to see that they are used like things
> spent in a great potlatch, this Texas barbecue
> of Asia, Africa, and all the Americas,
> And the professional military behind him, thinking
> to use him as they thought to use Hitler
> without losing control of their business of war. . . .

This poem is no good at all as far as I'm concerned. It's interesting to compare these opening stanzas of "Up Rising" to Levertov's "Tenebrae," the poem that annoyed Duncan so much:

> Heavy, heavy, heavy, hand and heart.
> We are at war,
> bitterly, bitterly at war.
> And the buying and selling
> buzzes at our heads, a swarm
> of busy flies, a kind of innocence.
> Gowns of gold sequins are fitted,
> sharp-glinting. What harsh rustlings
> of silver moiré there are,
> to remind me of shrapnel splinters.
> And weddings are held in full solemnity
> not of desire but of etiquette,
> the nuptial pomp of starched lace;
> a grim innocence.
> And picnic parties return from the beaches

burning with stored sun in the dusk;
children promised a TV show when they get home
fall asleep in the backs of a million station wagons,
sand in their hair, the sound of waves
quietly persistent at their ears.
They are not listening.
Their parents at night
dream and forget their dreams.
They wake in the dark
and make plans. Their sequin plans
glitter into tomorrow.
They buy, they sell.
They fill freezers with food.
Neon signs flash their intentions
into the years ahead.
And at their ears the sound
of the war. They are
not listening, not listening.

Duncan charges her with bigotry for writing about women who are so much concerned about their gowns of gold sequins, and about wedding partners who have no genuine desire and TV watchers and hoarders of food, who are accused of not paying any attention to the world. Levertov's poem, which begins "bitterly bitterly at war," conveys how the experience engulfs our entire being, but, he writes, it degenerates into the "full solemnity of a political etiquette, or approved moral stand." Duncan has a point. He had a low opinion of Auden's poetry, but Auden's "Musée des Beaux Arts" is precisely the kind of poem that avoids such pitfalls; without moralizing it deals with the same indifference on the part of the public. In the end, Duncan was not being fair to Levertov. How many Americans lost sleep over the millions killed in Indochina? Not many, as we know, and she was understandably appalled. And so was he, when he wrote in an introduction to one of his books of poems:

> When in moments of vision I see back of the photograph details and the daily body counts actual bodies in agony and hear—what I hear now is the desolate bellowing of some ox in a ditch—madness starts up in me.[5]

The truth is that it was not only the war in Vietnam that came between them. Levertov had changed. She no longer needed Duncan as a mentor and that drove him to want even more to win her assent to his view of poetry. "Now Robert," she writes to him, "I'm risking a great deal in writing you this letter. You know you are a major person in my life & I cannot endure the thought of your being angry with me—but I cannot not write it & keep my self-respect." The cause of her irritation here is a nasty article Duncan wrote about her friend Hayden Carruth and a letter in which he objected to her increasing support of political violence in opposing the war. The phrase "Revolution or Death" in one of her poems shocked him. He accused her of preparing to wage war under the banner of peace and reminded her that all revolutions have been deeply opposed to the artist.

She replies that clearly he feels that the quality of her work has fallen off because of the time and energy she has spent in political involvements. He counters that by saying that her need to be of service to her cause was in conflict with the aesthetic concerns of the poems. There will always be wars, he tells her, as if that bit of wisdom could be any consolation to a woman whose son was in danger of being drafted and whose husband was about to stand trial and go to jail for being engaged with others in a conspiracy against the military draft law.

In one of the long letters before their final breakup, Levertov admits that, yes, hers is a naive, romantic, emotional point of view. Still, she says, she is impressed by the freedom and the courage and vision of the people in the revolutionary left. As for his accusation of sloganeering, she calls it bullshit and disgustingly elitist. She says in another letter that she has put up with his arrogance for years but has assiduously suppressed such feelings. Wearily, Duncan reminds her that he shares with her the spirit of rebellion and that as a homosexual he knows something about being among the cursed. As it usually happens in long quarrels, both parties took an increasingly dogmatic position until they reached a point where they had nothing more to say to each other. Duncan, to make matters worse, was a convinced Freudian who overanalyzed every word she wrote. He couldn't free himself of the suspicion that her noble sentiments hid some kind of base personal motive or demonic possession, and that was just too much for her to forgive him.

Levertov has left some truly magnificent poems and so has Duncan, though, in my opinion, not as many. However, their poems about the war are not memorable. He argued that poetry should transcend historical actualities and then contradicted himself when he sat down to write; she believed that it must confront them head on while admitting that poetry can only be socially useful if it's aesthetically sound. Charles Olson, who had an epic poet's view of things, pointed out, "it's not *either . . . or,* but *not only but also . . . and also."* Of course. Some of the best antiwar poems ever written don't even mention the subject directly. The lyric and didactic impulses in poetry have always been in conflict and have seldom been reconciled in a poem. Whitman, Pound, Jeffers, Lowell, and a few others managed to do the impossible on a few rare occasions, so we know it can be done, but not in any programmed way. No good poetry can be written to order, regardless of how worthy or pressing the cause. Duncan's and Levertov's letters are an invaluable historical document on how difficult it is to respond to such questions while innocent blood is being spilled. They seem to me even more eloquent and relevant today as we find ourselves living through another senseless war.

NOTES

1. *Conversations with Denise Levertov,* ed. Jewel Spears Brooker (University Press of Mississippi, 1998), p. 84.

2. Paul Christiansen, "Robert Edward Duncan," in *American National Biography* (Oxford University Press, 1999), vol. 7, p. 75.

3. *Robert Duncan: Scales of the Marvelous,* ed. Robert J. Bertholf and Ian W. Reid (New Directions, 1979), p. 86.

4. Denise Levertov, *The Poet in the World* (New Directions, 1973), p. 47.

5. *Bending the Bow* (New Directions, 1968), p. 1.

Angels on the Laundry Line

This huge, comprehensive edition of Richard Wilbur's *Collected Poems* represents the work of some sixty years. In addition to his most recent poems, it includes seventeen previous collections, five children's books, and translations from several languages. Over the length of his distinguished career, Wilbur has also published two books of literary essays and has translated the plays of Molière and Racine to high praise. For his accomplishments, he has been honored with a National Book Award, two Pulitzer Prizes, the Bollingen Translation Prize, and many other prestigious awards.

The critic Peter Stitt described him as standing apart from his literary age in at least three ways. Wilbur, he wrote, "exhibits a classic, objective sensibility in a romantic, subjective time; he is a formalist in the midst of relentless informality; and he is a relative optimist among absolute pessimists."[1] I agree with that, except for one minor quibble. All poets, if they are any good, tend to stand apart from their literary age. They either linger in the past, advance into some imaginary future, or live in some version of the present that is altogether their own. What is interesting about Wilbur is how faithful he has been over a lifetime to what may appear to some as a very odd choice.

Recognition came early to Wilbur with the publication of his first book of poems in 1947. With the exception of Robert Lowell, who was four years older and already had a small reputation, most of the poets of his generation, including such diverse figures as Anthony Hecht, Donald Justice, Denise Levertov, Louis Simpson, and Richard Hugo, were barely known to the

---

Review of *Collected Poems, 1943–2004,* by Richard Wilbur. From the *New York Review of Books,* April 7, 2005.

poetry-reading public. Eventually, they all became the ɑ
poets we know them to be, while often modifying or radɪ
tering the poetry they were writing—but not Wilbur. One ɑ
shuffle his poems, disregarding the order in which they first ɑ
peared, and mixing the earliest with the latest work, without con
fusing or displeasing the reader. The same cannot be said of any
other poet of this period. Most of them would now and then go
out on a limb and do something completely unpredictable and
risky. Needless to say, I'm exaggerating. Wilbur's later poems are
plainer and a little more personal, but are in truth not that
different from his earliest ones. Unlike others, he has been
happy to work within an older and well-established poetic tradition over these many years.

"It was not until World War II took me to Cassino, Anzio, and
the Siegfried Line," Wilbur later said, "that I began to versify in
earnest."[2] Earlier he had thought of a career in journalism since
his mother's father and grandfather had been newspaper editors. He was born in 1921 in New York City. His father, Lawrence
Wilbur, was a painter. He graduated from Amherst College in
1942. While still a student, he spent his summers hitchhiking and
riding the rails around the country. His mother encouraged him
to write and his father encouraged him to paint. Once he was in-
ducted into the army, his only occasional participation in leftist
causes caught the attention of federal investigators while he was
being trained as a cryptographer and he was demoted to a front-
line infantry position with "suspected of disloyalty" stamped on
his service record, and thus he saw action in Italy, France, and
Germany. After he was demobilized, he continued his studies at
Harvard and received an MA in English in 1947, the same year
his first book of poems was published. After Harvard, he taught
English at Wellesley College, then Wesleyan University, where he
stayed twenty years, and finally went to Smith College as a writer
in residence, where he remained till his retirement.

The Beautiful Changes and Other Poems was widely and by and
large favorably reviewed. Louise Bogan in the *New Yorker* de-
tected the influence of Marianne Moore, T. S. Eliot, John Crowe
Ransom, and Gerard Manley Hopkins. I would add Stevens and
Frost to that list. The general consensus was that Wilbur had the
talent to become a major poet. Rereading the volume today one

,ee. The poems are deftly crafted, at times verbally daz-
.ld as often weakened by the use of stale poetic language
.tock sentiments. Of course, unevenness in quality is what
  expects to find in every first book. I mention it here only
~ecause unevenness is a problem with all of Wilbur's books. His
best poems are usually so much better than the rest; one keeps
searching for an explanation. "Every poem of mine is auton-
omous, or feels so to me in the writing, and consists of an effort
to exhaust my present sense of the subject," he wrote of his own
work.[3] Fair enough. However, what that turns out to mean in
practice is a wide variety not so much of styles—which is com-
mendable—as of sheer quality. Here, for example, are the last
two stanzas of "Place Pigalle" from his first book:

> Ionized innocence: this pair reclines,
> She on the table, he in a tilting chair,
> With Arden ease; her eyes as pale as air
> Travel his priestgoat face; his hand's thick tines
> Touch the gold whorls of her Corinthian hair.
>
> "Girl, if I love thee not, then let me die;
> Do I not scorn to change my state with kings?
> Your muchtouched flesh, incalculable, which wrings
> Me so, now shall I gently seize in my
> Desperate soldier's hands which kill all things."

"Priestgoat" is nice, but the rest—which some critics claim to be
a parody of early Eliot—is simply dreadful no matter what the
intentions were. This is the same book that contains his much-
anthologized and truly masterful poem "Potato," which is free
of any such affectations, and one called "Cicadas," with its beautiful quiet beginning:

> You know those windless summer evenings, swollen to stasis
> by too-substantial melodies, rich as a
> running-down record, ground round
> to full quiet. Even the leaves
> have thick tongues.

Wilbur's first book reads at times like a collection of formal
exercises. He is interested not only in various meters and rhyme

schemes but also in exploring different kinds of vocabu.
was probably a wish to explore the effect of certain wor
occasioned a poem like "A Simplification," which is unlike
other in the book. This mock lament for the passing of the gre
orators and ranters of the past doesn't work entirely as a poem
but it begins delightfully:

> Those great rough ranters, Branns
> And catarrhal Colonels, who hurled
> Terrible taunts at the vault, ripped down Jesus' banns
> And widowed the world
> With Inquisitorial thunder, dammed-
> Up Biblical damnations, were
> The last with tongues to topple heaven; they hammed
> Jahweh away and here
> We are. . . .

The critical reaction to Wilbur's next book, *Ceremony and
Other Poems,* in 1950 was more or less along the same lines. The
reviewers continued to praise his extraordinary skill and to be
puzzled by his antiquarian approach. Wilbur wrote as if Whitman, Pound, Williams, and Cummings never existed, and that
pleased some and annoyed others. Even when he wrote about
topical issues like the recent war, he was emotionally detached.
"His manners and manner never fail,"[4] Randall Jarrell said of
his second book. The poems with their pretty surfaces and rejection of intimate confession recalled nineteenth-century
French Parnassians who disdained the effusiveness of Romantic
poetry. Compared to Wilbur, Frost, who also had no use for
modern idiom in poetry, was a downright rebel. Whatever the
merit of any of these complaints, critics have continued to this
day to disagree about his poetry. His most devoted supporters
argue that modern free verse was a historical aberration, that
true poetry was always about meter and rhyme, while his detractors continue to insist that his reluctance to take risks beyond the confines of his style and write like a contemporary is a
serious flaw. In his defense Wilbur said in a recent interview:

> The word "experiment" always introduces an element of
> stupor into any conversation about poetry, because it seems

ssible for us to get rid of the idea that technical inno-
on resembles scientific discovery, and involves some sort
progress, in the light of which some are stragglers and
others in the vanguard. It's a long time since there were theories and manifestos about how free verse should be done,
and for most of America's myriad free-versers the sole remaining technical consideration is where to put the line-
breaks; yet every damned one of them thinks that he is
experimental because it was anciently proclaimed that for-
ward-looking poetry was going to dispense with meter and
rhyme. What dreary rot. There can be, and are, good free
verse poems, but significant chance-taking in poetry is not a
matter of form alone but of concerting of thought, tone, diction, sound, cadence and all else that goes into a poem's
making.[5]

Reading his *Collected Poems,* I readily concede that there's
nothing troublingly retrograde about his use of meter and
rhyme and still have reservations about his work. In my view,
Wilbur's susceptibility to grandiloquence spoils too many of his
poems. It's seldom enough for him just to describe something,
recount an experience, construct an argument, and hint at
some idea; he also likes to hold forth, even though he is aware
of the dangers of doing so. In his essay on Emily Dickinson, he
writes that her taste for truth involved a regard for solid and
homely detail, remembering to include buckets, shawls, and
buzzing flies even in her most exalted poems. Wilbur, too, values the commonplace and reproaches Poe for scorning the real
and wanting to exclude from poetry all earthly business that
might detain the soul from its flight. He's right, of course. Still,
he frequently forgets Dickinson's warning that "too much proof
affronts belief."[6] She knew when to leave the poem alone and
let the imagination of the reader tie the loose ends.

A poet like Theodore Roethke, on the other hand, ruined
many a fine poem by tacking on some uncalled-for epiphany as
if the poem would be poorer without an outburst of wisdom.
Wilbur shares that weakness. My complaint is not that he is a
poet of ideas or even that he seeks to make pronouncements,
but that he is too fond of clichés:

Love is the greatest mercy,
A volley of the sun
That lashes all with shade,
That the first day be mended;
And yet, so soon undone,
It is the lover's curse
Till time be comprehended
And the flawed heart unmade.
What can I do but move
From folly to defeat,
And call that sorrow sweet
That teaches us to see
The final face of love
In what we cannot be?

There are many such lines in the *Collected Poems*. Even his rightly admired poem "Love Calls Us to the Things of This World" has a couple of false notes:

The eyes open to a cry of pulleys,
And spirited from sleep, the astounded soul
Hangs for a moment bodiless and simple
As false dawn.
Outside the open window
The morning air is all awash with angels.
Some are in bed-sheets, some are in blouses,
Some are in smocks: but truly there they are.
Now they are rising together in calm swells
Of halcyon feeling, filling whatever they wear
With the deep joy of their impersonal breathing;
Now they are flying in place, conveying
The terrible speed of their omni-presence, moving
And staying like white water; and now of a sudden
They swoon down into so rapt a quiet
That nobody seems to be there.
The soul shrinks
From all that it is about to remember,
From the punctual rape of every blessèd day,
And cries,
"Oh, let there be nothing on earth but laundry,
Nothing but rosy hands in the rising steam

And clear dances done in the sight of heaven."
Yet, as the sun acknowledges
With a warm look the world's hunks and colors,
The soul descends once more in bitter love
To accept the waking body, saying now
In a changed voice as the man yawns and rises,
"Bring them down from their ruddy gallows;
Let there be clean linen for the backs of thieves;
Let lovers go fresh and sweet to be undone,
And the heaviest nuns walk in a pure floating
Of dark habits,
keeping their difficult balance."

The title of the poem comes from a lovely passage in Augustine's *Confessions* which could serve as a rationale and plot summary for so many poems since the days of the Romantics:

> I have learnt to love you late, Beauty at once so ancient and new! I have learnt to love you late! You were within me, and I was in the world outside myself. I searched for you outside myself and, disfigured as I was, I fell upon the lovely things of your creation. You were with me, but I was not with you. The beautiful things of this world kept me far from you and yet, if they had not been in you, they would have no being at all.

The speaker of "Love Calls Us to the Things of This World" comes to a similar understanding. He awakes to the sound of pulleys wheeling the wash outside his window. In his drowsy state of mind they appear to him like angels spirited from his sleep (note the pun), freshly laundered, as it were, and hung bodiless on the line. Outside what is most likely a tenement window, the ordinary reality is miraculously transformed for a moment. The short-lived vision of lightness and cleanliness is ruptured by the "punctual rape" of the alarm clock. At that point, the poem is damaged for me by the lines that follow in which the soul groans at being cheated of such bliss and having to return to the body. I realize that the cry that there be nothing in life but such ecstatic flights is meant to be taken partly

tongue-in-cheek, but it still strikes me as literary retouch,
the experience, destroying, as far as I'm concerned, wha
verisimilitude it had.

Baudelaire could get away with conceits like that, but not
twentieth-century American poet. Denise Levertov, in her poem
"Matins," which describes a nearly identical early-morning experience, sends the speaker more plausibly to the bathroom afterward. In contrast, Wilbur's poem feels contrived, its meaning
manipulated at a crucial point, so that even the powerful con-
cluding lines about clean linen for the backs of thieves and the
difficulty of keeping a balance between the sacred and the pro-
fane, the real and the imaginary, do not have the impact they
ought to have.

"Some men write their poems in response to their agonies;
some, to their delights," Hyam Plutzik wrote in a review of
Wilbur's *Things of This World* back in 1956.[7] He went on to call
him that rare bird, a poet of joy who walks among the devils
that his fellow poets keep pointing out to him, although he
doesn't see them. In an interview, Wilbur has said that he wants
to simply celebrate the radical joyousness of this world while
at the same time rejecting the apostolic zeal of the ideologue
and the humanitarian: "The world is sufficient before I ever
trouble myself to say so. It's not raw material waiting for the
artistic kiss of life to revive it."[8] In his essay "Poetry and Happiness," he has his own theory on what makes poets write. There
are two impulses in poetry, according to Wilbur, the impulse to
name our reality and the impulse to discover and project the
self. "All poets are moved by both," he declares, "but every poet
inclines more to one than to the other." Here, as an illustration
of how these two impulses work together, is the title poem of
his 1961 collection:

Advice to a Prophet

When you come, as you soon must, to the streets of our city,
Mad-eyed from stating the obvious,
Not proclaiming our fall but begging us
In God's name to have self-pity,

ʎe us all word of the weapons, their force and range,
ɪe long numbers that rocket the mind;
Our slow, unreckoning hearts will be left behind,
Unable to fear what is too strange.

Nor shall you scare us with talk of the death of the race.
How should we dream of this place without us?—
The sun mere fire, the leaves untroubled about us,
A stone look on the stone's face?

Speak of the world's own change. Though we cannot
    conceive
Of an undreamt thing, we know to our cost
How the dreamt cloud crumbles, the vines are blackened by
    frost,
How the view alters. We could believe,

If you told us so, that the white-tailed deer will slip
Into perfect shade, grown perfectly shy,
The lark avoid the reaches of our eye,
The jack-pine lose its knuckled grip

On the cold ledge, and every torrent burn
As Xanthus once, its gliding trout
Stunned in a twinkling. What should we be without
The dolphin's arc, the dove's return,

These things in which we have seen ourselves and spoken?
Ask us, prophet, how we shall call
Our natures forth when that live tongue is all
Dispelled, that glass obscured or broken

In which we have said the rose of our love and the clean
Horse of our courage, in which beheld
The singing locust of the soul unshelled
And all we mean or wish to mean.

Ask us, ask us whether with the wordless rose
Our hearts shall fail us; come demanding
Whether there shall be lofty or long standing
When the bronze annals of the oak-tree close.

The subject of this poem is nuclear war and the destruction of
the planet. It addresses some prophet of doom, weary of re-
peating the obvious, who has failed to make himself heard by

the people he is trying to warn. The speaker advises him to avoid dry statistics about the power and range of weapons, their destructive capacities, and the horrors that await us afterward since we cannot fear what we find nearly impossible to imagine. The prophet, if he's to be believed, must remind people that impermanence is the very essence of their experience of the world and make them recall incidents from their lives that show that to be the case. A white-tailed deer slipping into shade or a lark flying beyond the reach of our sight—in these and countless other similar occurrences, we glimpse ourselves. "We are happy," Yeats said, "when for everything inside us there is a corresponding something outside us."

Undoubtedly, as Wilbur intimates in his poem, our conceptions of perfection and beauty and their transience all derive from such experiences. If the "live tongue" that calls our natures forth is ever silenced, and the annals of the oak tree closed, not only will history end, but so will our ability to speak about what most matters to us. This is what the prophet must make people understand: we rely on nature to tell us what we are. On a razed planet there will be no renewal. We will be left— if we are left at all—with our slow, unreckoning hearts, lacking even a soul.

As one can see from this unsettling and forceful poem, *Collected Poems, 1943–2004* is still an indispensable book despite my reservations. In addition to the poems I have already cited, I count at least two dozen others that seem to me first-rate. Among them are "Juggler," "For the New Railroad Station in Rome," "Exeunt," "A Black November Turkey," "To Ishtar," "In the Smoking-Car," "Two Voices in a Meadow," "Thyme Flowering Among Rocks," "The Mind-Reader," "Teresa," "A Shallot," "The Fourth of July," "The Writer," "Under a Tree," and this hard, imagistic poem that steers clear of artifice and whose one classical allusion at the end is well earned:

Stop

In grimy winter dusk
We slowed for a concrete platform;
The pillars passed more slowly;
A paper bag leapt up.

The train banged to standstill.
Brake-steam rose and parted.
Three chipped-at blocks of ice
Sprawled on a baggage-truck.

Out in that glum, cold air
The broken ice lay glintless,
But the truck was painted blue
On side, wheels, and tongue,

A purple, glowering blue
Like the phosphorous of Lethe
Or Queen Persephone's gaze
In the numb fields of the dark.

The book also contains many splendid translations Wilbur
made over the years. There are poems by Baudelaire, Valéry,
Brodsky, Nerval, Apollinaire, and a number of other poets.
Wilbur may be our finest translator since Pound. He doesn't
range as widely among languages and literatures as Pound did,
nor does he permit himself the liberties the older poet took
with the originals. Especially when he's translating from the
French, Wilbur frequently manages to accomplish the impossible by re-creating not only the meter and rhyme, but even
some of the wordplay and the music. According to him, any
translator unwilling to be slavish to the original is in the wrong
racket. He is right about that. What follows is one of the several
marvelous translations of the great fifteenth-century French
poet François Villon, in which the colloquial flow, the swagger,
and the lyricism are all preserved:

Ballade of Forgiveness

Brothers and sisters, Celestine,
Carthusian, or Carmelite,
Street-loafers, fops whose buckles shine,
Lackeys, and courtesans whose tight
Apparel gratifies the sight,
And little ladies'-men who trot
In tawny boots of dreadful height:
I beg forgiveness of the lot.

Young whores who flash their teats in sign
Of what they hawk for men's delight,
Ape-handlers, thieves and, soused with wine,
Wild bullies looking for a fight,
And Jacks and Jills whose hearts are light,
Whistling and joking, talking rot,
Street-urchins dodging left and right:
I beg forgiveness of the lot.

Excepting for those bloody swine
Who gave me, many a morn and night,
The hardest crusts on which to dine;
Henceforth I'll fear them not a mite.
I'd belch and fart in their despite
Were I not sitting on my cot.
Well, to be peaceful and polite
I beg forgiveness of the lot.

May hammers, huge and heavy, smite
Their ribs, and likewise cannon-shot.
May cudgels pulverize them quite.
I beg forgiveness of the lot.

It may be unavoidable that the virtues of every poet's work are in the end responsible for its defects. As perceptive as Frost was, he noticed little of American life outside of his rural New England. The pet theories of Stevens and Pound have a way of driving even their greatest fans nuts. Wilbur's fastidious craftsmanship is also a straitjacket. His love of tradition comes at a cost. Many of his poems sound timid to anyone who has seen what his more imaginative and inventive contemporaries can do.

Am I being unfair to him? I don't think so. Wilbur does well some of the hardest things in poetry and not so well with some of the others. He leaves me—as he does many of his readers and critics—with a mixture of profound esteem and disappointment. His books of essays, *Responses* (1976) and *The Catbird Song* (1997), are filled with sensible, cautionary observations on poets and poetry which for reasons that I do not understand he doesn't always adhere to when he sits down to write. Whatever the answer, his best work, like this fairly recent poem of his, is astonishingly good and will continue to be read:

A Barred Owl

The warping night air having brought the boom
Of an owl's voice into her darkened room,
We tell the wakened child that all she heard
Was an odd question from a forest bird,
Asking of us, if rightly listened to,
"Who cooks for you?" and then "Who cooks for you?"

Words, which can make our terrors bravely clear,
Can also thus domesticate a fear,
And send a small child back to sleep at night
Not listening for the sound of stealthy flight
Or dreaming of some small thing in a claw
Borne up to some dark branch and eaten raw.

NOTES

1. *Richard Wilbur in Conversation with Peter Dale* (Between the Lines, 2000), p. 96.

2. Donald L. Hill, *Richard Wilbur* (Twayne, 1967), p. 13.

3. Richard Wilbur, *Responses* (Harcourt Brace Jovanovich, 1976), p. 118.

4. *Richard Wilbur's Creation*, ed. Wendy Salinger (University of Michigan Press, 1983), p. 46.

5. *Richard Wilbur in Conversation with Peter Dale*, p. 35.

6. Wilbur, *Responses*, p. 4.

7. Salinger, *Richard Wilbur's Creation*, p. 66.

8. Frances Bixler, *Richard Wilbur: A Reference Guide* (Hall, 1991), p. 204.

How I Found the
Philosopher's Stone

One night in New York, it was so hot and humid in a bookstore where I was reading my poems, I was soaked with sweat, my pants kept sliding down, so I had to constantly pull them up with one hand while I held the book in the other. A fellow I knew told me afterward that he was enthralled. He and his companion were sure I'd forget for a moment and let them fall down. Another time in Monterey, California, I was reading in a nearly empty auditorium of the local college adjoining one in which the movie *King Kong* was being shown to a packed audience. At one point, during one of my most lyrical love poems, I could hear the great ape growl behind my back as he was on his way to strangle me. Back in the 1960s, in some youth center in some miserable little town on Long Island, I was put on the program between an amateur magician and a fellow who was a mind reader and the audience of local punks was not told who I was and what I was supposed to be doing. I recall their bewildered expressions as I was reading my first poem. In Detroit, I had a baby howl while I read and then a lapdog someone had sneaked in started to yelp. I was so drunk in Geneva, New York, I demanded that all the lights be turned off except the one on my lectern, and then I proceeded to read for two hours, some of the poems twice, as I was told the next day. In the 1970s, after hearing my poem "Breasts," a dozen women walked out in Oberlin, Ohio, each one slamming the door behind her. In a high school in Medford, Oregon, I was introduced as the world-famous mystery writer, Bernard Zimic. In San Jose, I lost the fellow I was supposed to be following in my

From *Mortification* (Fourth Estate, 2003).

at the peak of the rush hour traffic and realized I had no idea where the reading was. I drove ahead thinking he would realize I was not behind him and stop by the side of the road. I went past all the downtown and suburban exits and finally figured the hell with him, I'm going home to San Francisco. Since I had to go back the way I came from, I decided on the spur of the moment to take one of the exits and ask, except there was no one to ask at eight in the evening in a neighborhood of small apartment houses and tree-lined streets. After circling for a while, I saw an old Chinese man walking alone. I stopped the car and asked him, very conscious of how ridiculous I was, did he happen to know of a poetry reading? Yes, he said, in the church around the corner. In Aurora, New York, on beautiful Lake Geneva I gave the shortest reading ever. It lasted exactly twenty-eight minutes, whereas the crowd and the organizers expected a full hour. I had an excellent excuse, however. I squeezed the reading between the first and final quarter of an NBA playoff game and ran back to my motel outracing a couple of women who wanted me to sign books. In Ohrid, Macedonia, I read into a dead mike to an audience of thousands who would not have understood me even if they had heard me, but who nevertheless applauded after every poem. Now, I ask you, how much more can one ask from life?

The Memory Piano

They say that Donald Justice, who died in August 2004 at the age of seventy-nine, never published a bad poem in his life. Still, his work was not as familiar to readers of poetry as that of Allen Ginsberg, James Merrill, Robert Bly, John Ashbery, Robert Creeley and several others of his contemporaries, even though he had been honored through the years with the Lamont, the Pulitzer, and the Bollingen prizes and had a following of devoted admirers. One reason for that may be that he was not very prolific. Only four collections of his poetry and some additional poems in two earlier versions of selected poems appeared over a span of more than forty years.

The publication of *Collected Poems* comes as a revelation, a book that compels us not only to reassess his stature as a poet, but to mull over the related questions of what it means to be a modern, traditional, and even an original poet. What makes this an issue worth thinking about is that Justice was a most unusual kind of poet. He was both a formalist and a committed modernist at a time when these two aesthetics seemed incompatible. He wrote sestinas and villanelles, but he also liked free verse and surrealism. Despite these ways of writing being poles apart, his poems have been rightly praised for their consistency of style and their quiet virtuosity. I must admit that I did not fully appreciate how much fine poetry he wrote until I read this book.

Although he lived most of his life in Iowa City, where he taught at the University of Iowa Writers' Workshop, Justice was a Southerner. He was born in Miami, Florida, in 1925 and remained

Review of *Collected Poems,* by Donald Justice. From the *New York Review of Books,* February 24, 2005.

nful in much of what he wrote to that part of the country. His ther was a carpenter who had grown up on a farm in southern Alabama and spent his youth drifting through parts of Georgia and northern Florida learning his trade. Justice was an only child. They lived modestly. His parents didn't have much schooling and yet they made him take weekly piano lessons and he was encouraged to read widely. As he told an interviewer, "I have only recently come to realize, it was a happy childhood, for which I have my parents to thank."[1]

In high school, he read Twain, Poe, Dreiser, Dostoevsky, and discovered T. S. Eliot and Ezra Pound. After graduating in 1942, he received a scholarship to play clarinet in the band and study music at the University of Miami. A bone disease that he suffered in his childhood kept him from the army during the war. One of his teachers at the university was the composer Carl Ruggles, whose seriousness and devotion to the highest artistic ideals, Justice later said, left a profound impression on him. Nevertheless, after a couple of semesters, Justice came to the conclusion that he had limited musical talent and switched to English, which he described as being a good deal less fun and hardly more practical. "I had a kind of basic artistic . . . desire," he explained in another interview. "Reading a lot, playing a lot of music and trying to write music, I began to write a few other things, little stories and poems."[2]

He received his degree in 1945 and after a year of knocking around New York and working at odd jobs, he entered the University of North Carolina to study for an MA in English. At Chapel Hill, he met the poet Edgar Bowers and the novelist Richard Stern, and most importantly his future wife. The subject of his MA thesis was the Southern Fugitive-Agrarian poets. He tried to demonstrate how the ideas found in their critical writing influenced their poems. After graduating in 1947, and teaching at the University of Miami for a year, he moved on to Stanford with the intention of studying under Yvor Winters. That did not happen owing to some bureaucratic snag. Justice returned to Miami with the expectation that he would teach freshman composition for the rest of his days, writing verses on weekends and a novel or two to make a bit of extra money. The only other career he could imagine for himself at that time of

his life was that of a professional gambler working the ra
in the afternoons and the greyhounds in the evenings.

As it turned out, the year a chapbook of his poems, *The
Bachelor and Other Poems* (1951), was published, he lost his teac
ing job. Acting on the advice of friends, he applied to the Ph.D.
program in creative writing at the University of Iowa in the
spring of 1952. He found himself in illustrious company. John
Berryman, Robert Lowell, and Carl Shapiro were his teachers
and his fellow students were Jane Cooper, Henri Coulette,
Philip Levine, W. D. Snodgrass, and William Stafford. In 1954
he got his degree and was awarded a Rockefeller Foundation
fellowship in poetry, which made it possible for him and his
wife to travel to Europe for the first time. After his return, he
eventually settled in Iowa City, where, except for extended absences to teach in Syracuse and at the University of Florida, he
made his home. Over the years, he taught and influenced at
least a couple of generations of young poets, a few of whom
went on to become far better known than he ever was.

While still an instructor, Justice had been publishing poems
in many of the country's most prestigious journals—*Poetry,* the
New Yorker, Harper's, the *Hudson Review,* and the *Paris Review*—
and two of his short stories were included in the O. Henry Prize
Stories annual collections. In 1960, when he was thirty-five years
old, Wesleyan University Press brought out his first full collection of poetry. *The Summer Anniversaries* had six reviews. One was
disparaging, calling the poems imitative, while the others were
not only favorable but perceptive. Howard Nemerov wrote in
the *American Scholar:*

> Mr. Justice is an accomplished writer, whose skill is consis-
> tently subordinated to an attitude at once serious and unpre-
> tentious. Although his manner is not yet fully disengaged
> from that of certain modern masters, whom he occasionally
> echoes, his own way of doing things does in general come
> through, a voice distinct although very quiet, in poems that
> are delicate and brave among their nostalgias.[3]

The volume was selected by the Academy of American Poets
as the Lamont Poetry Selection for that year. Reading it today,

...ed how well the poems hold up. Justice was a master of ...ef lyric. He understood the power of self-restraint, mat-...-fact delivery, and the impact of a striking image or two. ...mething small, perfectly turned out like a sonatina is what he ...imed for, claiming that he was convinced that a prior model existed for the poem he was writing, a sort of Platonic script which he had been elected to transcribe. *The Summer Anniversaries* is a book of many finely turned-out poems. Here's one:

The Poet at Seven

And on the porch, across the upturned chair,
The boy would spread a dingy counterpane
Against the length and majesty of the rain
And on all fours crawl in it like a bear,
To lick his wounds in secret, in his lair;
And afterward, in the windy yard again,
One hand cocked back, release his paper plane,
Frail as a mayfly to the faithless air.
And summer evenings he would spin around
Faster and faster till the drunken ground
Rose up to meet him; sometimes he would squat
Among the foul weeds of the vacant lot,
Waiting for dusk and someone dear to come
And whip him down the street, but gently, home.

Because of the ease with which the words flow, one may not at first notice that this is a sonnet. Another curious thing about the poem is that some of its lines sound familiar. Like many of Justice's poems, "The Poet at Seven" is in part an adaptation of another poet's work. In this case, the poet is Arthur Rimbaud and it is his poems "Seven-Year-Old Poets" and "The Drunken Boat" that are being echoed. Eliot and Pound were both good at this kind of ventriloquism. They appropriated lines from the work of other poets and after a bit of tinkering passed them off as their own.

Justice's "The Poet at Seven" is not a translation or imitation of an entire poem, but an improvisation on some familiar lines from Rimbaud. He's like a composer who uses a melody of another composer to compose a variation on a theme. To give just one example, at the conclusion of Rimbaud's "The Drunken

Boat" a child full of sadness squatting on the sidewalk as the night descends launches a paper boat over a cold, black puddle in the street, while in Justice's poem, another dreamy child releases a paper plane frail as a mayfly to the faithless air. For him, it made no difference whether poetry came from actual experience or from books. If one cares a lot about somebody else's words in a poem, one may as well do something with them. What matters is the poem one ends up with, its quality and novelty, not the source of inspiration, or some underlying theory of what is authentic and what is not.

In addition to "The Poet at Seven," Justice's first book contains other much-anthologized poems like "Counting the Mad," "On a Painting by Patient B of the Independence State Hospital for the Insane," and "Sestina on Six Words of Weldon Kees." He was not a fussy formalist. A thirteen-line sonnet may be just dandy. "There seems to me no obligation," he said in an interview, "to carry on with a proper villanelle when it may mean including one or two stanzas less good than the others."[4] He admitted that he was never good at rhyming. His interest in intricate forms, he explained, was connected to a wish to displace the self from the poem, not to obliterate it entirely, but not to have it stand center stage. "I want to treat the personal stuff as impersonally as if I were making it all up,"[5] he said.

His experiments with chance in *Night Light* (1967) served the same purpose. He wrote words and passages that he heard on TV or read in newspapers on three-by-five note cards and then shuffled the cards over and over again like the gambler that he was until he found a phrase that he could use in a poem. Unlike his friend John Cage, who gave him the idea, he did not leave intact what chance had served up. He cheated and used only what he liked and could revise. As someone said, chance is fine when you're dealt five aces or at least four queens. Otherwise, forget it. Justice liked elegant writing and Cage's method did not lead to elegance.

His insistence on minimizing the role of the self may give the impression that his poems lack a point of view or emotion. This is not the case. Justice has a compassionate eye and a conscience. Old people, poor people, lonely people as well as children are everywhere. They do not dominate the poems; the landscape nd the weather are given an equal part. One of Justice's subjects is America. "The spirit and space, / the empty spirit / In vacant space," as Stevens says. He was one of Justice's heroes. The other was William Carlos Williams. There are poems of his that imitate Stevens's lush language and others where Williams's laconic style is the model. However, in some, he pays homage to both. Here's an example from one of his later books:

First Death
June 12, 1933

I saw my grandmother grow weak.
When she died, I kissed her cheek.

I remember the new taste—
Powder mixed with a drying paste.

Down the hallway, on its table,
Lay the family's great Bible.

In the dark, by lamplight stirred,
The Void grew pregnant with the Word.

In black ink they wrote it down.
The older ink was turning brown.

From the woods there came a cry,
The hoot owl asking who not why.

The men sat silent on the porch,
Each lighted pipe a friendly torch

Against the unknown and the known.
But the child knew himself alone.

June 13, 1933

The morning sun rose up and stuck.
Sunflowers strove with hollyhock.

I ran the worn path past the sty.
Nothing was hidden from God's eye.

The barn door creaked. I walked among
Chaff and wrinkled cakes of dung.

In the dim light I read the dates
On the dusty license plates

Nailed to the wall as souvenirs.
I breathed the dust in of the years.

I circled the abandoned Ford
Before I tried the running board.

At the wheel I felt the heat
Press upward through the springless seat.

And when I touched the silent horn,
Small mice scattered through the corn.

Justice admired Walker Evans and even wrote a poem on one of his photographs, and one can easily see why. Theirs is an America of back roads seen from a car. They both liked to find the extraordinary among the ordinary, then leave it pretty much as it was, confident that it was—if anything ever was—enough. "The air of the casual is reassuring,"[6] Justice said about Williams. He confessed that he hoped that some of his poems would end up being like a treasured photo that we take out from time to time to look at again. In the last decades of his life he learned how to paint. The four paintings which are reproduced on the cover of *Collected Poems* have that same sparse quality that we find in Evans and a painter like Hopper. Here is an example of what Justice called the art of limited means:

The Small White Churches of the Small White Towns

The twangy, off-key hymn songs of the poor,
Not musical, but somehow beautiful.
And the paper fans in motion, like little wings.

This is the entire poem. As expected, he preferred Dickinson to Whitman. He also approved of Frost, Crane, Ransom, Auden, and Weldon Kees. Together with Stevens and Williams, all these influences would have made him perhaps a more predictable poet if not for his abiding interest in nineteenth-century and modern European and South American poetry. I've already mentioned Rimbaud, but that's just the beginning. There are poems, like his famous "The Man Closing Up" and "Hands," that are closely based on the work of the French minimalist poet Guillevic. In *Departures* (1973) Justice has adaptations of poems y the Spanish poets Federico García Lorca and Rafael Alberti and the Peruvian poet César Vallejo. In *The Sunset Maker* (1987) Rilke, Baudelaire, and Laforgue are used as props and even Kafka and Henry James. Here's how that works:

American Scenes (1904–1905)

1. CAMBRIDGE IN WINTER

Immense pale houses! Sunshine just now and snow
Light up and pauperize the whole brave show—
Each fanlight, each veranda, each good address,
All a mere paint and pasteboard paltriness!
These winter sunsets are the one fine thing:
Blood on the snow, some last impassioned fling,
The wild frankness and sadness of surrender—
As if our cities ever could be tender!

The next three sections of the poem are entitled: "2. Railway Junction South of Richmond, Past Midnight," "3. St. Michael's Cemetery, Charleston," and "4. Epilogue: Coronado Beach, California." Undeniably, these many impersonations allowed Justice to write poems he could not write otherwise. They also raise the obvious question of to what degree such poems are to be regarded as original work.

Asked by Philip Hoy about the Scottish poet Robert Crawford's remark that as far as politics is concerned, the poet's most important work is to fiddle while Rome burns, he readily agreed. Still, Justice did write political poems. The best-known one is an antiwar poem written in February of 1965 and ironically dedicated to McNamara, Rusk, and Bundy:

To the Hawks

MCNAMARA, RUSK, BUNDY

Farewell is the bell
Beginning to ring.

The children singing
Do not yet hear it.

The sun is shining
In their song. The sun

Is in fact shining
Upon the schoolyard,

On children swinging
Like tongues of a bell

Swung out on the long
Arc of silence

That will not seem to
Have been a silence

Till it is broken,
As it is breaking.

There is a sun now
Louder than the sun

Of which the children
Are singing, brighter,

Too, than that other
Against whose brightness

Their eyes seem caught in
The act of shutting.

The young schoolteacher,
Waving one arm in

Time to the music,
Is waving farewell.

Her mouth is open
To sound the alarm.

The mouth of the world
Grows round with the sound.

Justice's America is pretty to look at, but the appearances are deceiving. There's an air of unhappiness about these small towns and suburbs. While outwardly prosperous and contented, these men and women he writes about don't sleep well.

"Already it is midsummer / in the Sweden of our lives," Justice writes in "Elsewheres." The long green shutters are drawn, the rooms are dark, a razor lies open on the cool marble washstand. There's the sound of something dripping on the floor. Is

ter or blood? The poet doesn't tell us and the reader can
ny guess. A poem like "Men at Forty" has the grimness and
poignancy of a Cheever story. Here's the way it starts and the
way it ends:

> Men at forty
> Learn to close softly
> The doors to rooms they will not be
> Coming back to.
>
> At rest on a stair landing,
> They feel it moving
> Beneath them now like the deck of a ship,
> Though the swell is gentle.
> . . . .
> Something is filling them, something
>
> That is like the twilight sound
> Of the crickets, immense,
> Filling the woods at the foot of the slope
> Behind their mortgaged houses.

A subject Justice returned to obsessively is his childhood.
This is especially true of his later poems. I can think of plenty of
other poets who go back to that period of their lives, but not for
the same reason that he does. There was never any history, he
says of his growing up in Miami, only hurricanes and tabernacle
tents that sprang up overnight on circus grounds where preach-
ers blessed the faithful. It is not some isolated traumatic event
that troubles him again and again in his childhood poems or a
longing for a happier time, but an indefinable, ineffable something he cannot quite name.

It is always late afternoon in his recollection, the light is turning golden, there are vast clouds in the sky, and the shadows are
lengthening. The speaker is alone playing or listening to grown-
ups whispering on the porch, their long melancholy silences
casting a spell on him. "Certain moments will never change nor
stop being," he says in "Thinking About the Past." The sadness
without a cause of a solitary child and the continuing memory
of it are the riddle he is trying to solve. The secret of his iden-

tity and his identity as a poet, he suspects, is to be found there.
In "Sonatina in Yellow," he writes:

> The faces fade, and there is only
> A sort of meaning that comes back,
> Or for the first time comes, but comes too late
> To take the places of the faces.
> Remember
> The dead air of summer. Remember
> The trees drawn up to their full height like fathers,
> The underworld of shade you entered at their feet.

What kind of meaning? Justice was not a closet transcenden-
talist. The spiritual meant little to him. He was brought up as a
Southern Baptist, but lost his faith. It's the visible, the mortal,
and the fleeting that he's interested in. The experience he's trying to recall can only be described as aesthetic since it doesn't
really have much other content. He remembers some moment
when everything worn-out and old appeared new and beautiful
to him. Paradoxically, the power of these poems comes from
their narrow range and their repletion. It's like being inside the
head of an insomniac or listening to a neighbor play the same
tune on the piano every night. The same images, the same notes
recur, casting one deeper and deeper into the mood. "Eternity
resembles / One long Sunday afternoon," he wrote. We know
what he is talking about. He has in mind those long-ago afternoons and evenings when our boredom and our sadness con-
spired to make a kind of happiness we can never bring ourselves
to forget. Justice convinces us that all our childhood reveries are
worth revisiting again not only to find out who we are but to become poets once more.

Writing about the American poet Weldon Kees, who disap-
peared mysteriously in 1954 leaving his car in the parking lot
near the Golden Gate Bridge and whose poems Justice collected
and rescued from oblivion, he describes what attracted him:

> The style was almost anonymous and therefore classical, as I
> saw it then and still today see it. It may be hard for some read-
> ers now to imagine the impression of simple purity the Kees

style could engender. It does not resound with the high ambition of an Eliot or Pound, it is not half so refined as the Stevens style, not so pugnacious as that of Williams. It is clearly not the style of a writer desperate for novelty, as so many current styles seem to me to be, but instead the style of an honest, plainspoken man, who finds himself impinged upon by a terror special to his time and with which he deals, hopelessly enough, by writing poems. I think it is in large part the very absence of flash that endears Kees to a good many of us—and there will always be those who do not understand that.[7]

Much of this, of course, is true of Justice himself, although he's a better poet than Kees ever was. He endeavored to write poetry that has ties to its long tradition, that is not afraid to grapple with some of its toughest formal requirements, but that avoids sounding contrived. The usual American manner in poetry, all earnestness and raw emotion, did not attract him in the least. Justice never strikes poses or indulges himself in being difficult. He thought the poet's presence ought to be discreet and discernible only in his style. This is not an easy ambition to fulfill since sooner or later one's autobiography inevitably intrudes into the work. Still, that was his ideal. The great Polish poet Zbigniew Herbert used to say that there are two kinds of poets on earth—the ox poet and the cat poet. The ox poet went out every morning and plowed his field while the cat poet lay around all day napping and hunting only when he was hungry. In an interview with Larry Levis, Justice was asked which kind of poet he was. His reply was, "I'm the kind of cat who envies the ox."[8] We ought to be glad that he was that, a cat stretched on a piano, looking out of the window, watching the rain as the last bus comes, letting dark umbrellas out that open into black flowers, many black flowers.

NOTES

1. *Donald Justice in Conversation with Philip Hoy* (Between the Lines, 2001), p. 20.
2. Donald Justice, *Platonic Scripts* (University of Michigan Press, 1984), p. 63.

3. Autumn 1960.

4. Justice, *Platonic Scripts*, p. 105.

5. *Donald Justice in Conversation with Philip Hoy*, p. 45.

6. Justice, *Platonic Scripts*, p. 207.

7. Donald Justice, *Oblivion: On Writers and Writing* (Story Line Press, 1998), pp. 103–4.

8. Justice, *Platonic Scripts*, pp. 79–80.

UNDER DISCUSSION
David Lehman, General Editor
Donald Hall, Founding Editor

Volumes in the Under Discussion series collect reviews and essays about individual poets. The series is concerned with contemporary American and English poets about whom the consensus has not yet been formed and the final vote has not been taken. Titles in the series include: